Life History

AND THE

Historical Moment

BY ERIK H. ERIKSON

Childhood and Society (1950, 1963)
Young Man Luther (1958)
Insight and Responsibility (1964)
Identity: Youth and Crisis (1968)
Gandhi's Truth (1969)
In Search of Common Ground (1973)
(with Huey P. Newton and
Kai T. Erikson)
Dimensions of a New Identity (1974)

ERIK H. ERIKSON

Life History
AND THE
Historical
Moment

W · W · NORTON & COMPANY · INC · *New York*

*   *   *

THIS BOOK was composed in Linotype Janson. Composition, printing, and binding were done by Vail-Ballou Press, Inc.

FIRST EDITION

Library of Congress Cataloging in Publication Data
Erikson, Erik Homburger, 1902–
    Life history and the historical moment.
    Includes bibliographical references and index.
    1. Psychoanalysis. 2. History. I. Title.
BF175.E74   1975   309'.01'9   74–20574

ISBN 0–393–01103–8

1 2 3 4 5 6 7 8 9 0

To Staff and Students of
Soc. Sci. 139 and 133,
The Human Life Cycle,
Harvard University,
1960–1970

Contents

Preface

THIS BOOK is made up of reflections offered to diverse gatherings during a decade of academic teaching and traveling. The main essay in each section was first presented at one of the symposia convoked by *Daedalus*, the journal of the American Academy of Arts and Sciences. Here men and women from a variety of fields come together to work on one theme. It was my double task to clarify for the participants from other fields something of the special nature of psychoanalysis and, thus, of the kind of light it could throw on the main theme, and yet also to ask myself and those conversant with my field what we may yet have to investigate when confronted with such new tasks. Thus, when representatives of the natural and the social sciences discussed the emergence of innovative concepts in their or their colleagues' careers, I was asked to reflect on the origin in my life of the concept of identity crisis. When historians discussed the nature of charismatic leadership, I reflected on my ongoing studies of Gandhi's emergence as a leader. And in a timely disputation on The Embattled University, I spoke of the students' struggle for inner liberation.

But each section also contains communications of a more diverse nature. My autobiographic reflections are followed by two book reviews of Freud's posthumous works. The section on Gandhi is concluded with an address given to students in South Africa where Gandhi's leadership began. In the section on modern liberation, there is a response to a former student who had asked me to look back on what I had written on women in the past.

Can I possibly claim that one over-all theme "orchestrates" all these occasions? I think that the book's title states it: it is the relationship of *life histories* to the *historical moment*. This concerns the life histories of great leaders to the historical moment of their emergence and the life histories of those who decided to follow them; it concerns the awakening of whole groups of contemporaries (young people, modern women) to a need for inner as well as political liberation; and it concerns, throughout, the life histories of us, the observers, defined as we are by our own past, by the history of our field, and by the tasks of the times. The reader is invited, then, to consider—if ever so critically—where and how our approach touches on his own life and work.

Personal Acknowledgments

There are few good thoughts in these pages which did not first emerge in conversations with Joan Erikson, and wherever a word seems just right, it is usually hers.

The editors of *Daedalus*, Stephen Graubard and Geno Ballotti, are devoted hosts to emerging ideas. For this and for the permission to re-edit my contributions to their symposia, my warmest thanks.

Pamela Daniels, always a thoughtful critic, helped me with the selection of the essays and the editing. She was also the last of the head section leaders in my course at Harvard: Ken Keniston, Gordon Fellman, and Dorothy Zinburg preceded her. They and the section leaders (a proud list, could I name them all) helped me to stay in touch with the students in those turbulent years. Now, I can only offer them and the erstwhile students this more formal dedication.

Time to travel and to reflect was provided by fellowships in the Center for Advanced Study in the Behavioral Sciences and in the Field Foundation.

Elizabeth Resnik and Sherrill Brooks, neighbors and friends in East and West, prepared the final draft.

And at long last, I wish to thank my lifelong publisher and helpful critic, George P. Brockway.

Tiburon, California

Acknowledgments

THE PRESENTATIONS, all re-edited for this volume, were first published in the following magazines and periodicals:

" 'Identity Crisis' in Autobiographic Perspective" and "Postscript and Outlook" first appeared in *Daedalus: Journal of the American Academy of Arts and Sciences*, Fall, 1970.

"A Historic Friendship: Freud's Letters to Fliess" appeared in the *International Journal of Psychoanalysis*, vol. 36, no. 1, 1955.

"A Questionable Cooperation: The Wilson Book" first appeared in the *New York Review of Books*, vol. 8, no. 2, 1967, and in the *International Journal of Psychoanalysis*, vol. 48, no. 3, 1967.

"On the Nature of 'Psycho-Historical' Evidence," parts 1 and 3, appeared in *Daedalus*, Summer, 1968.

"His Own Witness: The Leader as a Child" first appeared in *The American Scholar*, vol. 35, no. 4, 1966.

"Freedom and Nonviolence" was published under the title "Insight and Freedom" as the ninth T. B. Davie Memorial Lecture, University of Cape Town, 1968.

"Reflections on the Revolt of Humanist Youth" appeared in *Daedalus*, Winter, 1970, and in the *International Journal of Psychoanalysis*, vol. 51, no. 1, 1970.

"Once More the Inner Space" is appearing simultaneously, in somewhat different form, in Jean Strouse, ed., *Women and Analysis*, Grossman Publishers, New York, 1974.

PART ONE

Backgrounds and Origins

I

"Identity Crisis" in Autobiographic Perspective

It is in the nature of psychoanalytic inquiry that I should apply the very concept which has been suggested for discussion to the history of its emergence in my life and work experience; and that I should do so in some self-analytic detail: for in this way I may also be able to illustrate some *motivational dimensions* in the formulation of a new idea.

This, however, raises the question whether "identity crisis" can, indeed, claim to be an innovative concept in my own field, psychoanalysis. Another representative of my profession might well assert that the concept is not, strictly speaking, psychoanalytic, because it deals with matters too close to the "social surface" to remain sufficiently grounded in the theory of the dynamic depth. To him, such judgment would only be confirmed by the fact that identity concepts have secured themselves rather quickly a place of familiarity in the thinking or, at any rate, the vocabulary, of a wide range of readers in a number of countries

First presented at a *Daedalus* symposium on the "biography" of innovating ideas in the twentieth-century sciences, at the Villa Serbelloni, Lake Como, in 1969.

—not to speak of its appearance in cartoons which reflect what is intellectually modish. But then, the term has also begun to denote a universal, if often controversial conflict of general relevance. Thus, it was reported in the press that the Pope in a recent speech recommended the steadfastness of a newly sainted sixteenth-century Spaniard of Jewish descent to the young priests of our time—"a time when they say the priesthood itself suffers . . . a crisis of identity." The use of this term, I am told, may be related to the fact that some young priests in Rome were reading *Il Giovanne Lutero*.

I must postpone for another occasion the question of how concepts and terms dealing with human development and motivation may be absorbed into the ethical (and pseudo-ethical) climate of their time. Here, I will once more restate why and how the assumption of a phychosocial identity appears to be a conceptual necessity; and why and how it may, in fact, be relevant to the motivational nature of innovation.

Let me begin by presenting a kind of glossary which will, if not define, at least circumscribe for our present purposes what an identity crisis "is." Here I take heart from the reassurance of Stuart Hampshire, who has stated approvingly that I "leave [my] much misused concept of identity undefined" because it primarily "serves to group together a range of phenomena which could profitably be investigated together." [1] He understood, it seems, the difficulty of establishing the nature and the position of something that is both *psycho* and *social*. For we have as yet no unified social counterpart comparable to natural science. In each of the social sciences, in fact, the workings of identity appear in different contexts of verifiability. To say, then, that the identity crisis is psycho *and* social means that:

1. It is a subjective sense as well as an observable quality of personal sameness and continuity, paired with some belief in the sameness and continuity of some shared world image. As a quality of unself-conscious living, this can be gloriously obvious in a young person who has found himself as he has found his com-

munality. In him we see emerge a unique unification of what is irreversibly given—that is, body type and temperament, giftedness and vulnerability, infantile models and acquired ideals—with the open choices provided in available roles, occupational possibilities, values offered, mentors met, friendships made, and first sexual encounters.

2. It is a state of being and becoming that can have a highly conscious (and, indeed, self-conscious) quality and yet remain, in its motivational aspects, quite unconscious and beset with the dynamics of conflict. This, in turn, can lead to contradictory mental states, such as a sense of aggravated vulnerability and yet also an expectation of grand individual promise.

3. It is characteristic of a *developmental period*, before which it cannot come to a head, because the somatic, cognitive, and social preconditions are only then given; and beyond which it must not be unduly delayed, because the next and all future developments depend on it. This stage of life is, of course, *adolescence and youth*. The advent and solution of the identity crisis thus partially depends on *psychobiological* factors, which secure the somatic basis for a coherent sense of vital selfhood. On the other hand, *psychosocial* factors can prolong the crisis (painfully, but not necessarily unduly) where a person's idiosyncratic gifts demand a prolonged search for a corresponding ideological and occupational setting, or where historical change forces a postponement of adult commitment.

4. It is dependent on the *past* for the resource of strong identifications made in childhood, while it relies on new models encountered in youth, and depends for its conclusion on workable roles offered in young adulthood. In fact, each subsequent stage of adulthood must contribute to its preservation and renewal.

The "socio" part of identity, then, must be accounted for in that communality within which an individual finds himself. No ego is an island to itself. Throughout life the establishment and maintenance of that strength which can reconcile discontinuities and ambiguities depends on the support of parental as well as communal models. For youth depends on the ideological coherence of the world it is meant to take over, and therefore is sensitively aware of whether the system is strong enough in its traditional form to "confirm" and to be confirmed by the identity process, or so rigid or brittle as to suggest renovation, reformation, or revolution. Psychosocial identity, then, also has a *psycho-historical* side, and suggests the study of how life histories are inextricably interwoven with history. The study of psychosocial identity, therefore, depends on three complementarities—or are they three aspects of one complementarity?—namely, the personal coherence of the individual and role integration in his group; his guiding images and the ideologies of his time; his life history—and the historical moment.

All this sounds probable enough and, especially when shorn of its unconscious dimension, appears to be widely, and sometimes faddishly, acceptable in our day. The unconscious complexities often ignored can be grouped thus:

1. Identity formation normatively has its dark and negative side, which throughout life can remain an unruly part of the total identity. Every person and every group harbors a *negative identity* as the sum of all those identifications and identity fragments which the individual had to submerge in himself as undesirable or irreconcilable or which his group has taught him to perceive as the mark of fatal "difference" in sex role or race, in class or religion. In the event of aggravated crises, an individual (or, indeed, a group) may despair of the ability to contain these negative elements in a positive identity. A specific rage can be aroused wherever identity development thus loses the promise of an assured wholeness: an as yet uncommitted delinquent, if denied any chance of communal integration, may become a "confirmed" criminal. In periods of collective crisis, such potential rage is shared by many and is easily exploited by psychopathic leaders, who become the models of a sudden surrender to total doctrines and dogmas in which the negative identity appears to be the desirable and the dominant one: thus the Nazis

fanatically cultivated what the victorious West as well as the more refined Germans had come to decry as "typically German." The rage aroused by threatened identity loss can explode in the arbitrary violence of mobs, or it can—less consciously—serve the efficient destructiveness of the machinery of oppression and war.

2. In some young people, in some classes, at some periods in history, the personal identity crisis will be noiseless and contained within the rituals of passage marking a second birth; while in other people, classes, and periods, the crisis will be clearly marked off as a critical period intensified by collective strife or epidemic tension. Thus, the nature of the identity conflict often depends on the latent panic or, indeed, the intrinsic promise pervading a historical period. Some periods in history become identity vacua caused by the three basic forms of human apprehension: *fears* aroused by new facts, such as discoveries and inventions (including weapons), which radically expand and change the whole world image; *anxieties* aroused by symbolic dangers vaguely perceived as a consequence of the decay of existing ideologies; and, in the wake of disintegrating faith, the *dread* of an existential abyss devoid of spiritual meaning. But then, again, a historical period may (as, for example, the American Revolution did) present a singular chance for a collective renewal which opens up unlimited identities for those who, by a combination of unruliness, giftedness, and competence, represent a new leadership, a new elite, and new types rising to dominance in a new people.

If there *is* something to all this, why would insights concerning such universal matters first come from psychoanalysis, a clinical science? The fact is that in all periods of history, mental disturbances of epidemiological significance or special fascination highlight a specific aspect of man's nature in conflict with "the times" and are met with by innovative insights: as happened to hysteria in Freud's early days. In our time, a state of *identity confusion*, not abnormal in itself, often seems to be accompanied by all the neurotic or near psychotic symptoms to which a young person is prone on the basis of constitution, early fate, and malignant circumstance. In fact, young individuals are subject to a more malignant disturbance than might have manifested itself during other stages of life, precisely because the adolescent process can induce the individual semi-deliberately to give in to some of his most regressed or repressed tendencies in order, as it were, to test rock bottom and to recover some of his as yet undeveloped childhood strengths. This, however, is safe only where a relatively stable society provides collective experiences of a ceremonial character, or where revolutionary leaders (such as Luther) provide new identity guidelines which permit the adolescent individual to take chances with himself. Historical crises, in turn, aggravate personal crises; and, indeed, many young people have in the recent past been judged to suffer from a chronic malignant disturbance, where we now know that an aggravated developmental crisis was dominant. This, then, is the clinical anchorage for the conception of an identity crisis.

To make the emergence of this clinical conception plausible in terms of my field and of my life, I will now give an account of my clinical training, and then describe my origins. Here I will be descriptive in order to let the cast of contending identity elements announce themselves.

I am about two years younger than the twentieth century, and I therefore can speak roughly of the decades of my life as coinciding with those of the calendar. I was graduated from the Vienna Psychoanalytic Institute in my (and the century's) early thirties.

The very beginning of my career marks me as one of those workers in my field who had quite heterogeneous professional origins. I was an artist before I studied psychoanalysis, and can otherwise boast only of a Montessori diploma. Psychology as such did not attract me. In fact, if William James could say that the first lecture in psychology he ever took was the first one he gave, I must concede that the first course in psychology I ever took was also the first (and the last) I flunked. But, for reasons to be given presently, I was attracted to and became acceptable to the Vienna Psychoanalytic Institute, which was the training arm of a private society not connected with and often opposed and belittled by both academic departments and professional organizations in that city, and beyond. Although Sigmund Freud was a doctor and medical school lecturer, he had taken it upon himself to create a new tradition in the selection of the original circle of men and women (most of them medically trained, some not) who had been willing to learn his methods according to his prescription. For this, they had to be prepared by a general erudition and gifted with a certain rare perceptiveness for the nonrational; which means that they had to be both sane enough to survive such dangerous dealings with the uncharted inner world and just "odd" enough to *want* to study it. For them, Freud had created simultaneously a training institute, a clientele, a publishing house, and, of course, a new professional identity.

The truly transforming scientific and therapeutic orientation created by Freud had been based on a radical change in the concept of the role and the self-perception of the healer as well as of the patient. If the "classical" hysterical patients, as Freud had concluded, were far from being the degenerates they were judged to be by his medical contemporaries, he could only conclude that the authoritative methods used to cure them violated what alone can in fact free a person from inner bondage—namely, the conscious acceptance of certain truths about himself and others. He advocated that the psychoanalytic practitioner himself undergo treatment so as to come to terms with his own unconscious and to acquire the capacity to explain, and not to evade or to condemn. The "analysand," whether patient or trainee, was asked to verbalize all his available thought processes, and thus to become co-observer as well as client; while the analyst, as observer, continued to observe himself as he observed the patient's trend of thought. They were thus to become collaborators in the job of becoming conscious of (and of learning to verbalize) that reservoir of unconscious imagery and affect which soon proved not only to be festering in individual patients but also to have been repressed in all past history by the whole race—except for seers and prophets, dramatists and philosophers. The atmosphere thus created in the Vienna circle was one of intense mutual loyalty and a deep devotion to a truly liberating idea, if often also of deeply ambivalent mental upset. Here much fascinating material is awaiting the historian who manages to become a historian of ideas and to resist the temptation merely to turn early psychoanalysis against itself in a polemic manner.

My own training psychoanalysis was conducted by Anna Freud, who accepted me as a fellowship candidate on the basis of the fact that she and her friends had witnessed my work with children both as a private tutor and as a teacher in a small private school. Anna Freud had founded the Vienna version of the subspecialty of child analysis, and I, too, was to be primarily trained as a psychoanalyst of children, although such training included the supervised treatment of adolescent and adult patients. The reader will appreciate the complex feelings aroused by the fact that my psychoanalyst was the daughter of the then already mythical founder, who was apt to appear in the door of their common waiting room in order to invite his analysand into his study. But this is only one special circumstance within the peculiar bonds and burdens of a training psychoanalysis. While such a preparation is of the essence in this kind of work, and while this essence can up to a point be comprehended in a systematic and disciplined way, it stands to reason that the generational succession of teachers, so important in all fields, will remain a specific treasure and a specific burden in the life of the maturing psychoanalyst—including the conceptualizations he may later feel called upon to confirm or to disavow. Even the most venerable training psychoanalyst is (and must be) experienced both as a liberating agent and as a potential indoctrinator, as an identity model and yet also as a powerful personality from whom one must learn to differentiate oneself. For in all pursuits which attempt to gain a rational foothold in man's pervasive irrationality, insights retain an unconscious significance which can only be clarified by lifelong maturation.

The systematic clinical acquaintance with the unconscious can convey a certain ceaseless surprise about the creative order that governs affects never before faced and a certain sense of liberated sanity just because of the chaos experienced. This is probably hard to comprehend except through the experience itself; and yet some of it must be visible in the impact of psychoanalysis on other fields and in the augmented access it has provided to a wealth of data previously not envisaged or not comprehended. Considering the revolutionary ingredients of such data, it should not be surprising that it will take generations to find proper forms of verification as well as the range and limits of application, which, in turn, will lead to transformations in the professional identity of the psychoanalyst. In the meantime, it may be possible also to see analogies between this novel training situation, extreme in what we may call a *disciplined subjectivity*, and more or less latent interpersonal factors in more objectively scientific courses of study.

But before I continue my account of psychoanalytic training as I experienced it, I must come to the question of how a wandering artist and teacher came to find in it an occupational identity and a field for the use of his given capacities. Here it must be said first that in the Europe of my youth, the choice of the occupational identity of "artist" meant, for many, a way of life rather than a specific occupation—or, indeed, a way of making a living—and, as today, it could mean primarily an anti-establishment way of life. Yet, the European establishment had created a well-institutionalized social niche for such idiosyncratic needs. A certain adolescent and neurotic shiftlessness could be con-

tained in the custom of *Wanderschaft;* and if the individual had
some gifts into the bargain, he could convince himself and others
that he should have a chance to demonstrate that he might have
a touch of genius. There were, of course, youth movements with
varying political and religious involvement for those who wanted
to abandon themselves to some collective utopia or political
ideology; but much of what young people today display in
alienated and concerned groups was then more commonly experienced in an isolation shared only with a few like-minded
friends. To be an artist, then, meant to have at least a passing
identity, and I had enough talent to consider it for a while an
occupational one. The trouble was, I often had a kind of work
disturbance and needed time. *Wanderschaft* under those conditions meant neurotic drivenness as well as deliberate search,
even as today dropping out can be a time either of tuning in or
of aimless negativism. But somehow, when we did not work, we
had a deep and trusting relationship (often called "romantic"
today) to what was still a peasants' Nature; we kept physically
fit by interminable hiking; we trained our senses to changing
perspectives, and our thoughts to distilled passages of, say, Ange-
lus Silesius and Lao-tse, Nietzsche and Schopenhauer, which we
carried in our knapsacks. I will not describe the pathological
side of my identity confusion, which included disturbances for
which psychoanalysis seemed, indeed, the treatment of choice;
no doubt such disturbances assumed at times what some of us
today would call a "borderline" character—that is, the borderline between neurosis and adolescent psychosis. But then, it is
exactly this kind of diagnosis to which I later undertook to give
a developmental perspective by calling it an aggravated identity
crisis of varying diagnostic types. No doubt, my best friends
will insist that I needed to name this crisis and to see it in everybody else in order to really come to terms with it in myself.
And they could, indeed, quote a whole roster of problems
related to my *personal* identity.

There is first of all the question of origin, which often looms large in individuals who are driven to be original. I grew up in Karlsruhe in southern Germany as the son of a pediatrician, Dr. Theodor Homburger, and his wife Karla, née Abrahamsen, a native of Copenhagen, Denmark. All through my earlier childhood, they kept secret from me the fact that my mother had been married previously; and that I was the son of a Dane who had abandoned her before my birth. They apparently thought that such secretiveness was not only workable (because children then were not held to know what they had not been told) but also advisable, so that I would feel thoroughly at home in their home. As children will do, I played in with this and more or less forgot the period before the age of three, when mother and I had lived alone. Then her friends had been artists working in the folk style of Hans Thoma of the Black Forest. They, I believe, provided my first male imprinting before I had to come to terms with that intruder, the bearded doctor, with his healing love and mysterious instruments. Later, I enjoyed going back and forth between the painters' studios and our house, the first floor of which, in the afternoons, was filled with tense and trusting mothers and children. My sense of being "different" took refuge (as it is apt to do even in children without such acute life problems) in fantasies of how I, the son of much better parents, had been altogether a foundling. In the meantime, however, my adoptive father was anything but the proverbial stepfather. He had given me his last name (which I have retained as a middle name) and expected me to become a doctor like himself.

Identity problems sharpen with that turn in puberty when images of future roles become inescapable. My stepfather was the only professional man (and a highly respected one) in an intensely Jewish small bourgeois family, while I (coming from a racially mixed Scandinavian background) was blond and blue-eyed, and grew flagrantly tall. Before long, then, I was referred to as "goy" in my stepfather's temple; while to my schoolmates I was a "Jew." Although during World War I, I tried desperately to be a good German chauvinist, I became a "Dane" when Denmark remained neutral.

The general setting was that of an old state capital of a Lutheran principality (we lived on the castle square) with a sizable Catholic population. I do not remember having been interested in the old Luther of the state church or, for that matter, in the young one; and yet years later I was to choose young Luther as a matter of course for the presentation of some views on youth and history. At the time, like other youths with artistic or literary aspirations, I became intensely alienated from everything my bourgeois family stood for. At that point, I *set out* to be different. After graduation from the type of high school called a humanistic *Gymnasium* (where one then acquired a thorough classical *Bildung* and a true sense for languages), I went to art school, but always again took to wandering. I now consider those years an important part of my training. Sketching (as even a man like William James experienced) can be a fundamental exercise in tracing impressions. And I enjoyed making very large woodprints: to cut stark images of nature on this primary material conveyed an elemental sense of both art and craft. And in those days every self-respecting stranger in his own (northern) culture drifted sooner or later to Italy, where endless time was spent soaking up the southern sun and the ubiquitous sights with their grand blend of artifact and nature. I was a "Bohemian" then.

If this was a "moratorium," it certainly was also a period of total neglect of the military, political, and economic disasters then racking mankind: as long as one could expect some financial support from home, and did not perish in some cataclysm, one lived (or so one thought) by the measure of centuries, not of decades. Such cultural and personal narcissism obviously could be a generation's and, certainly, a young person's downfall unless he found a compelling idea—that is, one with minute meaning for everyday life as well as for the history of ideas—and the stamina to work for it.

It was my friend Peter Blos (who also was to become a psy-choanalyst and who is now so widely known for his classical writings on adolescence [2]) who came to my rescue in my late twenties. During our youth in Karlsruhe, he had shared his father with me—a doctor both prophetic and eccentric (he first told us about Gandhi)—and we had been friends in Florence. Now he invited me, with the encouragement of the founder, Dorothy Burlingham, to join him in that small school in Vienna, which he led. With his help, I learned to work regular hours, and I met the circle around Anna Freud—and Freud.

It must be more obvious now what Freud came to mean to me, although, of course, I would not have had words for it at the time. Here was a mythical figure and, above all, a great doctor who had rebelled against the medical profession. Here also was a circle which admitted me to the kind of training that came as close to the role of a children's doctor as one could possibly come without going to medical school. What, in me, responded to this situation was, I think, some strong identifica-tion with my stepfather, the pediatrician, mixed with a search for my own mythical father. And if I ask myself in what spirit I accepted my truly astounding adoption by the Freudian circle, I can only surmise (not without embarrassment) that it was a kind of positive stepson identity that made me take for granted that I should be accepted where I did not quite belong. By the same token, however, I had to cultivate not-belonging and keep contact with the artist in me; my psychoanalytic identity there-fore was not quite settled until much later, when, with the help of my American wife, I became a writing psychoanalyst—if in a language which, again, had not been my own.

But as I ask myself once more how an artist and teacher could find a place in a clinical and scientific movement so in-tensely verbal, three impressions stand out. One is that my first acquaintance with the psychoanalytic view of childhood coin-cided with a period of daily contact with children, and my first study of dreams with the observation of children's play. And children, the moment one learns to listen and to look while facilitating their self-expression in word and play, express matters of utmost complexity for adults with configurational directness. Secondly, I soon detected in Freud's writings vivid manifestations of an indomitable visual curiosity, which sent him hurrying to Italy and through her city squares and museums whenever his work permitted. His description of his patients' memories and dreams also reveal that he deeply empathized with their imagery before he entered what he had heard and seen into the context of verbal nomenclature. And, finally, I remember something that Anna Freud said once, rather early in the game. To quote one's analyst is always beset with hazards of self-deception, but this memory seems genuine. When I declared once more that I could not see a place for my artistic inclinations in such high intellectual endeavors, she said quietly: "You might help to make them see." As I continue with a conceptual account of my training, this simple mandate must be assumed to shine through the (to me) often obscure attempts to make a science out of the data observed in the psychoanalytic setting. When, several decades later, I wrote my first book (*Childhood and Society*), I think I found that clinical writing lent itself to artistic as well as theoretical expression.

But to return briefly to the stepson theme: one might suspect that later on I had to succeed in making a professional life style out of my early existence on what Paul Tillich has described as a life on boundaries, for throughout my career I worked in institutional contexts for which I did not have the usual credentials—except, of course, for my psychoanalytic training proper. But, as pointed out, psychoanalysis then almost methodically attracted and collected at least a few men and women who did not quite belong elsewhere, and some of my most outstanding colleagues had followed similarly improvised life plans. What is to be demonstrated here, then, is not singularity of either deviation or achievement, but the configurational affinity of life history and the history of professions.

However, I must also acknowledge the dangers of such a course of life, both for a person's character and for his concepts. That a stepson's negative identity is that of a bastard need only be acknowledged here in passing—and by myself. But a habitual stepson might also use his talents to avoid belonging anywhere quite irreversibly; working between the established fields can mean avoiding the disciplines necessary for any one field; and, being enamored with the aesthetic order of things, one may well come to avoid their ethical and political as well as their methodological implications. If one can find all these weaknesses in my work, there are also some pervasive attempts to counteract them, and this exactly in a conceptual turn to social and historical implications and—possibly inspired by my great compatriot Kierkegaard's differentiation of the aesthetic and the ethical life—to religious actualists such as Luther and Gandhi.

That much about the themes I recognize as reaching from my childhood into my professional identity. If it seems all too obvious, however, that such an early life would predispose a person to a severe identity crisis, this must be said to be only partially true; for in my instance the more obvious identity conflicts concerned my *personal* identity and *psychosocial* choices which were relatively clearly delineated. If the malignancy of the identity crisis is determined both by defects in a person's early relationship to his mother and by the incompatibility or irrelevance of the values available in adolescence, I must say that I was fortunate in both respects. Even as I remember the mother of my early years as pervasively sad, I also visualize her as deeply involved in reading what I later found to have been such authors as Brandes, Kierkegaard, and Emerson, and I could never doubt that her ambitions for me transcended the conventions which she, nevertheless, faithfully served. On the other hand, she and my stepfather had the fortitude to let me find my way unhurriedly in a world which, for all the years of war and revolution, still seemed oriented toward traditional alternatives, and in which threatening cataclysms could still be ascribed to the episodic transgressions of criminal men and evil nations or classes. What I eventually came to describe as the malignant forms of identity crisis, both in groups and in individuals, was probably of quite a different order from what we then experienced. All the warring ideologies of my young years harbored some saving scheme which was to dominate forever after just one more war, just one more revolution, just one more New Deal. It is only in our lifetime that faith in change has gradually given way to a widespread fear of and superficial adjustment to change itself —and a suspiciousness concerning faith itself. Identity problems and even the symptoms of identity confusion have changed accordingly. At any rate, the comparative study of the nature of identity crises at different periods of history (and in different groups during the same period) may well turn out to be a historical as well as a clinical tool, provided that the uses of such concepts are themselves submitted to historical scrutiny.

During the years of my training, Freud no longer taught and never appeared at public functions. I sometimes met him in the Burlinghams' house or garden, or, one summer, on mushroom hunts on the Semmering, but rarely addressed him—not only out of shyness and conventional deference, but because of the pain that all attempts at speaking seemed to cause him. He was in his early seventies; a radical upper jaw operation had done away with a cancerous affliction years before, but the "infernal prosthesis" which covered the roof of his mouth led to repeated fresh outbreaks and fresh operations. His daughter also functioned as a combination of nurse and private secretary, intellectual companion and ambassador, both to the old guard of the psychoanalytic movement and, on rare ceremonial occasions, to the public. Some of the writings which Freud published during these years were of a markedly philosophical bent, or what the Germans call *weltanschaulich*. In his *Autobiographical Study*,[3] which he wrote in his sixty-eighth year (about the age, it seems, for reminiscing), he himself ascribed this trend to "a phase of regressive development" reverting back to his pre-medical and, in fact, adolescent interest in the problems of culture—or, rather, *Kultur*. Theoretically, it all culminated in the concept of the *death instinct*—a grandiose contradiction in terms, and yet an acknowledgment of the all-enveloping duality of life and death, otherwise (until recently) neglected in psychoanalysis.

At that time in Vienna, all training took place in the evenings in what today might be called a free psychiatric university. Again, only those who have attended similarly autonomous study groups of men and women serving what they feel to be a truly transforming idea—and serving at a sacrifice of income, professional status, and mental peace—will know of the devotional atmosphere in which no clinical detail was too small and no theoretical insight too big to merit intensive presentation and debate. Clinical writings rarely reflect the high degree of common sense and humane humor pervading the joint study of ongoing treatments and the regular and exhaustive comparison of treatment histories. Clinical conferences close to the data are the heart of the matter, for they freely reflect the interplay of the therapist's and the patient's mentalities. Nowhere is the art in the clinical art-and-science more apparent.

At the same time, our training continued to impress on us in all their clinical immediacy the five conceptions which Freud in the same autobiographical study had called "the principal constituents of psychoanalysis." These five have remained fundamental to theory and psychoanalytic technique and thus to the clinical study of identity problems as well. The most fundamental is *inner resistance*, a term which was never meant to be judgmental in the sense of an inner recalcitrance or of a conscious lack of cooperation. Some memories and thoughts are unconsciously "resisted" even by one who has every reason to recover them, whether out of personal despair or out of scientific curiosity. For such inner resistance, Freud blamed *repression*, a defensive quality of the organized mind which marks the *unconscious* as much more than simply not conscious. In fact, if Freud found in his patients' symptoms repressed drives and wishes, memories and fantasies, he did so by recognizing complex symbolic disguises and imaginative elaborations which subsequently proved to be at the core of mythological and artistic creativity as well. His Victorian data, of course, permitted him a special access to what he called the *etiological significance of sexual life*—that is, the pathogenic power of repressed sexual impulses. He, of course, called "sexual" a wide assortment of impulses and affects never previously included in such designation. It was the burden of the libido theory to show how much in life is codetermined by derivatives of repressed and, indeed, sublimated infantile sexuality. Freud, therefore, considered systematic attention to the *importance of infantile experiences* an intrinsic part of his method and his theory: and we now know how his and Karl Abraham's first findings opened up a whole new view of the stages of life and, thus, of life histories.

I would add to these five points the prime importance of what Freud calls *transference*—that is, a universal tendency to experience another person (often unconsciously, of course) as reminiscent of an important figure of the preadult past as experienced *then*. Such transference serves the inadvertent reenactment of infantile and juvenile wishes and fears, hopes and apprehensions, and this always with a bewildering "ambivalence"—that is, a ratio of loving and hateful tendencies which may coincide dangerously or alternate radically.

All the mental qualities enumerated here as dominant aspects of the data observed in the psychoanalytic setting, however, must also be recognized in the observer's responses to such data —wherefore we also speak of the psychoanalyst's *countertransference* to his patient. Thus, a psychoanalytic science making the clinical encounter communicable, accountable, and classifiable is of a very special kind. Nevertheless, it is clear that such transferences (of childlike trust, or childish ambivalences), which in the training analysis and in clinical work move into the center of attention, also exist in daily life, and especially where work arrangements are the basis for intense experiences of leadership and followership and of fraternal or sororal rivalry. The question as to where and when such tensions support or hinder the inventiveness, solidarity, and altruism demanded of co-workers is a vital one. The answer seems to be that mutual emotional involvement, even of the kind called transference, can, under favorable conditions, evoke powers of parental and filial loyalty as well as ambivalence, and thus, when attached to ideological fidelity and equipped with competence, support personal growth and creative innovation. If psychoanalysis uses this power (David McClelland unhesitatingly calls it religious) for therapeutic purposes, it only puts to systematic use what Mircea Eliade [4] has described in primitive rites which seek rebirth in a return to origins: and Eliade rightly recognized a parallel in the (often quite ritualized) faith on which modern psychotherapy is founded.

This, however, does not justify the frequent assumption that psychoanalysis is primarily "faith healing." To Freud and his followers, the consulting room has always been not only a healer's sanctuary but also a psychologist's laboratory. For what was thus observed, one had to seek and find a classification, a terminology, and a methodology which would make therapeutic techniques increasingly adequate in dealing with a widening range of pathological conditions and would help formulate a body of insights amounting to a theory of human motivations. That in some of Freud's first co-workers idiosyncratic gifts as well as ideological predilections often seemed to obscure the ground plan for which he thought he alone had a firm sense of schedule—that is certainly not surprising. A truly historical study of these developments is still difficult, but it could throw much light on the influence of such personal passions and such residual pathology as those aroused when man's central motivations are submitted to observation and conceptualization. Yet it sometimes seems that such passions are never truly absent even from the most controlled laboratory work, especially when assumptions that have contributed to the stability of a classical world image are being questioned, and when the transformation of ideas becomes a matter of competition between individuals and schools.

Here it is interesting to note that (as I think Freud's letters to Fliess strongly suggest) his original metapsychology absorbed the methods of thinking acquired in medical training. Every student of psychotherapy is (or should be) impressed with the hiatus between the unfathomable richness of the data and the stingy parsimony of theorizing. Thus, our training made it incumbent on us to learn to "locate" any given clinical observation on a number of coordinates which Freud called "points of view." I have discussed these in greater detail in my account of the nature of clinical evidence.[5] Here I need only summarize these points of view: there is a *topographic* one which would "locate" a given item in a spatial model of the mind and its inner divisions. A *dynamic* point of view takes account of the energy conflicts between these inner domains. An *economic* point of view, in turn, attempts to conceptualize the householding of energy in man's instinctual life. Later, the *genetic* point of view permitted the reconstruction of the origin and the development of all these structures, functions, and energy distributions and thus, of course, contributes most to case history and life history. Although Freud called his points of view his *meta*-psychology and assigned to them a level of abstraction not accessible to direct observation, it is hard to overcome the impression that they had served as the bridge by which he, a fervent and painstaking medical researcher before he became the first psychoanalyst, could apply the traditional anatomical, physiological, pathological, and developmental modes of observation to the workings of the mind. As though the elemental sweep of his discoveries had aroused a sense of hybris in the medical researcher, he seems to have determined, in his metapsychology, to reconnect his vast findings with the disciplined thought patterns which in his young manhood had commanded his fidelity and helped establish his occupational identity. It is often overlooked that even his preoccupation with an all-pervasive libido was related to a scientific commitment to think in terms of energies "equal in dignity" to the forces found in physics and in chemistry. On their neurological home ground, however, such modes of thinking had been based on visible, observable, and verifiable facts, while in the study of the mind they sooner or later served, especially in the hands of dogmatic followers, as unchecked reifications—as if the "libido" or the "ego" had, after all, become measurable entities.

The intellectual milieu governing the many evenings spent in small intensive seminars (and some were so small that we could comfortably meet in our teachers' homes) is best characterized by a listing of these teachers. All but the first two later came to this country to preside over the strange fate of a psychoanalysis that in exile became influential in medical training, lucrative in practice, and popularized in the media.

My training in child analysis took place in the famous *Kinderseminar* led by Anna Freud; that in the treatment of juvenile disturbances (including delinquency) was directed by August Aichhorn. Helene Deutsch and Edward Bibring supervised my first adult cases. Heinz Hartmann was the leading theoretician, and his thinking, which later culminated in his monograph on the adaptive function of the ego, influenced me deeply. Anna Freud's clarification of the defensive mechanisms employed by the ego against the drives [6] and Hartmann's explorations of the ego's adaptive response to the environment challenged theoretical thinking at the time.[7] One of the most obscure and yet fascinating teachers was Paul Federn, and it is possible that in his seminar on the boundaries of the ego I first heard the term "identity" mentioned in one of its earlier usages. The preoccupation with the ego was then replacing that earlier attention to the id which was based on Freud's original determination to find the whole extent of man's enslavement to sexuality.

What survived from that first period was a strangely ascetic preoccupation with all the big and small manifestations of Eros, a kind of intellectual bacchanalia. Nothing seemed to be further from the mind of those early workers (not even the followers of Wilhelm Reich) than that psychoanalysis might someday be used as an argument for sexual license outside the rules of a rationally enlightened bourgeoisie or, for that matter, some new proletarian convention. Both Reich and, as visitor, Siegfried Bernfeld, who was deeply involved in problems of youth, I remember as very inspiring teachers already then driven to a certain tragic isolation by their belief that Freud's "libido," which sounded so tangibly quantitative, would *have* to be found and isolated physiologically. On the other hand, the student could not help sensing in the didactic milieu a growing conservatism and especially a subtle yet pervasive interdiction of certain trends of thought. This concerned primarily any idea which might be reminiscent of the deviations perpetrated by those earliest and most brilliant of Freud's co-workers (such as Rank, Adler, and especially Jung) who had been separated from the movement before World War I. In other words, the psychoanalytic movement was now already working under the impact of its own prehistoric trauma, its own rebellion against the father-founder. The possible merits and decisive demerits of those deviations the student could not judge.

I must admit that, after such intense training under such complex conditions, the idea of moving on and working independently seemed an invigorating as well as politically advisable idea. Vienna at that time chose not to foresee the power of National-Socialist advances, not to speak of the total disruption that would soon separate the regions of Europe, as well as the old country and the New World. And if I should now briefly indicate what rather vague uncertainty and curiosity I took with me when my graduation coincided with my emigration from

Europe, I would grievously oversimplify it in the following way. Psychoanalysis had broken through to much that had been totally neglected or denied in all previous models of man: it had turned *inward* to open up man's inner world, and especially the unconscious, to systematic study; it searched *backward* to the ontogenetic origins of the mind and of its disturbances; and it pressed *downward* into those instinctual tendencies which man thought he had overcome when he repressed or denied the infancy of individuals, the primitivity of man's beginnings—and evolution. That (as Darwin, too, had discovered) was the territory to be conquered, the origins to be acknowledged. But conquerors so easily lose themselves in the discoveries of the new territory; how to reassimilate them to what is already known— that is the job of the second stage. The question remained, I felt dimly, whether an image of man reconstructed primarily on the basis of observation and reconstruction in the clinical laboratory might not lack what, in man's total existence, leads *outward* from self-centeredness to the mutuality of love and communality, *forward* from the enslaving past to the utopian anticipation of new potentialities, and *upward* from the unconscious to the enigma of consciousness. All of this, however, seemed to me always implicit in Freud's own writings: if not in the shifting focus of his grim pursuit, then in the grand style of its communication—the style for which, in those very days, he received the Goethe Prize as the best scientific writer in the German language.

To Freud, the *via regia* to mental life had been the dream. For me, children's play became the first *via regia* to an understanding of growing man's conflicts and triumphs, his repetitive working through of the past, and his creative self-renewal in truly playful moments. I identified with Freud, then, not so much as the former laboratory worker who insisted on a terminology made for the observation of transformable quantities of drive enlivening inner structures, but as the discerner of verbal and visual configurations which revealed what consciousness wanted to enlarge upon, and what it attempted to disguise—and revealed. To put it bluntly, I have always suspected (maybe because I do not really understand these things) that what sounded most scientific in psychoanalysis in terms of nineteenth-century physicalism was more scientism than science, even though I understood that psychology and social science, in attempting to free themselves from philosophy and theology, had no choice but to try, for a while, to think in the scientific imagery of the century. But Freud's phenomenological and literary approach, which seemed to reflect the very creativity of the unconscious, held in itself a promise without which psychoanalytic theory would have meant little to me. This may be one reason why, in later years, I proved inept in theoretical discussion and was apt to neglect ruefully the work of my colleagues—and not only where they seemed to take Freud at his most atomistic and mechanical word, or where they turned neo-Freudian. All this may well have an admixture of a particular and maybe peculiar identification with Freud's freedom and enjoyment of inquiry. But then, he was the father of it all—a fact which I probably tried to objectify in my later studies of great men, as well as in a few essays on Freud himself.[8]

I was barely graduated, then, when I settled in this country to begin private practice, eager to see what I could do by myself —although by no means alone. For in Vienna I had met and married Joan Serson—Canadian-born, American-trained—then a dancer and teacher, later also a craftswoman and writer; she, too, had taught in our small school. At about the time when Hitler came to power in Germany, we had left Vienna for Copenhagen. I had first attempted to regain my Danish citizenship and to help establish a psychoanalytic training center in Copenhagen. When this proved then impractical, we had emigrated to the United States and settled in Boston, where a psychoanalytic society had been founded the year before. Since my graduation in Vienna had made me a member of the International Psychoanalytic Association, I was welcomed in the American association as well. Although the medical professionalization of psychoanalysis in the United States would soon thereafter lead to the exclusion of further non-medical candidates from training, I remained one of the few non-medical members, hoping that the quiet contributions of non-physicians would sooner or later impress American psychoanalysts with the wisdom of Freud's conviction that this field should not be entirely subordinated to medical professionalism. Personally, I was, of course, ready to abide by the medical and legal cautions necessary in therapeutic work; and I cannot say that my being a non-physician has ever interfered with my work.

In fact, to an immigrant with a desirable specialty (and the term "immigrant" had not yet given way to "refugee"), this country proved, indeed, a land of unlimited possibilities. Harvard, and later Yale, did not hesitate to provide medical school appointments, and thus a vastly expanded clinical experience. At Harvard there was Harry Murray's Psychological Clinic, where an intensive study of students proved a valuable guide to the characteristics and values of American academic youth, while Murray's style of thinking conveyed something of the grand tradition of William James. And there was a flowering of interdisciplinary groups, led and financed by imaginative men like Lawrence K. Frank of the General Education Board and Frank Fremont-Smith of the Josiah Macy, Jr., Foundation, and vigorously inspired by such wide-ranging observers as Margaret Mead and Kurt Lewin. Each participant was expected to make himself understood at these small and intense meetings, and I think that this also taught me (as I slowly learned to speak and write in English) to address myself to an interdisciplinary audience, an effort which, in turn, may have had some influence on my choice of concepts. After World War II, we made contact again with receptive colleagues from all over Europe in the Child Study Group of the World Health Organization—men such as Julian Huxley, Konrad Lorenz, and Jean Piaget—while

Alexander Mitscherlich invited me to return to the lost scene of my childhood: on Freud's one hundredth birthday, in 1956, I was to find myself addressing a new German youth, in the city of my birth, Frankfurt, in the presence of the scholar-president of Germany. The *Daedalus* conferences have since assumed the important role of interdisciplinary meetings in my professional life.

But let me sketch my deepening encounter with identity problems by summarizing the decades. In the thirties, I was first of all a practicing psychoanalyst, working primarily with children and making frequent excursions to clinical conferences in the medical area of Harvard. I did some graduate work in psychology on the side, but when the Yale Medical School gave me a full-time research appointment, I decided to weather the future without belated degrees. The Yale Institute of Human Relations offered then a remarkable interdisciplinary stimulation under the leadership of John Dollard; and my job permitted me my first field trip (with Scudder Mekeel) to the Sioux Indians in South Dakota. I spent the forties in California, having been invited to abstract the life histories of a cross section of Berkeley children then being studied in the Institute of Child Development, under the directorship of Jean MacFarlane. From there, I made my second field trip (with Alfred Kroeber) to the Yurok Indians in California. Later, having been appointed a training psychoanalyst, I resumed private practice in San Francisco, but continued to act as a consultant in various public clinics, including a veteran rehabilitation clinic toward the conclusion of World War II. My first professorship, in the University of California, Berkeley, was short-lived because of the loyalty oath controversy during the McCarthy era. As one of the few non-signers, I was fired before the first year was up, and after being reinstated as politically dependable, I resigned because of the firing of others who were not so judged. As I think back on that controversy now, it was a test of our American identity; for when the papers told us foreign-born among the non-signers to "go back where we came from," we suddenly felt quite certain that our apparent disloyalty to the soldiers in Korea was, in fact, quite in line with what they were said to be fighting for. The United States Supreme Court has since confirmed our point of view.

It would seem almost self-evident now how the concepts of "identity" and "identity crisis" emerged from my personal, clinical, and anthropological observations in the thirties and forties. I do not remember when I started to use these terms; they seemed naturally grounded in the experience of emigration, immigration, and Americanization. As I summed the matter up in my first book, which appeared in 1950:

We begin to conceptualize matters of identity at the very time in history when they become a problem. For we do so in a country which attempts to make a super-identity out of all the identities imported by its constituent immigrants; and we do so at a time when rapidly increasing industrialization threatens these essentially agrarian and patrician identities in their lands of origin as well.

The study of identity, then, becomes as strategic in our time as the study of sexuality was in Freud's time. Such historical relativity in the development of a field, however, does not seem to preclude consistency of ground plan and continued closeness to observable fact. Freud's findings regarding the sexual etiology of a mental disturbance are as true for our patients as they were for his; while the burden of identity loss which stands out in our considerations probably burdened Freud's patients as well as ours, as re-interpretations would show. Different periods thus permit us to see in temporary exaggeration different aspects of an essentially inseparable whole.[9]

Identity problems were in the mental baggage of generations of new Americans, who left their motherlands and fatherlands behind to merge their ancestral identities in the common one of self-made men. Emigration can be a hard and heartless matter, in terms of what is abandoned in the old country and what is usurped in the new one. Migration means cruel survival in identity terms, too, for the very cataclysms in which millions perish open up new forms of identity to the survivors. In retrospect, I had also recognized something of a national identity problem in that most surrounded great nation in Europe, once defeated and humiliated Germany, then hypnotized by a fanatically unadult leader promising a thousand years of unassailable super-identity.

In the Roosevelt era, we immigrants could tell ourselves that America was once more helping to save the Atlantic world from tyranny; and were we not hard at work as members of a healing profession which—beyond the living standards it accustomed us to—contributed to a transforming enlightenment apt to diminish both the inner and the outer oppression of mankind? What now demanded to be conceptualized, however, called for a whole new orientation which fused a new world image (and, in fact, a New World image) with traditional theoretical assumptions. I could not look at my patients' troubles any more in (what I later came to call) "originological" terms—that is, on the basis of where, when, and how "it all started." The question was also what world image they were sharing, where they were going from where they were, and who was going with them. And if something like an identity crisis gradually appeared to be a normative problem in adolescence and youth, there also seemed to be enough of an adolescent in every American to suggest that in this country's history fate had chosen to highlight identity questions together with a strangely adolescent style of adulthood—that is, one remaining expansively open for new roles and stances—in what at the time was called (as it had been at the very beginning of the republic) a "national character." This, incidentally, is not contradicted by the fact that today some young adults are forcefully questioning the nation as to what generations of Americans *have*, indeed, *made* of themselves by claiming so irreverently to be self-made; what, indeed, has become of their now old New World identity; and what they have made of their continent, of their technology, and of the world under their influence. But this also means that problems of identity become urgent wherever Americanization spreads, and that some of the young, especially in Americanized countries, begin to take seriously not only the stance of self-made men but also the question of adulthood, namely, how to *take care* of what is being appropriated in the establishment of an industrial identity.

At any rate, the variety of my clinical and "applied" observations now helped me to see a nexus of individual and history as well as of past and future: the Berkeley children, in the particular setting of their parents' Californization, could be seen approaching a special and yet also normative identity crisis, which seemed to be built into the human life plan. A different version of such a crisis, which then, in fact, seemed permanent, could be seen in the American Indians, whose expensive "reeducation" only made them fatalistically aware of the fact that they were denied both the right to remain themselves and the right to join America. I learned to see traumatically renewed identity crises in those returning veterans of World War II who had broken down with what were alternately called symptoms of shock or fatigue or of constitutional inferiority and malingering. And I could later, in the fifties, verify the symptoms of acute and aggravated identity confusion on my clinical home ground—that is, in the young patients of the Austen Riggs Center in the Berkshires, where I turned after the University of California debacle. There also I found my critic and friend David Rapaport, who professed to see a place for my concepts (in the conceptual vicinity of Heinz Hartmann's) in the edifice of psychoanalytic ego psychology [10]—but not without having added to the dynamic, structural, economic, and genetic points of view an "adaptive" one, relating the ego to the environment.

In the sixties, I suspended my clinical work in order to learn how to teach my whole conception of the life cycle—including the identity crisis—to people normatively very much in it: Harvard and Radcliffe undergraduates. I should emphasize here, however, that in my course at Harvard, identity crisis was always treated as one crisis embedded in a sequence of life stages

—from birth to death, or, as the students had it, "from bust to dust." But this is another chapter, as is the more systematic pursuit of historical problems by myself and by my colleagues during this decade, and the further search for the structure of the ideological world images which form the framework for all identities.

Clinical verification, as I have indicated, is always of the essence in any conceptual shift in psychoanalysis, because it confirms that (and why) a syndrome such as "identity confusion" is not just a matter of contradictory self-images or aspirations, roles or opportunities, but a central disturbance dangerous for the whole ecological interaction of a human person with the "environment"—and man's environment, after all, is nature transformed into a shared social universe.

Psychosocial identity thus proved to be "situated" in three orders in which man lives at all times.

1. The *somatic order*, by which an organism seeks to maintain its integrity in a continuous reciprocal adaptation of the *milieu intérieur* and other organisms.

2. The *personal order*—that is, the integration of "inner" and "outer" world in individual experience and behavior.

3. The *social order*, jointly maintained by personal organisms sharing a geographic-historical setting.

The methods by which each of these orders can be studied are, then, complementary to each other. Much of man's creative tension as well as his debilitating conflict will be seen to originate in their incomplete adjustment to each other. For these orders seem to wholly support each other only in utopian schemes; while man seeks forever the restorative means to correct, at intervals, the accrued dangers to health, sanity, or social order. The study of the identity crisis in adolescence, therefore, is strategic because this is the stage of life when the organism is at the height of its vitality and potency; the person must integrate wider perspectives and more intensive experience; and the social order must provide a renewed identity for its new members, in order to reaffirm—or to renew—its collective identity.

At this point, it must be rather apparent why the concept of identity crisis also helped me to recognize one of the transforming functions of the "great man" at a certain junction of history. As I put it in my book on young Luther: deeply and pathologically upset, but possessed both by the vision of a new (or renewed) world order and by the need (and the gift) to transform masses of men, such a man makes his individual "patienthood" representative of a universal one, and promises "to solve for all what he could not solve for himself alone."

Finally, after all the new insights that totalitarianism, nuclear warfare, and mass communication have forced us to face, it can no longer escape us that in all his past man has based his ideologies on mutually exclusive group identities in the form of "pseudo-species": tribe, nation, caste, region, class, and so on. The origin of man's identity problem thus is to be found in evolution itself. The question is: Will mankind realize that it is one species—or is it destined to remain divided into "pseudo-species" forever playing out one (necessarily incomplete) version of mankind against all the others until, in the dubious glory of the nuclear age, one version will have the power and the luck to destroy all others just moments before it perishes itself?

Psychoanalysis represents a very special admixture of "laboratory" conditions, methodological climate, and personal and ideological involvement. Other fields may claim to be governed by radically different admixtures and certainly by much less subjective kinds of evidence. But I wonder whether they could insist, at any time, on a total absence of any one of the ingredients described here.

II

Freud's Posthumous Publications: Reviews

An impressive photograph
exists of Sigmund Freud's arrival, on June 5, 1938, in a
Paris railroad station, en route to his exile in London.
Frail-looking, he is flanked by a maternally supportive
princess, Marie Bonaparte, and by a dapper American
ambassador, William C. Bullitt. Their appearance as
guardian angels is genuine, for both were highly influential in saving Freud and his closest family from
arrest and in securing permission for his emigration
from Nazi-occupied Vienna. If we see also an element of possessiveness in that splendid welcome, it
may only be because we now know that Marie
Bonaparte was then in possession of one of Freud's
posthumous works, his newly discovered letters and
memoranda to Wilhelm Fliess, first to be published
in German in 1950; and that Bullitt's files contained
a mysterious manuscript jointly begun by him and
Freud in 1930, and not to be published until 1967.
My original reviews of these two books follow here,
because the first one shows how, at the very time
when we came to face problems of identity, we had
to take new cognizance of Freud's loneliest years,
when he created what is now our profession; while
the second review records what happened to Freud's
first secret attempt to engage in a psycho-historical
analysis of a living political leader, Woodrow Wilson.

A HISTORIC FRIENDSHIP:
FREUD'S LETTERS TO FLIESS

THE TRANSLATION into English of Sigmund Freud's personal and scientific communications to Wilhelm Fliess * has now followed their publication in German. Where the German edition only allowed that this correspondence conveys something *out of* the beginnings of psychoanalysis, the translation is more bluntly titled *The Origins of Psycho-Analysis*. And, indeed, such directness is deserved, for these letters and drafts, in the words of the editors, "amplify the prehistory and early history of psychoanalysis in a way that no other available material does; provide insight into certain phases of Freud's intellectual processes from his first clinical impressions until the formulation of his theory; throw light on the blind alleys and wrong roads into which he was diverted in the process of hypothesis-building; and furnish a vivid picture of him in the difficult years during which his interest shifted from physiology and neurology to psychology and psychopathology." No reviewer could improve on the inclusiveness of this one-sentence preview; for better or for worse, he can only enlarge upon it.

The man who wrote these letters had indicated twice that he wished them destroyed: first by way of a pact with his correspondent, whose letters he himself did not preserve; and again when the letters, having survived Fliess's death and his family's emigration from Nazi Germany, found their way into the hands of one of the editors, Marie Bonaparte. She took them to Vienna, but, although she was in analysis with Freud at the time, determined to save them—first from him and then from the Nazis—by entrusting them (being a Danish princess by mar-

* Sigmund Freud. *The Origins of Psycho-Analysis. Letters to Wilhelm Fliess, Drafts and Notes: 1887–1902*, edited by Marie Bonaparte, Anna Freud, Ernst Kris. Authorized translation by Eric Mosbacher and James Strachey. Introduction by Ernst Kris. London: Imago Publishing Company, 1954; New York: Basic Books, 1954.

riage) to the Danish diplomatic service. As if to counteract their valiant revolt against Freud's wishes and probably because they shared his fear of undue publicity, the editors attempt to limit the readership and to determine the use of this volume by suggesting in their preface that the material here released "contains nothing sensational." To the English translation they add a special paragraph warning the (American?) reader that these letters, like earlier revelations concerning Freud's life, lay bare only "certain aspects of his interests and preoccupations at the time," and certainly not his life's "secrets." In the meantime, however, Ernest Jones, in his official biography, has made extensive use of these letters, offering his own translation and unhesitatingly calling the correspondence dramatic and the friendship revealed in it "the only really extraordinary experience in Freud's life." [1] In the face of these (and other) contradictory evaluations, the appearance of the English translation provides us with an opportunity to take stock, once more, of the kind of material which this book puts before the world, and particularly before the worker in the field.

About 450 pages long, the book contains a lengthy introduction by Ernst Kris, about 250 pages of letters, and 150 pages of scientific "drafts," including a major "project": a "Psychology for Neurologists." Kris's introduction is most scholarly and restrained, offering essential background material on both Fliess's and Freud's life situations and scientific development and previewing the material in the light of what subsequently became of psychoanalysis. In establishing the connection between Freud's early struggles and more recent developments in psychoanalysis, the introduction somewhat prejudices this basic material: it is as if one introduced an account of Columbus' embarkation on the *Santa Maria* with a description of Manhattan. The reader does well to keep his mind fresh for the full impact of black nights on uncharted seas: "Instead of the passage we are seeking, we may find oceans, to be fully explored by those who come after us."

Of the original items of the correspondence, 284 in all, we are

permitted to see 168. Ernest Jones, who has seen them all, reassures us that "the letters and the passages omitted in publication refer to uninteresting details about arranging meetings, news
about the health of various relatives and patients, some details of
the efforts Freud made to follow Fliess's 'law of periods,' and a
number of remarks about [Freud's early collaborator] Breuer
which show that Freud harboured more vigorously critical opinions about him than had generally been supposed" (Jones, p.
288).

The letters and drafts published are all Freud's; Fliess's answers can, on occasion, be surmised, not more. Kris compares
the reader's experience to listening in on one party's contribution
to an animated telephone conversation. And indeed, although the
dates indicate long and eventful intervals between some of the
letters, their simple sequence creates a special temptation for the
psychoanalyst, namely, to follow his occupational habit of reading and treating even such a one-sided record as if it were a
set of free associations, and this all the more so since these letters
and drafts *are* governed by great freedom in the description of
moods and in improvisations of thought. I will give some examples later; here I want to underscore the fact that this is part
of an exchange of letters. A correspondence of long standing is
a *rituel à deux*. It develops and cultivates particular levels of
mood, selected confessions, and habitual admissions; it is apt to
indulge in expressions of admiration and even plaintive comparison with the unseen recipient's person or fate, and, of course, in
fervent hopes for a reunion; in other words, it invites some kind
of mutual correspondence transference. All of this, of course,
varies with the meaning of personal mail, that great achievement
of intimacy over space and time. At any rate, some of the passion of intellectual intimacy and some of the mutual aggrandize-
ment notable in these letters must be acknowledged as familiar
features of intellectual correspondence of the past centuries.

This particular correspondence was, furthermore, subsidiary
to another *rituel à deux* developed by the two men, namely, to

what they called their "congresses." After detailed preparations and with much anticipation, they would get together in some city or town where long and leisurely walks (*Spaziergänge*) would add ambulatory vigor and visual perspective to the intense controversies and the intimate meeting of minds. Plans, tastes, and feelings would be exchanged in intimate and yet undoubtedly again clearly circumscribed areas. The correspondence thus promises to reveal new aspects of Freud only to the extent to which it challenges the analyst to study correspondence as a medium of communication and to understand intellectual friendship as a traditional and highly important form of sublimated homoeroticism. The letters present us with a truer or clearer picture of Freud only to the extent to which we are able to recognize in them a correspondence personality of an almost deliberate moodiness, indulgent dependence, and radical self-doubt, which (as both Jones's biography and Freud's published dreams indicate) overlapped with but did not wholly characterize either Freud's actions or even his dream life at the time. These letters, then, stand somewhere between the relative transparency of Freud's published dreams and the formal discipline of his other writings. They are characterized, as are other of Freud's many utterances, by that frank and playful deliberateness with which he could immerse himself in any form of communication, with himself or with others, and by that zestful curiosity with which he would follow new perspectives.

These are general impressions. The reviewer chooses as his theme an elaboration of the way in which this correspondence between intellectual friends is, on Freud's part, drawn into a radically new kind of interchange, a specifically psychoanalytic style of awareness.

The introduction by Ernst Kris, and the papers of Bernfeld to which he refers, indicate that Freud, at the age of thirty, simultaneously needed a new colleague, a new friend, and a new ideal. He had married only a year before and had, for financial reasons, abandoned the academic laboratory for the private office; he was, for the first time, self-employed. To give up the laboratory meant to relinquish a work discipline and a work ideology to which he had been deeply committed. When, at the age of seventeen, Freud had chosen medicine in preference to law and politics, he had done so with a nature-philosophic passion for which he found what is known as Goethe's "Ode to Nature" representative: the unveiling of nature's mysteries, not the healing of the sick, provided the first self-image as a doctor. But soon he had, as many bright young people must do, become deeply committed to less fanciful and more ascetic pursuits, of which men like Brücke and Meynert were the masters: pursuits of an almost monastic service to painstaking physicalistic physiology. The ideology of this important movement was represented in the oath "to put in power this truth: No other forces than the common physical chemical ones are active within the organism . . . One has either to find the specific way or form of their action by means of the physical mathematical method, or to assume new forces equal in dignity to the chemical physical forces inherent in matter." When, at age thirty, Freud was forced to exchange the academic monastery for the medical parsonage, he had fully developed a style of work, a manner of publication, and a personal bearing which would have sufficed for an impressively productive, if maybe not creatively unique, lifetime. The letters make clear that now, in abandoniug pure science, Freud left a whole future (or, as we would say today, a professional identity) behind him; and, since we know so little about the ego's relation to early work commitments, we may well pay attention to the symptomatic unrest which ensued.

But now what later would appear to have been a prolonged moratorium, a delay of destined career which characterizes the beginnings of many a creative worker, was over, and for the moment Freud found himself, of all things, a practicing specialist in the neurotherapeutic methods of his day. This role was compatible neither with the ideal of the researcher, committed to the point of "therapeutic nihilism" to an ascetic devotion to truth, nor with that other ideal which Freud now mourned as irretrievably missed, namely, the general practice of medicine with its Hippocratic attention to "the whole patient" (57). The not quite either-or role of a practicing specialist, chosen for purposes of making a living where a Jewish doctor could expect one, was not in agreement with what Freud called his need for an inner tyrant; i.e., a great principle and its total work discipline.

Freud had been closely associated with one man to whom he liked to refer as a "practicing physician," a man who had, in fact, taught him how to find a laboratory in the very practice of neurology: Breuer. But just at that time the bond with Breuer, for a variety of reasons, was weakening. Breuer had been able to follow Freud in his speculations regarding the sexual nature of hysterical disturbances only because of the respectable assumption of a law of constancy—which meant that normal psychic life is characterized by a tendency to keep the general level of excitation constant. Both hysterical and sexual states provided outstanding examples of energy storms with dramatic patterns of emergence, climax, and termination: they both obviously called for quantitative formulations concerning the charge and discharge of some highly transformable energy. Thus, epidemiological facts (the prevalence of hysteria in women) and patterns of scientific thought converged on sexuality as a vital field of inquiry; and insofar as sexuality promised to be good and remain one energy among others to be studied with scientific detachment in traditional professional settings, it was admissible as subject matter. Freud, as did Breuer, darkly felt that the matter was more important and more dangerous; and Freud resolved to challenge that danger, while Breuer recoiled from it. It was at this point that Freud met Fliess, also a practicing physician, in whom far-reaching ideas about the role of sexuality in normal and abnormal states, and in the very cycles and rhythms of the universe, were germinating. In him

Freud obviously saw a man to whom he could entrust those ideas which emerged from the new self-chosen and lonely discipline, i.e., a mixture of therapeutic experimentation, clinical observation, and scientific speculation; a man who could help him unfold those powers of disciplined and yet courageous speculation which alone would make the routine attention to patients bearable: "We cannot do without men with the courage to think new things before they can prove them" (137). [In German, Freud is more modest: "before they can *demonstrate* them."]

To this reviewer, the letters seem to indicate that Freud thus accepted Fliess as a friend in need, a companion on a voyage, while he obviously never completely accepted the development of Fliess's theories. There are indications that Freud's overestimation of Fliess as a theorist has been exaggerated. True, Freud attempts to go along with Fliess in the published correspondence; and we are told that some of the omitted letters show Freud's special efforts at following his friend into his theories. Yet all of this remains part of the correspondence. Freud seems to have been careful throughout not to let this so-called overestimation enter into writings destined for the public. Such phrases as he did use publicly ("magnificent simplicity," "grandiose conception") are noncommittal in regard to the scientific solidity of Fliess's theories, while Fliess's public references to his friend Freud seem to have been extraordinarily stingy. Even in the letters, Freud calls Fliess "a worse visionary [*Phantast*] than I." This is said jokingly and even tenderly; yet kidding references to Fliess's theories of the neurological connections between the nose and the genitals seem relentless throughout: Freud reports that "Breuer has accepted the whole of your nose" or adds to greetings to Fliess and his family greetings "to sexuality through the nose." Maybe his most obvious slur was a practical joke which he perpetrated on his friend, when on an outing in the Austrian Alps he entered Fliess's name in the guest book of a mountain hotel, naming as his profession "Universalspecialist" (285), obviously someone who knows less and less about more and more. It does not seem, then, that on the whole Freud overestimated Fliess's theories any more or any longer than he did some of his own speculations; while he stated with utmost frankness what he wanted from him: "In the first place, I hope you will explain the physiological mechanism of my clinical findings from your point of view; secondly, I want to maintain the right to come to you with all my theories and findings in the field of neurosis; and thirdly, I still look to you as the Messiah who will solve the problem I have indicated by an improvement in technique." Beyond this, Fliess seems to have had the personality and the education which permitted Freud to entrust him with "imaginings, transpositions, and guesses," and to make of him the representative of what can only be translated as "the Other" (298). In German, this is "*der Andere*," and if one finds it translated as "other people," one shudders to think how often the most crucial words in translation come to say the opposite of what they mean. With Fliess, Freud could institute that relationship of bipolarization which many creative men need in order to have the courage of their own originality. Such a relationship consists, to some extent, of a mutual casting in the double roles of benevolent authority and audacious co-conspirator, of applauding audience and cautioning chorus—roles which fortify both participants against the sense of guilt and against the fear of shame which might inhibit their innermost aspirations. What Freud wanted from Fliess, Jones calls "sanction," a fitting and significant designation. When completing his "project" of a psychology for neurologists, Freud thanks Fliess, in fact, for letting him take it so seriously.

That in the ensuing correspondence unrestrained terms of mutual lionization should appear; that Fliess should be made an Apollonian tower of calm strength while the writer becomes a driven Dionysian (and "shabby Israelite"); that figures of speech should occur which picture the writer as a womanly womb for the intellectual siring of the other—all of this gradually surpasses what might have been sanctioned as an intellectual and poetic friendship. True, men in development often appreciate in one another their early and innermost aspirations rather than what they are finally going to be: "I see," Freud wrote to Fliess, "that you are using the circuitous route of medicine to attain your first ideal, the physiological understanding of man, while I secretly nurse the hope of arriving by the same route at my own original objective, philosophy. For that was my original ambition, before I knew what I was intended to do in this world" (121). Against the background of such a friendship pattern, the outlines of that emerging transference can be recognized—the first transference in history to lead, through the discovery of its own nature, to its own self-therapeutic liquidation.

The correspondence starts slowly and warms up gradually. From the first five years (1887–92), only sixteen letters are preserved, only thirteen reprinted here. They are a doctor's letters to a doctor. By the end of this period, a solid friendship seems to have formed, partly owing to the circumstance that Fliess frequented Vienna to court a Viennese girl at the time when Freud's "battle with my collaborator," Breuer, gradually led to a deep personal enmity and to thorough theoretical estrangement. In the first "drafts," Freud shakes off the shackles of traditional inhibition and personal indebtedness and sends to his friend, up in the more forward-looking Berlin, a series of clear-cut if extreme formulations concerning the origin of various neurotic states in the sexual practices of his day. ("You will, of course, keep the draft away from your young wife.") These formulations are of a sweepingly epidemiological character and end with a prediction of doom reminiscent of the pessimism of the classical economists: "In the absence of such a solution [i.e., an innocuous method of preventing conception] society seems doomed to fall a victim to incurable neuroses which reduce the enjoyment of life to a minimum, destroy the marriage relation and bring hereditary ruin on the whole coming generation. The lower ranks of society know nothing of Malthusianism; but they are following along the same path and will eventually fall a victim to the same fatality." His conclusions are "that the neuroses can be completely prevented but are completely incurable. The physician's task is thus wholly concentrated on prophylaxis." There is as yet no inkling of the unbeaten paths into the inner unknown which would have to be pursued before widespread prophylaxis (today's mental hygiene) could be envisaged. The doctors send one another case abstracts, but Fliess seems to insist on his "nasal reflex neurosis," while Freud pursues a sexual etiology somewhere between social contamination and somatic excitation. True, Freud in 1893 refers to the nasal reflex neurosis as "one of the commonest disorders," but adds, "unfortunately I am never sure of the 'executive,' " meaning "how it works." In the meantime, he pursues his etiological formula according to which neurosis is a consequence of sexual experience in which a complete discharge was impossible, either because of the inadequacy of the sexual partner, or because of the limited potency of the patient himself, or (and this assumption now begins to gain ascendancy) because of a seduction at a time when discharge was developmentally impossible, i.e., in childhood.

But then, in the letter of April 19, 1894, an entirely new note appears. Freud apparently had consulted Fliess in regard to a variety of his own symptoms and moods, which he condenses in the word *"Herzelend,"* cardiac discomfort heightened into a general "heart misery." Fliess had cauterized his nose and had urged him to give up his beloved cigars. The intellectual communication appears jammed: "I have not looked at your excellent case histories. The reading was abandoned in the middle of a sentence . . ." Freud now reacts much like any patient, if one with a tragic sense of alarm over a change in relationship which he knew he should understand. "As everyone must have come under someone's suggestion, to escape his own criticism, from that time on three weeks ago today—I have had nothing lit between my lips." So says the translation; the German original says "nothing warm between my lips" and thus opens up a perspective on an elemental oral theme from infancy—a theme which then could be met by these men only with a negative transference which neither could understand. And indeed: "I am suspicious of you this time, because this heart trouble of mine is the first occasion on which I have ever heard you contradict yourself." To add an element of "acting out," Freud reports a visit to the estranged Breuer, with whom scientific cooperation was then coming to an end, to have *him* help clarify the question as to whether Freud was suffering "from a reasonable or a hypochondriacal depression" (83).

Whatever Freud's disturbance was clinically, he indicates one month later the kind of intellectual crisis which seems to be the cause and concomitant of his inner storms: "I have the distinct feeling that I have touched on one of the great secrets of nature" (83). This secret, of course, was the central importance in human life (and not only in psychopathology) of sexual affect as a quantity, and of differential defenses against it. That every step of his search led Freud both into oedipal guilt and into that sense of having challenged the gods which the Greeks call "hybris" is amply demonstrated throughout the letters. It can now be suggested that it is this very hybris which the young medical man, with his wide sweep of interests, had overcompensated for by applying himself to the ascetic concentration on the details of nerve structures; and that it is this same hybris (multiplied by the subject matter now emerging) which drove the maturing man deeper into neurotic conflict, and into a kind of transference (first positive, then negative) to his mentor-friend, who was also his physician and surgeon. For if now the approach to "Nature" was open again, so were all the dangers of a mutual aggravation of oedipal conflict (renewed by his father's impending death) and of a nature-philosophic speculation which now approached the hidden secrets of *human nature:* such overdetermination is the stuff these letters are made of.

The grandeur of Freud's aspirations then appears in a classi-

fication of the major neuroses and an outline of a theory bridg-
ing all of sexuality and psychopathology, with the intervening
concept of the principle of psychic constancy. In the meantime,
the letters convey a sense of two elemental truths which were
soon to be more consciously perceived and to be formulated in
this very correspondence: (1) that basic psychological insight
cannot emerge without some involvement of the observer's impulses and defenses, and (2) that such insights cannot be communicated without the ambivalent involvement of the participants. For the present, however, that element of father transference which had begun to blur the friendship with Fliess
sought refuge in a stubborn theory which would blame primarily the fathers for the neurotic suffering of generations: a theory
which was to be adhered to fatefully, and abandoned only after
another transference crisis.

The spring of 1895 finds Freud preparing himself for the
greatest intellectual effort yet, namely, a "Psychology for Neurologists." He now had found his "tyrant" (119): psychology.
"I am plagued," he writes, "with two ambitions: to see how the
theory of mental functioning takes shape if quantitative considerations, a sort of economics of nerve-force, are introduced into
it; and secondly, to extract from psychopathology what may be
of benefit to normal psychology." Moody references to fluctuat-
ing physical complaints continue, and yet it becomes clear that
Freud works best in what throughout the letters is hinted at as
an optimum state of mild painful discomfort. This compromise
seems to resolve the struggle against smoking: "I have started
smoking again, because I still missed it (after fourteen months'
abstinence), and because I must treat that mind of mine de-
cently, or the fellow will not work for me. I am demanding a
great deal of him. Most of the time the burden is superhuman."
With this return of ego equilibrium, a great harvest comes to be
garnered: in July he "exhaustively" analyzed the strategic dream
of his patient Irma and established wish fulfillment as the core of
dream life; in August he gained the understanding of pathologi-

cal defense: "the theory," he exclaims, "is bold and beautiful."
After another inspiring "congress," the great "Project" is jotted
down in the autumn, sent to Fliess in October—only to be
promptly recanted in November: "All I was trying to do was
to explain defence, but I found myself explaining something
from the very heart of nature. I found myself wrestling with the
problems of quality, sleep, memory—in short, the whole of
psychology. Now I want to hear no more of it."

This is the halfway mark of the correspondence, the time
when Freud began to evolve systematically what had originated
coincidentally and eruptively. This midway point shows a man
in many ways maturely settled in community, practice, and
family. There are many delighted—and untranslatably delight-
ful—references to his children. Yet he remains daimonically ob-
sessed with the inner necessity to reconcile the ideology of his
past discipleship in physiology and his now unavoidable approaching mastership in psychology. His discipleship (as is not
uncommon for originators) had been rather prolonged; certain
latent adolescent-homosexual trends universally connected with
it were now finding a not untraditional expression and yet also
a painful clarification in the friendship with Fliess. Now, so
daimonic conflict seems to demand, the utopian part of the ideology needed to be spelled out *ad absurdum*, so that the truly
revolutionary part of it might become free and live.

Freud introduces the "Psychology for Neurologists" with a
candid statement of purpose: "The intention of this project is
to furnish us with a psychology which shall be a natural science:
its aim, that is, is to represent psychical processes as quantita-
tively determined states of specifiable material particles and so
to make them plain and void of contradictions. The project involves two principal ideas:

"1. That what distinguishes activity from rest is to be regarded as a quantity (Q) subject to the general laws of motion.

"2. That it is to be assumed that the material particles in
question are the neurones."

Freud proceeds to develop a model of organization of these

"particles," a sensitive machine for the management (through defense, discharge, and action) of varying qualities and quantities of excitation, such as are aroused by external and internal stimuli. Physical concepts, such as the principles of inertia and the preservation of energy, are combined with histological concepts to create a neuronic golem, in which all those puzzling subjective phenomena of pleasure and pain, of consciousness, thought, and memory, are mechanistically demonstrable and explainable on the basis of an over-all principle of solipsistic inner constancy. As Freud put it later: "Everything fell into place, the cogs meshed, the thing really seemed to be a machine which in a moment would run of itself" (129). All this goes beyond the physical-biological ancestry often exclusively ascribed to Freud's configurations of thought and embraces mechanical and economic configurations. Freud grew up in an era of universal search for an inner equilibrium in a closed universe, as if enlightened and rational man now invested his faith in the certainty that not only nature but also the "nature of things" could be trusted somehow to maintain its own balance in the face of change and upheaval. In the economic sphere, too, self-preservation, pleasure-seeking, and profit hunger themselves were to be ennobled as "natural" parts of a self-correcting market. Decades before Freud, economists spoke of men in the aggregate as pleasure-and-pain machines (Edgeworth). "Human nature" as a psychological system was not as yet fully included in this, although the human organism was. When Freud, then, spoke of an inner economics of nerve force, he meant a much closer analogy to concepts of economics than is later implied in his much refined and specialized "economic point of view," which ascribes to mental life a householding of energy.

Freud's Project (or what he refers to mock-cryptically as his $\phi\psi\omega$), while sent to Fliess in 1895, is attached to the book as an appendix. As my attempt at abstracting some of the dominant ideas must have indicated, it is forbidding reading for all but a few. Ernest Jones in his biography has humanely offered a prepublication summary in English. This reviewer can only testify that it is highly rewarding for one who is not one of the few to try, with the help of one who is, to follow Freud's astonishing reasoning. He will thus participate in the persistence and courage of the high intellectual adventure attending the pursuit of *creative misconceptions*—a persistence which disposes of traditional assumptions not by abandoning them but by pursuing them to that bitter end where radically new assumptions may, because they must, emerge from the matrix of traditional configurations of thought.

The psychoanalytic reader gradually comes to feel that what these neurones are supposed to do is in fact what he has learned to assume the psychic apparatus does: he will imperceptibly replace a psychological for a neurological point of view, and yet suspect that the former would never have emerged without the latter. Secondly, he may come to feel (with Jones) that Freud's Project has significant relations to cybernetic theories of communication (which may or may not speak for either). Thirdly, he will find, in the neuronic discourse, surprising eruptions of configurations of thought which anticipate the preoccupations of our day.

Freud is certainly not the first to speak of an ego. What is surprising is to find in this mechanistic discourse a reference to the ego as an "organization," "a *group of neurones* which retains a constant cathexis" and thus "form part of the *domain* of the ego" (384). Here a field concept clearly overtakes that of pathways of facilitation.

A second quotation, in order to be appreciated, would have to be seen emerging from the up to then completely mechanistic exposition: "At early stages the human organism is incapable of achieving this specific action [i.e., toward a riddance of a given excitation]. It is brought about by extraneous help, when the attention of an experienced person has been drawn to the child's condition by a discharge taking place along the path of internal change (e.g., by the child's crying). This path of discharge thus acquires an extremely important secondary function—viz., of bringing about an understanding (*Verständigung*) with other people; and the original helplessness of human beings is thus the primal source of all moral motives" (379). Note that Freud here does not speak of the "mother," or the "environment," but of an "experienced person" ("*ein erfahrenes Individuum*"), who in the sentence immediately following becomes a "helpful" person *vis-à-vis* a "helpless" one. In one sentence, he seems to anticipate that source of a new morality, based on the mutuality of function, which in our time may well (again, because it must) evolve from psychoanalytic and ecological considerations.

One month after the dispatch of the Project, Freud called it a kind of delusion ("*Wahnwitz*"): "I no longer understand the state of mind in which I concocted the psychology." In the meantime, however, he feels that he has made fundamental headway toward an understanding of "the two neuroses" (anxiety neurosis and neurasthenia) and of dream life. As if freed from some consuming servitude, the doctor now comes into his own: "I am sure that both neuroses are radically curable now . . . I have lived some forty years not quite in vain." But now he must fill the "psychological gaps," must establish a *theory of neuroses*.

The elucidation of these gaps fills the letters for years to come: many small and dark headwaters are seen to combine with those broad streams which became *The Interpretation of Dreams, The Psychopathology of Everyday Life*, and the *Three Essays on the Theory of Sexuality*. The letters say little about technique, but in 1896 the word psychoanalysis quietly joins the vocabulary. The over-all impression is that the basically more passive stance demanded of the psychoanalyst in the face of the patient's "resistance" was understood and accomplished by Freud only against a host of resistances in himself—resistances emanating from traditional masculinity as well as from cherished work habits: for a man's (and his time's) ideal images of a sexual being and a worker are fatefully intermeshed. It was, then, not only the difficulty inherent in the subject matter, namely, a universally repressed and infantile sexuality, but requirements of the new method which made it necesssary for Freud to face his own "feminine" and infantile selves. By the same token, it seems that he defended himself against fact and method again with the old grandiose persistence in the physiological ways of looking for well-differentiated entities. It seems to be part of a creative man's beginnings that he can change the scope and the trend of his thinking while maintaining the modes of logic and work discipline which have become part of his first identity as a worker. Shaw, when he gave up office work, wrote five pages a day for five years and produced five novels: they were then unpublishable, but he had become a writer. Freud, as a clinical observer, went on "slicing" his material in endless series of obviously overstated dichotomies. Here are some examples: "I know three mechanisms: (1) conversion of affect (conversion hysteria); (2) displacement of affect (obsessions) and (3) transformation of affect (anxiety neuroses and melancholia)." "In hysteria it is a *psychical* excitation which takes a wrong path in an exclusively somatic direction, whereas in anxiety neurosis it is a *physical* tension which is unable to find a psychical outlet and continues along a physical path." "The neuroses of defense are pathological aberrations of normal psychical states of affect: of conflict (hysteria), of self-reproach (in obsessional neuroses), of mortification (in paranoia), and of grief (in acute hallucinatory amentia)." "In hysteria it is memories, in obsessional neuroses perverse impulses, and in paranoia defensive fictions which penetrate to the surface in a distorted form imposed by compromise." In all of these statements, we see most important intuitive insights emerge: Freud used these psychopathological "sections" for the gradual establishment of a genetic dimension, just as he had done with the brain sections of different developmental levels when he investigated the persistence and the differentiation of early structures in the brains of kittens and puppies, of embryos and infants. Only now the reconstruction of fetal origins is applied to individual (and soon to phylogenetic) *"prehistory,"* while the search for traumatic *scenes* replaces that of lesions, and the tracing of *memories* that of neuronic pathways. But since he was now dealing with psychological material, i.e., material with inescapable concomitants in the observer's unconscious, not only the conflicts intrinsic to his work associations but also the whole of his past life became inextricably interrelated with his intuitive search. To take a look at the "primary process," and to remain truthful, means to confront the Medusa: here a man is apt to clutch his accustomed weapons.

As localization of the trauma in childhood became the dominant pursuit, the seduction theory entered the crisis, which ended in its liquidation. It was during this period that Freud's father ailed and died, mourned by his son in a memorable letter, and yet leaving him with some intensified conflict with the father image. An incredibly stubborn search for the "paternal etiology" followed, a persistent attempt to pin the fantasy of seduction in childhood on an actual "scene" of perverse seduction by the father. This was a creative error which led to absurdities of reconstruction and to psychological blind spots which would persist for some time. Yet it eventually opened the way to the understanding of the infant's and child's impulses and vulnerabilities, and to a first formulation of periods of heightened impressionability and of relative latency.

Freud enlivens his letters with diagrammatic sketches which seem well worth close study, especially for one who has been using just such diagrams in order to demonstrate epigenesis, the step-by-step unfolding of inborn patterns. In the German edition, these sketches are reproduced in his handwriting (big and aggressively spiked), while the English edition renders them in print. One of these diagrams (Fig. 6, p. 164) does not seem to be transferred correctly. Freud here means to indicate that in hysteria the "scene" took place before the age of four, in obsessional neurosis between four and eight, and in paranoia between ten and fourteen. However, he speaks of a "reawakening" of these scenes, followed by repression during the "transitional periods" of eight to ten and thirteen to seventeen. In the English translation, such latencies are incorrectly allocated to the periods ten to fourteen and seventeen to X. Correctly transposed, the diagram would look as follows:

	IA Up to 4	IB Up to 8	A	II Up to 14	B	III Up to X
Hysteria	Scene		R *		R	
Obs. neur.		Scene	R		R	
Paranoia				Scene	R	

* R = repression

What finally evolves from this differentiation between the *periods* when "the event" occurs, the *quality* of the event, and later periods of "reawakening" and of *repression* is a time-space schema of the psyche, in which different memory traces (various species of "signs") are still ascribed to different neuronic systems, but are subject to "transcriptions" during successive epochs of life. In this gradual charting of the epigenetic character of human development, the erotogenic zones and the stages of libido are eventually recognized.

This step forward, however, remains shackled to the theory of "seduction by the father," which now replaces heredity as the primal and exclusive cause of all evil: "heredity is seduction by the father." Only gradually does this ruthless and perverse father figure become (more vaguely, more correctly, more suggestively) "the pre-historic, unforgettable other person who is never equalled by anyone later." Here, for once, capitalization would be indicated, because the German *"der Andere"* means, as we said, "the Other," a singular position reserved in these letters for friend and father, and somehow (so one senses) echoing both Devil and God. But according to his way of work, Freud had to make two detours before he could face and accept the fact that that prehistoric Other with his absurd deeds was a primal fantasy image which merged with a mother image of even earlier origin. One of these detours was into phylogenetic history: Why, he asks, were the confessions extracted from the "possessed" under torture in the ecclesiastical courts of the Middle Ages so very similar to his patients' "reports" under psychological treatment? He delves deeply and thoroughly into this "parallel with witchcraft." But he cannot penetrate this riddle without courting renewed emotional discomfort: "I am beginning to dream of an extremely primitive devil religion . . ."— obviously the underworld of anal-sadistic ruminations. He insists that these "intervening phantasies" arise from things *heard* but only understood *later*, still adding, "all the material is of course genuine" (196). His stubborn pursuit of this theory leads him to an almost dianetic absurdity: Hysterical fantasies go back to things heard from six to seven months onward! He goes so far as to speak of a patient's luck in that the "Almighty was kind enough to remove the father by death, before the child was eleven months old" (211). But his own outraged sense of reality now forced upon him the insight that he himself was the captive of a fantasy. A dream suddenly showed him "my wish to pin down a father as the originator of neuroses" (206). This wish, of course, could only be a neurotic one. He could not escape any longer his own analysis and, with it, an intensified transference to Fliess. It is in this context that he again becomes strangely submissive and almost religiously dependent. "You are flourishing, while I open all the doors of my senses and take nothing in . . . I am agape (*erwartungsvoll blöde*) as never before for what you have to say . . . I am empty and ask your indulgence." In German, in fact, he asks for the other's *Gnade* (mercy). But he recognizes the transference: "Something from the deepest depths of my own neurosis has ranged itself against my taking a further step in understanding of the neuroses, and you have somehow been involved."

At long last, in the historic and heroic letters of the autumn of 1897 the seduction theory is abandoned, the father image is recognized as part of the Oedipus complex (which in turn is recognized as a dominant theme in world literature), and Freud's self-analysis breaks through to the first "pre-historic Other" of them all: the mother, or rather the mother image, as shared by his natural mother and by his old *Kinderfrau* (nanny). She was both evil (she was a thief) and holy: she took him to his home town's churches, "told me a great deal about God and hell, and gave me a high opinion of my own capacities" (219). After prolonged work, Freud recognized his own resistance to his own self-analysis, and completed the personal groundwork on which today's training analysis rests: "Self-analysis is really impossible, otherwise there would be no illness . . . I can only analyse myself with objectively acquired knowledge (as if I were a stranger)."

It was here that Freud apparently began to realize fully the extent to which he had made Fliess "the Other," while he could make himself "the Stranger" only up to a point. He seems to have exploited the authoritarian conflict with his father beyond all reason not only because of the universal taboo against filial death wishes but also because of the inaccessibility, at the time, of a basic element of mother fixation in all transference, even in that to the man Fliess—a transference which had been behind, say, the querulous complaint over the forbidden warmth between the lips. He now acknowledges that infantile trust, that gratitude toward the "experienced person," which had made its surprise entrance in the middle of his φψω: "If I succeed in resolving my hysteria, I shall have to thank the memory of the old woman [the nanny] who provided me at such an early age [meaning when his mother gave birth to the first siblings] with the means for living and surviving." His personal recovery included a manly acceptance of error: "I am proud that after penetrating so far I am still capable of such criticism. Can these doubts be only an episode on the way to further knowledge?" (217). He now dares to utilize what, no doubt, before would have seemed a "feminine" mode of work: "I have to wait until things move inside me and I experience them." Here his German is lyrical, Rilke-like: "*bis es sich in mir rührt, und ich davon erfahre.*" Finally, he found his insights "beautiful" in the simple manner of all craftsmen.

The road is now open for an insight on Freud's part into the whole *tour de force* of his clinical research: Instead of his first "crude answer, at the time when I was still trying to take the citadel by storm," he now speaks of auto- and heteroerotic stages, of object relationship and of regression. Also, he takes a fresh look at his own relationship to his patients, admitting that days preoccupied with theory cause him to be "far away from things," while, in turn, full receptivity to patients dulls his interest for ideas. Foreseeing that someday soon he will apply himself to "patients' feelings as well as their ideas," he summarizes: "I have let myself be lured a long way from reality. . . . All this work has done a lot of good to my own mental life. I am obviously much more normal than I was four or five years ago" (280).

Thus another basic insight arose from creative misconception, namely, that at any given time the psychoanalyst's ability to conduct cures and to gain as well as to give insight depends on his consistent efforts at curing in himself whatever conflicts his work will awaken and reawaken.

The letters describe a number of depressive and anxious states, which Freud, never one to spare himself, refers to as neurotic and as "my *phobia.*" During these years, he apparently traversed certain mental states in which an exaggerated sense of the *passing of time*, of premature aging, and of the possibility of an early death is prominent throughout. The first of the letters to Fliess was written by what today we could consider a rather young man (thirty-one), the last one by a man certainly not old (forty-six); yet it is well to remember that expectation of life was much shorter then. Freud had not left his parents' household for good until he was twenty-seven, and had established his own only at thirty: he had taken his time with coming into his own. Now a monumental lifework began to arise before him, and yet in the letters he depicts himself more than once as being on the verge of giving up. We thus see both a post-adolescent search for a work ideology and the despair of early aging crowd into a decade which was busy enough with the generative problems of middle age, "of fresh possessions in children and knowledge": his wish for Fliess on *his* fortieth birthday. We witness, then, a high condensation of life problems and work problems, while the writer penetrates into his past by way of letting the past make contact with the acute present. The life cycle, its normative crises and its phasic pathology, here takes on new meaning.

There is, for example, Freud's "railroad phobia," mentioned often but never described. Whatever it was, Freud now traces it to infantile sources, the loss by migration of a "prehistoric" childhood milieu which had combined life in the Moravian countryside, relative economic safety, and, of course, people like the *Kinderfrau*. That her mediation between Freud's Jewish milieu and the devoutly Catholic environment had left a lasting imprint can be seen again from the fact that Freud locates the beginnings of his phobia at age three, when on traveling—migrating—with his mother, he had in the railroad station of Breslau seen the first gas jets: "which reminded me of souls burning in Hell." It was on this same trip that he remembers having seen his mother "in nudam," an improbable occurrence, considering Victorian travel, but significant as "cover memory" for fears and wishes later to recur in the theme of unveiling nature. Later, a patient taught him (yes, patients consistently taught him things about himself) that "my phobia, if you please, was a poverty, or rather a hunger phobia, arising out of my infantile gluttony and called up by the circumstance that my wife had no dowry (of which I am proud)" (306). In other words, the fear of impoverishment and abandonment first experienced during his family's economic crisis and move to

Vienna was renewed and intensified during that life crisis of professional displacement in which this correspondence originates: the time when Freud, after much procrastination, became self-employed and the head of a household. Subsequently, the letters persistently and ambiguously refer, on the one hand, to an infantile paradise lost, to a "prehistoric" period, and to an early wish world out of which come deferred fulfillments and with them the only happiness known; and they report, on the other hand, the economic pressures of his life circumstances, the influence on the income of medical specialists of that first Great Depression, that "paradox of poverty in plenty" which accompanied industrial expansion in Europe, and which hit some countries more than others, and Vienna significantly more than Berlin.

During the years of the letters, Freud's railroad phobia, then, was associated with acute fears of an early death. That he was "coming too late," that he was "missing the train," that he would perish miserably before reaching some promised land—these thoughts are clearly reflected in the letters. He cannot see how he can complete what he feels to be growing within him, if every single step takes so much "work, time, and error" (a scientist's counterpart to the Churchillian formula for war). Connected with this are, at first, references to dangers to the heart, that inner metronome and measure of endurance. The themes of time pressure, heart acceleration, and the aspiration of "getting there first" combine in the remark: "I picked up a recent book by Janet . . . with beating heart, and laid it down again with my pulse returned to normal. He has no suspicion of the clue."

This urgent theme of time first overlaps with and then is gradually replaced by a *geographic* restlessness: would time permit becoming a general practitioner, maybe in Berlin, in England, in America? And toward the end of the correspondence a strangely intense, a "deeply neurotic" urge to see Rome. At first, the dominant wish is to arrange for a "congress" there; then a persistent "we are not in Rome yet" or "I shall no more get to

Rome this Easter than you will" (328); and a mock-despairing "On the whole I am further away from Rome than at any time since we met, and the freshness of youth is notably declining. The journey is long, the stations at which one can be thrown out are very numerous, and it is still a matter of 'if I can last out' " (310). The last sentence is one of numerous references to a Jewish joke according to which a man, traveling without a ticket, and kicked out with increasing vigor at successive stations, is finally asked for his destination. "Karlsbad," he answers, "if my constitution permits."

Only when *The Interpretation of Dreams* is published, and the friendship with Fliess comes to an end, does Freud plan more firmly to spend Easter in Rome. "Not that there is any justification for it, I have achieved nothing yet [the German original, "*es ist nichts erreicht*," suggests a creative destination rather than "achievement"] and in any case external circumstances will probably make it impossible" (327). Rome, of course, was the Semitic warrior Hannibal's never consummated conquest, as Israel was Moses' never visited visionary land—this double theme clearly emerges as the core of Freud's identification in the matter of Rome. Beyond this, the Eternal City seems to mean many things, all of which are superbly condensed in the phrase "Next Easter in Rome" (317). Here is the humanistic German's nostalgia for the classical world; the homeless Jew's longing as expressed at Passover in the words "Next year in Jerusalem"; and most probably also the small child's wish (now repudiated by the rational man) to experience again the ceremonial splendor of the holiday of resurrection, and this in the Pope's own city.

Only at the very end of the correspondence does the writer's perspective of time and place fit what we now know to have been the future of the originator of psychoanalysis: "I have readers . . . ; the time is not yet ripe for followers." The last letter written in the nineteenth century contains a rather different complaint: "We are terribly far ahead of our time."

When Freud, then, spoke of a "railroad phobia," he obviously referred to an anxious state which did not keep him from traveling. When he wrote about his being unable to work, he was referring to that intellectual activity which really was above and beyond the call of duty of a practicing neurologist: thinking. He was never unable to take care of his practice, when there were patients; but he never felt that anything had been accomplished without some advance in creative thought.

In addition to this "phobia," the letters refer to numerous physical complaints, among which migraine-like headaches seem prominent. Yet, as we have noted, there is a tendency to welcome a certain amount of physical discomfort as necessary for intellectual work, while complaint follows only when the powers of concentration were drowned out by the pain. There are also dispersed over the years most instructive references to areas of mental functioning which did not keep pace with his superior equipment: Freud refers to "a very poor feeling for space" associated with what he calls his "two left hands," a "stunted acoustic sensibility," and a lack of "the slightest mathematical ability" as well as of "memory for numbers and for measurements."

The destination envisaged in all these ruminations is, in retrospect, clear enough. In 1898 all other pursuits are dropped in favor of "*the dream book*." As far as can be seen, no preliminary drafts are sent to Fliess: in fact, drafts solely meant for Fliess's attention do not accompany the letters in the second half of the correspondence. Fliess receives completed chapters for criticism and prompt return. The letters themselves now move more freely from travel vistas to case episodes and literary discussions. It is as if the complete and systematic breakthrough to the rich mines of symbolism and of inner dynamics had set Freud free to go in many directions at once; gradually (but not before one more significant crisis) he also comes to the conclusion that he must go it alone. He is now a psychologist: "Beyond a feeling of conviction (concerning the organic basis of mental life) I have nothing, either theoretical or therapeutic, to work on, and so I must behave as if I were confronted by psychological factors only." The letters now move freely into metapsychology, a term he chooses because his psychology "leads behind consciousness" into "psychomythology," including the psychology of religion and nationalism; into "clinical psychology," and the connection of psychopathology with "conflict and life"; and into the psychoanalysis of literature. The case episodes now become, as it were, more three-dimensional, and it occurs to him how much like a "clever work of fiction" a case history really is. At this time, then, Freud's ability to discern the forms of life with creative pleasure, as well as to say truer things more perfectly, develops to its full stature. When, finally, the dream book nears completion, "the finest—and probably the only lasting—discovery that I have made," he significantly describes it to his friend as a bit of daring perambulation: "The whole thing is planned on the model of an imaginary walk. First comes the dark wood of the authorities (who cannot see the trees), where there is no clear view and it is very easy to go astray. Then there is a cavernous defile through which I lead my readers—my specimen with its peculiarities, its details, its indiscretions, and its bad jokes—and then, all at once, the high ground and the prospect, and the question: 'Which way do you want to go?' "

On November 4, 1899, Freud announces the publication of "the book," adding immediately that only after publication had he become aware of a slip: "Hannibal's father's name was Hamilcar, not Hasdrubal" (302). In reporting how, as a boy, he had noted his father's meekness in a confrontation with an anti-Semitic ruffian, and had concluded that this father would not have been a worthy ancestor to a Hannibal, a Semitic would-be conqueror of Rome, he had given to Hannibal's father the name of Hannibal's brother. Since this slip seems to question both a brother's and a father's worthiness, it is prophetic for the breakup of the brotherhood with Fliess which was to follow.

The grumbling of a deep discord with Fliess, as we saw, becomes noticeable early, but reaches a gradual crescendo only as

The Interpretation of Dreams progresses. True, Freud continues to write of himself as a "flickering light" and of Fliess as a "steady flame," and envies him for dealing "with light, not darkness, with the sun and not the unconscious." He compares himself with Nansen, "who discovers something new by a false route and finds that it is not so big as he expected." But when he adds, "Fortunately, the secure harmony of your nature preserves you from that" (260), some slur in the compliment is unmistakable, for it implies that Fliess's Olympian harmony prevents him from making creative errors—and from recognizing them. And, indeed, Fliess was gradually succumbing to nature-philosophy and a kind of speculative mathematics; he attributed not only conception and the sex of infants but also the very date of death to laws of periodicity. When to this list he added nervous breakdowns and their cures, he blithely overrode exactly what advance of reason and technique Freud had labored so painfully to achieve.

Paradoxically, when it comes to the final breakup, we have Fliess's description—in a polemic against several authors, published in 1906—but not Freud's. Freud's letters contain some determined attempts at a confrontation of issues and feelings, but they also indicate that he must at least have worn Fliess down with the gratuitous interpretation of the ambivalence revealed in his own slips and dreams. "Absurdity in dreams! It is astonishing how often you appear in them. In the *non vixit* dream I find I am delighted to have survived you." After all, Fliess had not cultivated the correspondence for purposes of self-analysis, and his amusement at the tricks of Freud's unconscious could at best have been sour-sweet. In fact, Fliess accuses him of "thought-reading his own conflicts into his patients"; and Freud naturally retorts that with this assumption Fliess tries to cover his own resistance. Freud does not believe Fliess's theory of left-handedness, and Fliess indicates that Freud may be left-handed himself—which Freud discusses most circumspectly, admitting that he had, in fact, "two left hands." There is no use looking for blame here: men who first lionize one another are later apt to turn on each other in the defense of their intellectual offspring. But it is noteworthy how here for the first time interpretations concerning the correspondents' unconscious motivations enter the argumentation ad hominem. On Freud's part, the partial understanding of his own irrational motivations appears to have contributed to a new sense of the tragic in human affairs (fate understood yet not escaped), while Fliess seems to have maintained a certain conventional indignation, followed years later by a more paranoid public defense of his priorities.

With ordinary men, this is where the unsavory matter would come to a gradual, forever uncomfortable rest. Freud's nature, and the nature of this friendship, led to the expression and documentation of one more significant crisis. Utterly disappointed over the fact that *The Interpretation of Dreams* was met with complete silence by colleagues and public ("not a leaf has stirred"), Freud seems temporarily to have despaired of his new way of life: and "When I am not . . . master of myself . . . every single one of my patients is a tormenting spirit to me." In March of 1900, again with the approach of Easter time, another deeply moving letter goes out to Fliess: "I must not smoke heavy cigars, alcohol does not mean anything to me, I have finished with begetting children, and I am cut off from contact with people." The reference to his "finished" procreative activities has suggested to some that, for Freud, who considered the then available contraceptives unbearable, this meant a cessation of marital relations altogether. Fliess offers a congress at Easter time, but this time Freud refuses. "It is more probable that I shall avoid you . . . I conquered my depression with the aid of a special intellectual diet, and now . . . it is slowly healing. In your company . . . your fine and positive biological discoveries would rouse my innermost (impersonal) envy . . . I should unburden my woes to you and come back dissatisfied . . . no one can help me in what depresses me, it is my cross, which I must bear . . ." (314).

The particular nature of this "cross," namely, the necessity to conquer major laws of psychology against mankind's unconquerable resistance, again becomes clear one month later. For he suddenly reports that he has recognized his patients' universal tendency to prolong the treatment and the dependence on the analyst as "an inherent feature and . . . connected with the transference . . . such prolongation is a compromise between illness and health which patients themselves desire, and . . . the physician must therefore not lend himself to it." It is clear that he has now recognized the "secondary gain" in his friendship as well; and that he will refuse to permit himself a further indulgence into the transference to Fliess although he will sorely miss him as *"mein einziges Publikum"* ("my one audience"). With this, he sacrifices the deepest kind of friendship, for "there can be no substitute for the close contact with a friend which a particular—almost feminine—side of me calls for" (318).

Freud now had to become his own father, and, as it were, the father of a people of his own. No other conclusion would, I think, do justice to the turn which this last crisis takes in the letters. It is as if Freud now had to take upon himself a depressively resigned orientation not uncommon for much older Jews who feel that they have wanted (and conquered) too much of a world that would never be theirs to keep. In some kind of filial integrity crisis, they have to take the curse of their people upon themselves. Calling himself a "shabby old Jew" (*"Israelit"* is the German word, with a stronger connotation of geographic displacement), he speaks with the words of a latter-day Moses: "It will be a fitting punishment for me that none of the unexplored regions of the mind in which I have been the first mortal to set foot will ever bear my name or submit to my laws" (318).

In July of 1900, one more congress takes place. Fliess reports later that Freud now expressed a shockingly violent opposition to Fliess's contention that periodicity, rather than psychic causes, brought about sudden deteriorations or improvements in the patients. Fliess interpreted it all as an outcome of that envy which he had noticed at some earlier time in Vienna, and which he had, at the time, reported to his wife and to "Frau Hofkapellmeister [Mrs. Imperial Musicmaster] Schalk, née Hopfen, who will gladly confirm it."

In September, 1901, Freud visits Rome. His tender and sober description of this much delayed old wish (which can be seen to represent a most personal and yet also a cultural dream) is the second to the last long letter in the (published) correspondence. The last is the report on the steps which Freud subsequently took to assure himself of that clinical professorship which was to put the practice of his specialty on a sound social and economic basis. "Others are just as clever, without having to come to Rome first," an obvious allusion to those colleagues who had undergone baptism for reasons of advancement: one of the opportunistic uses of religion so obnoxious to Freud's mind that they did much to spoil religiosity for him. The last letters, now again letters of one doctor to another, do not reach into that time of Freud's life when the empire of psychoanalysis itself replaced the vision of Rome (*"die römischen Träume"*) in his aspirations.

In the course of this review, I have found it necessary to correct the translation of a few strategic passages. I should make it clear that the translation, on the whole, is readable and accurate. It establishes, in these many-layered communications, a safe level of discourse, and sticks to it; to be more accurate would have meant to be less readable. Yet the lovers of Freud's German style, which, at times, becomes relaxedly Viennese in these letters, will mourn the loss of many an astonishing turn of phrase. Of English-speaking psychologists, only William James could have matched the manly abundance and tender strength of expression, the courage of precision, the play of literary allusions, colloquialisms, and neologisms that make up Freud's German— for which, after all, he received the Goethe Prize. Some of Freud's Goetheisms, such as *"Dämmergedanken, Schleierzwei-*

fel," are not translatable. And if I may be permitted a side remark or two to lovers, native or adoptive, of the Viennese idiom,
such phrases as "*eine zwanzig Individuen starke Kinderjause*" are
not conducive to translation into *any* other language. Viennese
readers will smile resignedly when "*eine grantige Periode*" becomes "a fit of gloom." As it is, the pleasantly even translation,
for the most part, is like a good reproduction in black and white
of a many-colored print.

In some parts, however, more essential tones and shades are
missed. I have referred to Freud's poignant use of "the Other,"
which contains an existential predicament not rendered by "other
people." In one of the last letters, he dramatically appeals to the
fading friend: "*Jetzt sieh einmal an*" ("Now look here"). The
translation says: "You see what happens" (272). The very salu-
tations of the letters, which in German climb from the equiva-
lents of "honored" and "esteemed" to those of "dearest," in
English range from a formal "dear" to a more formal "my dear."
And not even a marginal Viennese would conclude his letters
to an intimate friend with "heartiest" greetings.

The translation contains a considerable number of phrases
that Freud could not have uttered. For example, he could not
have said, "Happy is he who does not outlive his reputation"
(81); and, indeed, he says that such a deceased one is "enviable."
He could not have said to Fliess, "I can hardly tell you how
many things I (a new Midas) turn into—filth" (240). He said,
instead, "How many things . . . become filth to me" ("*was
sich mir in Dreck auflöst!*"). It would seem inconceivable that
Freud could say, "When I am not afraid I can take on all the
devils in hell" (183). And, indeed, this bit of translation does
injustice to the man *and* to his theory, for he wrote, "When I
happen to be free of anxiety." My criticisms are meant to indicate in how many different ways a translation can fail to fathom
all the nuances of Freud's surprising personal style, and that he
who wishes to quote in order to make a point had better first
consult the German. This does not apply to Mr. Strachey's both

accurate and felicitous translation of the difficult theoretical parts, the original style of which is, of course, more impersonally precise.

To summarize a summary, the letters and drafts contained in this volume show the reflection in a correspondence of the stuff that truly creative thought is made of. We see mirrored in a correspondence personality the relationship of a man's thoughts to the main currents of his time and that of a man's genius to his inner motivations. This correspondence does much to dispel that nebulous uncertainty which surrounded the origin of psychoanalysis and all too easily led to the impression that our science had issued from Freud's head as did Athene from Zeus'. Since from such an image we have derived some reflected omnipotence, this book is somewhat traumatic, albeit beneficial if slowly absorbed. To neutralize its immediate impact, we may feel tempted to highlight the neurotic in it or the creative, the infantile or the great, the emotional or the intellectual, the medical or the psychological. To this, Freud, if he cared, could say with (Cornford's) Pythagoras: "What is your warrant for valuing any part of my experience and rejecting the rest? . . . If I had done so, you would never have heard my name."

A QUESTIONABLE COOPERATION: THE WILSON BOOK

No READER acquainted with Freud's writings could open a page in the main section of this book * without asking himself how it could have been written—and how, indeed, published. There is, to be sure, an introduction unmistakably Freud's: a most

---

* Sigmund Freud and William C. Bullitt. *Thomas Woodrow Wilson: Twenty-Eighth President of the United States. A Psychological Study.* 307 pp. Boston: Houghton Mifflin, 1967.

welcome document for all those interested in an application of psychoanalysis to history and politics. The bulk of the book, however, is characterized by an amateurish jargon, topped only by the petty distaste with which Wilson's enigmatic (and, to many, by no means likable) personality is demeaned page after page.

The origin, then, and the nature of the co-authorship of Freud and the American diplomat become the central issue. Bullitt has played a brilliant and significant role in American matters of state. Most important, for this review, is the fact that he attended the Paris Peace Conference in 1919 and at that time was entrusted by Wilson with a mission to Lenin's Moscow. There he felt he secured vital information, only to be ignored by the President on his return to Paris. He resigned in a manner which, besides personal irritation, showed courage and foresight; and, indeed, Roosevelt later appointed him this country's first ambassador to Russia when that country was recognized in 1933. But how his profound dislike for Wilson could find expression in a decidedly bad book which carries the name of Sigmund Freud as senior author and a subtitle raising the issue of the American presidency itself becomes a matter of intense curiosity—and of concern. It is of concern to those who are carrying on Freud's work and recognize its fundamental grandeur even where it is most dated and most open to question. It is of concern to historians as well as psychoanalysts who do not wish to shirk the task of taking a new look at the deep and dangerous ambiguities of political leadership. But, above all, it has a certain desperate relevance for all those who are aware of the indispensability of psychological insight in matters of war and peace—including the question of the wide personal margin permitted to the American president and his advisers.

Perhaps nothing characterizes the tone of this book so well as the obsessive frequency with which Woodrow Wilson is referred to as "little Tommy":

Tommy Wilson always tried to be on the side of the angels: he en-
deavored to think about serious matters and he attempted to express his
thoughts in distinguished phrases. Those were exceptional attributes in
the United States after the Civil War, when most men of ability were
concentrating on the acquisition of wealth. They gave Tommy Wilson
both prestige and an endearing idealism. He was so serious about himself
that others took him seriously. To make fun of him was easy: to ignore
him was impossible. He was a prig: a prime prig. (9) [2]

In spite of the glaring incongruity of such passages with
Freud's style, his alleged senior authorship is unhesitatingly ad-
vertised as the principal authorship of this work. An advance
selection was thus announced on the cover of *Look*.[3] Such mis-
representation, however, is not only good for sales; it also provides a chance to be amused for otherwise literate people. "This
time," one of them exclaims triumphantly about a book nearly
thirty years old, "this time, Dr. Freud, you have gone too far!" [4]
And the chestnut of "Freudulance" will be rewarmed again.

This word, as it turns out, does have a certain tragicomic
significance here, for it is not at all certain which parts of the
body of this book, if any, were written by Sigmund Freud himself. Mr. Bullitt's own preface, in fact, does not claim that Freud
"wrote" any of it. He only speaks of Freud as having written
"the first draft of portions of the manuscript" (vii). And he describes a "collaboration" extending over eight of the most dramatic years in history and in the lives of both collaborators; for
the rest, Mr. Bullitt rightly accepts responsibility, although he
clearly is not aware of the weight of it. And Bullitt has Ernest
Jones's word for it that he, as "the only person privileged" to
read the original manuscript, had found it easy "to distinguish
the analytical contributions of the one author from the political
contributions of the other." [5] I will later quote some of these
"analytic contributions," as now printed. In the meantime, I can
only surmise respectfully that Jones on a visit to New York in
1956 was so awed by the occasion (he was permitted to peruse

for two hours a diplomatic manuscript brought to him by an armed guard) and so taken with the potentialities of this psycho-political approach that his judgment was somewhat strained.

Bullitt's preface describes the collaboration as having begun in Berlin, where Freud had gone for a "small operation." Freud was in Berlin in 1930 for the readjustment of his "infernal" oral prosthesis which had replaced his whole upper jaw. For eight weeks he underwent (as Dr. Schur tells us) four or five hours of minute fittings every day—"extremely taxing and painful." That Freud was "depressed" is more than likely; that he would have spoken of his mind as "emptied" maybe less so. But Freud may, indeed, have "come to life" when he heard Bullitt was writing about the Treaty of Versailles, and when the opportunity seemed to offer itself to apply psychoanalytic knowledge to the life history of one of its perpetrators. To be fascinated by the fact that he and Wilson were born in the same year is a "chronological" quirk not foreign to Freud. And Bullitt seemed to have the facts. He produced the relevant books, selecting "all that I considered worthy of his attention" (vii). With Freud's encouragement, Bullitt left for the United States for extensive interviewing and came to Vienna some months later with a mass of private information from individuals who had known Wilson. "Without exception," Bullitt reports, they wanted to remain anonymous. Was no "good" information of any kind sought or given, one wonders, no information at all which the informant would have been quite willing to sign with his name? All this, we would now say, seems to violate one rule of psycho-historical study: that there be at least a rough indication of how the data were collected. But it also partially explains the totally un-Freudian bias which causes the "facts" reported consistently to disintegrate into a petty denigration of the man under study. There is nothing analogous in Freud's published work. There *are* a few analogies in his letters and reported conversations which may throw some light on how the manuscript came into being. Were Freud's contributions memoranda and letters—that is, notes in conceptual shorthand? As others have done before the book was published, I have made every effort to find out the whereabouts of those "first drafts of portions of the manuscript" which Freud is said to have written—presumably in his own militant, oversized handwriting, for Freud never typed anything. But it appears that *all* original drafts have been, to use a neutral word, lost.

What Bullitt calls the resulting "amalgam" of joint writing was apparently ready to be typed in final form in 1932. But since Bullitt could not accept some of Freud's additions (they seem significantly to have concerned a psychoanalytic evaluation of Christianity or, at any rate, of Wilson's Presbyterianism), both agreed to let the matter rest and to initial each chapter of what Mr. Bullitt calls the "then unpublishable manuscript." As have others, I have tried in vain to learn the whereabouts of this manuscript and of the initialed pages. Nobody known to me seems to have seen them; but then Freud himself had treated the matter with utmost discretion, conceivably because he believed that the news of their joint effort might hurt Bullitt's then resumed diplomatic career. Thus, there are good reasons to conclude that with the exception of the introduction (of which only a typed copy was turned over to the Freud Estate), all of Freud's original contributions, in whatever form, have disappeared.

The main point to be made here is that Bullitt either transcribed or wrote, translated or caused to be translated, every word of the bulk of the book. He "showed Freud the final text" in London in 1938, eight years after the beginning of the collaboration. Freud was in the last year of his life. He was a desperately sick man (a new neoplasm had been found in August, 1938), and an émigré, by then deeply grateful to Bullitt for reasons about which Bullitt is modestly silent. When Hitler occupied Vienna, it seems to have been Bullitt who asked President Roosevelt to intervene in Freud's and his closest family's behalf. It becomes understandable that, on a number of grounds, Freud was in no mood to prolong the struggle for alterations, and at the very end formally signed this book, thus committing his estate to its publication in some form. The date for publication was left to Bullitt. When it drew near, numerous amendments in the final manuscript were suggested by Freud's heirs, but none were acceptable to Bullitt.

Freud's introduction was written at the very beginning of the collaboration in the twilight between the two world wars. It explains his interest in the adventure in the frankest terms. He declares that the figure of the American President "as it rose above the horizons of Europeans, was from the beginning unsympathetic" to him and that this feeling increased "the more severely we suffered from the consequences of his intrusion into our destiny." These words carry the weight of more than a personal gripe or prejudice. Anyone who lived in Europe in those days can remember Wilson's "rise over the horizon" as a bewildering spectacle akin to a mystical experience. Could it be that a semblance of Christian charity had survived the first mechanized slaughter of history? Could it be that the destruction or the dehumanization of mankind by the unrestricted use of super-weaponry might be checked by the creation of a world democracy? That flash of bright hope made the gloom that followed only more dismal—and, indeed, was to help prepare Nazism.

In the twenties, Freud had written *The Future of an Illusion*, and, in 1930, *Civilization and Its Discontents*, both of them one-sided yet measured documents of a firm skepticism. What Freud felt when he heard from Bullitt some details of Wilson's Presbyterian background and motives—a religious heritage familiar to Bullitt but essentially unfamiliar to Freud—was evidently a Moses-like indignation at all false "Christian" prophecy. A proud man brought up in skeptical Judaism, even if surrounded by the folklore and display of Catholicism, which, as the Fliess letters show, touched him deeply as a child, persists in the grim conviction that as yet no Messiah has appeared. When such a man observes the man-made suffering sanctioned by the spokesmen of Christianity, and foresees rightly that the growth of industrial nationalism can only multiply it, the incantations of fumbling Christian statesmen must sound profoundly offensive.

In the days of Versailles, Wilson's oratory caused the saying to be circulated in Europe that "Wilson speaks like Jesus Christ, but acts like Lloyd George." This duplexity was a quality of which Clemenceau, for example, could be scornful, while he himself attended to his own rational belief in the traditional "safeguards" of open or secret treaties. But Freud saw man's only hope in the gradual replacement of high-minded hypocrisy with a new kind of insight that would make "the content of our psychic inner world" amenable to the logic of natural science, and would make man accept "the real outer world." What he heard from Bullitt about Wilson (with whom Bullitt had broken in Paris, as the book recounts) convinced Freud that Wilson's policies represented the epitome of "Christian science applied to politics." He judged Wilson himself to be like a doctor "who wishes to restore the eyesight of a patient but does not know the construction of the eye and has neglected to learn the necessary methods of operation." The patient was Western civilization itself.

One may wonder about this medical simile and about Freud's willingness to accept Bullitt's mediation. As a young man and before he became a doctor, so Freud himself tells us, he had wanted to be a statesman. His deep identification with Moses can be clearly read in his work. Did Bullitt awaken in the old and ailing man the fading hope that his lifework, psychoanalysis, might yet be destined to become applicable to statesmanship? Bullitt brought him at least a semblance of the kind of "data" which Freud had illuminated in his case histories. And Freud the "pessimist" was on occasion (as we saw in the case of Fliess) quite naïvely trustful.

In the introduction, Freud also speaks frankly and passionately as one who neither knows nor trusts America. Occasionally he too had been seduced into the wish that she would fulfill her often proclaimed world mission. He had visited the States only once, receiving his one and only honorary degree from Clark University and sharing frankfurters roasted in a bonfire at his friend James Putnam's camp in the Adirondacks (James's daughter, Marian, has described to us how on that occasion Freud the Austrian, Jung the Swiss, and Ferenczi the Hungarian were greeted by a row of bloomer girls who sang the German national anthem). Grateful for the acceptance of his ideas in America, he nevertheless left the country in a skeptical mood, not later corrected, one may be sure, by the free associations of his American patients—psychic refugees, as it were—or by the rapid expansion of psychoanalytic professionalism in the States. But it would be a pity if what is personal and temporal in Freud's admitted prejudice (for example, the testy-sounding analogy between Wilson and the Kaiser as "chosen darlings of Providence") were to make the reader forget the chronic ambivalence in foreign countries—even in those dependent on her—toward America's "invasion into our destiny." For many countries have learned to expect the arrival from America of messages promising a world made safe for democracy—together with threats of military escalation or of isolationist withdrawal. We may not care to accept foreign ambivalence toward us, but we must learn for the sake of peace to read our messages for what they sound like to intelligent foreigners.

I have focused so far on the introduction because it is a prologue to matters far beyond this book—matters, in fact, betrayed by the book's content. Freud, in being frank and clear, at least fulfills the first rule of a "psycho-historical" study, namely, that the author should be reasonably honest about his own relation to the bit of history he is studying and should indicate his motives without undue mushiness or apology. That Freud's personal involvement and trust in the collaboration with one once closely engaged in current events were to cloud his objectivity we must accept as well as we can, knowing that the greater the man, the

greater his mistakes appear. But the introduction does not support Jones's or anybody else's claim that the division of labor
was clean and clear throughout. Bullitt, Freud states, "has prepared the Digest of Data on Wilson's Childhood and Youth"
(xiv). For the "analytic part," Freud declares himself and Bullitt
"equally responsible"—certainly an amazing concession to a
diplomat by the founder of psychoanalysis, and yet also a disavowal of sole responsibility for what might emerge.

But now, at last, to the book itself. The first chapter outlines
Wilson's development as a child. His father is said to have had
"two great passions: words and his son, invariably called
Tommy." His mother was an "under-vitalized woman." This
chapter contains some fascinating fragments and fleeting descriptions of a child and young man brought up as a Presbyterian
in the South of the Civil War and after. But the items are strung
together relentlessly on a thread of vindictiveness which does not
let "little Tommy" get away with anything, certainly not with
the fact that "he never had a fist fight in his life," and least of all
with having been called little Tommy and desperately wanting
to be known as Woodrow Wilson. Not even that the boy "drew
a veil of forgetfulness" over some painful impressions of his
childhood is forgiven in this psychoanalytic study.

The book thus blurs exactly what could have been most fruitful to investigate, namely, what was typical and what was excessive in this particular version of a southern Presbyterian background. And what was its true influence on the personality of a
man who in all his remoteness came to impress generations of
bright students as the best teacher they ever had, who came to
be chosen by his compatriots as worthy of the presidency, and
who was able to induce the world to trust him as a peacemaker?
His success is glibly explained: "in order to be a man, he had to
be a statesman." Nor does the book see Wilson's "Christ complex" against the background of what Robert Bellah (paraphras-
ing Rousseau) calls the "civil religion in American tradition," a

messianic tradition which made it incumbent on all would-be presidents to declare themselves tools of God's will on a continent obviously set apart for American destiny. Only melancholy Lincoln cautiously called the American people an "*almost* chosen people."

I could only make matters worse if I were to condense what is already a "digest" of monotonous condemnation. Wilson's appearance as a child is described as ugly and sickly, and later as bearing "the sterilized, disinfected expression which characterized ministers and Y.M.C.A. secretaries" (30). Even Wilson's "nervous breakdowns" in his youth or later are treated entirely as demeaning: "he crept back to the shelter of the Manse in Wilmington." That he eventually chose a wife who was congenial is described as "the greatest stroke of luck." To her touching words, "I am the only one who can rest him," the book adds: "That was true. He could rest on her shoulder with as complete confidence as ever he had had as an infant sleeping on the breast of his mother." When she died, it is recounted he wanted to be dead. But "he did not die . . . he married again. He could not do without a woman on whose breast he could rest."

The admittedly enigmatic personality of Wilson, then, appears here in stereotypes which are intended to introduce the second chapter, an outline of "the facts which psychoanalysis has found to be true with regard to all human beings." This, if Ernest Jones was right, must be the chapter clearly attributable to Freud. And, indeed, there are many passages here which sound like approximate translations of what Freud might have noted down or said in an attempt to explain psychoanalysis to a layman. One must even concede that some of the formulations are reasonable facsimiles of Freud's early theories, which ascribed to a somewhat mythological libido certain quantitative properties in the manner of the physicalistic physiology of the nineteenth century. Strikingly un-Freudian, however, is the use of such terms as "accumulator" or the Kinseyan "outlet":

We have noted that the libido of the child charges five accumulators. Narcissism, passivity to the mother, passivity to the father, activity toward the mother and activity toward the father, and begins to discharge itself by way of these desires. A conflict between these different currents of the libido produces the Oedipus complex of the little boy (39).

There follows a gradual crescendo in the use of this model and of the word "outlet," which on the first page of Chapter X appears ten times, to be topped by the phrase "evacuation of libido." What these words could possibly have been in Freud's German I can only guess ("discharge"?), but it was probably not for such phrases that Freud received the Goethe Prize in the very year when this book was begun. Freud firmly agreed with Goethe that one should speak for the moment, but write for posterity. But it should be a warning to all of us to see how a habitual use of theoretical shorthand can result, in the minds of those who attempt to reproduce our words, in a reification of the concept of the libido in hydraulic terms and of an ego endowed with astonishing virtuosity:

The ego of a little boy who has no sister is compelled to force his libido to cross with one leap the chasm between his mother and the outside world . . .

To indicate what to the publishers and some critics appears as genuine Freudian history, let us follow only one interpretational theme, namely, the transfer of little Tommy's father and brother images on the presidency of Princeton, the presidency of the United States, and the abortive job of savior of the world. It is exactly because filial and fraternal transferences *are* basic Freudian themes that we must take cognizance of their corruptibility. And as we know from that other posthumous volume, the letters to Fliess, Freud at one time *could*, to the point of absurdity, hold on to the thesis that fathers cause their children's neuroses. Only by suffering an almost spiritual uncertainty and, in fact, recognizing the central importance of father and brother transferences which had taken possession of his friendships as well as his identification with historical figures could he clarify the matter for himself—and for mankind. Nevertheless, even as Bullitt's mechanization of psychic forces only caricatures a trend which does exist in the literature, so do the following excerpts only render more obviously absurd a kind of formulation not always absent from newer applications of psychoanalysis to history.

Here is the basic father complex:

The portion of his libido which charged passivity to his father was far greater than the portion which charged aggressive activity toward his father; and it is obvious that his Ego employed the method of repression to handle the conflict between his powerful passivity and his relatively feeble aggressive activity (59).

This extends to God, Christ:

The God whom Thomas Woodrow Wilson worshipped to the end of his days was the Reverend Joseph Ruggles Wilson, the "incomparable father" of his childhood . . . if his father was God, he himself was God's Only Beloved Son, Jesus Christ (61).

But there was a brother, also:

His little brother Joe may have been the original much loved betrayer who was followed many years later in his unconscious by Hibben and House. The original emotion involved was, of course, Tommy Wilson's passivity to his own father; but it seems to have reached his friends by way of his brother Joe (69).

So he did not have a chance:

He was in the full vigor of his young manhood—17 at the beginning of that period, 27 at the end—but he clung to the habits of his childhood and remained a virgin full of dyspepsia, nervousness, headaches and ideals (81).

But there was a hero, Gladstone:

He refound the "incomparable father" of his early childhood in Mr. Gladstone. . . . Adolescent Tommy then destroyed Mr. Gladstone by the cannibalistic method of identification and announced: "That is Gladstone, the greatest statesman that ever lived. I intend to be a statesman, too" (83–84).

Cannibalism works thus:

We have seen, however, that in his unconscious, to become a statesman meant to identify himself with the "incomparable father" of his childhood who wore the face of Gladstone and thus by "cannibalistic" identification to destroy the old man. We may, therefore, suspect that in his unconscious the "something" he wished to "do" was to annihilate the Reverend Joseph Ruggles Wilson (104–5).

Now Gladstone lives on—inside:

His feeling for West had by this time turned into hostility, and when West was elected Dean of the Graduate School in 1901, Wilson began to employ him as a father representative upon whom the flood of his hostility to his actual father could be loosed. . . . When he was elected President of Princeton he became, in his unconscious, Gladstone (110–11).

But there was always Christ:

In that address he spoke for Christ; in his unconscious he was Christ: the flow of his passivity through his identification with Christ swept unimpeded into the ears of his auditors (117–18).

. . . and Judas:

The outlet of his identification with Christ was further enlarged by his turning Hibben [friend, enemy, later successor as president of Princeton] into Judas Iscariot (127).

And then there was Colonel House:

It was easy for Wilson in the summer of 1916 to diminish somewhat the quantity of his libido which found outlet by the way of House. He had just enormously increased the quantity of his libido directed toward his unconscious identification with Jesus Christ. Both his love for House and identification with the Saviour were outlets for the same great source of libido, his passivity to his father. Therefore, as his unconscious identification with Christ increased, his need to love House decreased (216).

Thus House was slipping:

. . . it is clear that in Wilson's unconscious until the armistice House still represented little Tommy Wilson although he was no longer quite a perfect little Tommy Wilson (219).

As to Versailles (where Wilson's behavior indeed would bear psychoanalytic scrutiny), it is all foredoomed:

Throughout the day of April 7, he had seemed so utterly determined to fight that even House was astonished by the completeness of his surrender on the afternoon of April 8. . . . And one is tempted to imagine that he lay awake that night, facing the fear of a masculine fight which lurked in the soul of little Tommy Wilson (260).

And so it remains when he returns and attempts to convince America of his mission:

When he set out in 1919 for the West . . . it is clear that he was driven to destruction by the old conflict . . . between his activity toward his father and his passivity to his father (291).

As he dies, he reverses the stages of this life-historical fairy tale:

As he drew closer to death he talked less and less about his days as President of the United States and more and more about his days as President of Princeton. Again and again he refought his fight with West and grew emotional over the "treachery" of Hibben, forgetting his fight with Lodge and the "treachery" of House. Again and again he retold the old, old stories about his "incomparable father" (295).

It is a pity; for one does find in the childhoods of great men and women of messianic bent and historic performance a comparable relation of parent and child, which makes it incumbent on the child to fulfill the parent's ideal image and to redeem his —and the child's—shortcomings. Some of the more primitive dynamics of such relationships are strongly suggested in this book. Conversely, one can find in and between the lines of this book suggestions regarding the infantile origins of such desperate overcompensations and reaction formations as are apt to put in jeopardy the efforts of the most powerful peacemakers. Yet the decisive factors in any historical study are not only how the parent could coerce the child, and the child convince the parent, but how the child became a man who could convince his contemporaries that he was filling a place waiting for him and that he was, indeed, a principal force in history. About this, the book says nothing.

I will confess to having looked forward to this book, for I had often thought that if I had another life or two I would like to trace each of the Big Four of Versailles through their individual lives in their respective milieus and nations to their fateful confrontation around that peace table. Something like this seems to have been in Bullitt's mind when he convinced Freud of the desirability of collaboration; and one can only wish he had stuck to it and endowed it with his rare knowledge of international personalities and power struggles. For when in subsequent chapters he permits himself to let the brilliance and the militancy of his younger years speak out, the style often becomes vivid and clear enough to justify a fleeting fascination with the incredibly personal equations in the game of diplomacy. The "joint" attempt, however, to treat the whole scene at Versailles as a stage for the *danse macabre* of one man's father complex does not clarify the workings of history.

To review the historical part of this book—that I must leave to scholars acquainted with international events. I cannot see how this book reveals anything about Wilson that has not been described and analyzed incomparably better by the Georges in their pioneering study *President Wilson and Colonel House*.[6] No doubt they will join me in wishing that this book had not been written. Do I wish that, once written, it had not been published? By no means. It could have been responsibly released with a historical introduction outlining in the light of contemporary psychoanalysis the moment when the book was conceived: where Freud stood (and sovereignly erred) when he consented to this collaboration, where Bullitt stood, and what were the methodological and conceptual problems encountered in the completion of the manuscript.

One would not want, even if one had the facts, to turn on Bullitt the method he employs on others; but one is reminded of what George Kennan once called his "passionate indiscretion." Certainly, if any junior worker ever succeeded, for whatever motivation, in making his senior's theories sound absurd, here it is. In thus permitting some readers the satisfaction of seeing in print, under Freud's name, what they want to believe attempts at psychoanalyzing history would look like, the book spares them the shock value it should have, namely, that of bringing readers up sharply against some of the fatal dangers of political leadership which do call for "analysis."

Considering what the book fails to accomplish and its general effect on the large audience who may be eager to believe that Sigmund Freud would indulge or knowingly collaborate in a psychoanalytic belittling of any person, great or small, this publication can only be deplored. For regardless of what profound mistakes psychoanalysis may have made, how "mechanistic" some of its early concepts may have sounded, or how fashionable and faddish may have been some of its triumphs, it is undeniable that Freud's revolutionary and abiding respect for his patients has had a decisive influence on the honesty of "dialogue" in all manner of relations among men. And the book lacks the corollary in Freud's work, namely, systematic self-analysis as a basis of insight. For example, Freud long ago revealed—for the circumscribed purpose of explaining his own dream life—his own version of a Victorian man's ambivalent friendships:

. . . my warm friendships as well as my enmities with contemporaries went back to my relations in childhood with a nephew who was a year my senior . . . All my friends have in a certain sense been reincarnations of this first figure who . . . "long since appeared before my troubled gaze" (Goethe, *Faust*, Dedication). They have been *revenants*. My nephew himself re-appeared in my boyhood, and at that time we acted the parts of Caesar and Brutus together. My emotional life has always insisted that I should have an intimate friend and a hated enemy. I have always been able to provide myself afresh with both, and it has not infrequently happened that the ideal situation of childhood has been so completely reproduced that friend and enemy have come together in a single individual—though not, of course, both at once or with constant oscillations, as may have been the case in my early childhood.[7]

It is not without a sense of tragic empathy, then, that Freud could write about any man's failure in friendship; nor that in the introduction of this book he could come to the general conclusion:

Fools, visionaries, sufferers from delusions, neurotics and lunatics have played great roles at all times in the history of mankind and not merely when the accident of birth had bequeathed them sovereignty. Usually they have wreaked havoc; but not always. Such persons have exercised far-reaching influence upon their own and later times, they have given impetus to important cultural movements and have made great discoveries. They have been able to accomplish such achievements on the one hand through the help of the intact portion of their personalities, that is to say in spite of their abnormalities; but on the other hand it is often precisely the pathological traits of their characters, the onesidedness of their development, the abnormal strengthening of certain desires, the uncritical and unrestrained abandonment to a single aim, which give them the power to drag others after them and to overcome the resistance of the world (xvi).

The mandate to continue psychoanalytic inquiry into the phenomenon of the "charismatic" influence of the chosen on the masses, and of the masses on the chosen—a mutual influence in which the most rational and the most irrational aspirations of man meet—that difficult and, no doubt, hazardous mandate is only renewed by the appearance of this book.

III

Postscript and Outlook

As ONE TURNS from the dim past of a new field to the history of its establishment, it sooner or later appears to have become "classical"—a word that denotes both mature form and finiteness. And if in such a field, the "classical" approach is identified totally with one man, it stands to reason that in his lifetime or right after his death even the most necessary conceptual transformations become associated with emotions of filial or sororal loyalty or heresy. Thus, often quite in contrast to the founder's own irreverent beginnings, the followers' thinking comes under the shadow of the question of what "he" would have approved of or would have disavowed, as if even the greatest among men could (if, indeed, they would) guarantee the purity of their creation once it enters the domain of history. Such imagery would probably have to be considered, if one were to investigate what the word "classical" really implies in all its logical and emotional ramifications. Each field has its own classical stance; and yet, in any given historical period, there must also be a mutual assimilation of all the concepts deemed classical in various fields. For even as the individual needs a livable orientation in the multi-

Conclusion of remarks presented to the 1969 *Daedalus* symposium, on the "biography" of ideas (see p. 17).

plicity of experience, so must a civilization strive to integrate all transforming ideas into a coherent universe. Such a process is, of course, more obvious in religio-ideological and medico-humanitarian pursuits because they must simplify as well as unify and vitalize in order to be able to guide, cure, and teach. But even in the hallowed objectivity of science, truly transforming ideas seem to have a fate which not only leads from scientific incredulity to verification, but also from philosophical repugnance to a new sense of classical coherence, proving once more that "God does not play dice with mankind." And who could be greater, even if he is only very partially understood, than the modest scientist who takes a daring new look behind appearances and returns to affirm that God knows what He is doing?

Because of the marked ideological-humanitarian aspects of psychoanalysis, however, the development of a revolutionary approach into a classical and even an orthodox one—and into the resulting heresies—took little time. I, at least, could witness it in one lifetime; although I must admit that my primary interest in the flux of phenomena left little impetus either to find safety in orthodoxy or escape in heresy.

Being somewhat of an expert in play, I must add here that while we remember great men usually as severe creators, they are certainly also the ones in whom a divine playfulness is undiminished in its capacity to transcend in new formulae some of the traumatic discrepancies of the times. To me, Freud, too, had throughout his decades played so sovereignly with so many types of conceptualization (from nature-philosophy to economics) that I could not see how he could have thought of himself as anybody but the one who had to try out the thought patterns of the centuries on the entirely new task which he first envisaged, namely, a systematic method of self-knowledge and a new art-and-science of healing.

In Freud, however, one can trace a continuous struggle between the doctor role and such powerful identity fragments as liberator, scholar, writer. These he permitted himself to cultivate only sparingly, for he was, above all, a physician who would cure man of the curse of the past whether it originated in evolution, in primitive history, or in early life history—all three aspects of man's life discovered in Freud's very century by the Darwinists, the archeologists and anthropologists, and by himself: his many analogies between the mind's layers and archeological research come to mind here. Freud's antiteleological concern with the past as encapsulated and entombed in the mind has led, in both practice and theory, to astonishing discoveries; and if it is true that the mood of this kind of mastery of the past resembled somewhat the ritual re-enactment of beginnings (creation, spring, birth), then it would seem plausible that psychoanalysis appealed above all to people who had lost their origins in soil, ritual, and tradition. For it will not do to explain human phenomena by their origins in childhood without asking why and how the social environment initiates, reinforces, and aggravates selected childhood conflicts and makes their outcome part of the positive and negative identity fragments which will vie with each other in adolescence. By an exclusive emphasis on origins, psychoanalysis has in fact contributed to a world image pervaded by a new sense of ontogenic predestination, which, it sometimes seems, can be alleviated only by a dogmatic faith in psychoanalysis.

Freud's combination of a retrospective and introspective approach in psychoanalysis is often referred to as his "fatalism"; while I am only too aware of the fact that later concepts such as mine are welcomed by many as a more "optimistic" promise of life chances not doomed by childhood experience. But identity concepts only emphasize for one stage of life what is true for all—namely, that periods of rapid growth and of a widening range of cognition permit, in interaction with living institutions, a renewal of old strengths as well as an initiation of new ones. That, however, does not in itself provide a more benign outlook. Rather, it demands new and ruthless insights into the functioning and malfunctioning of society and this especially in a world of rapid and unpredictable change.

Are such conceptions as the identity crisis, then, mere additions to the classical scheme, or do they call for a transformation in clinical and theoretical outlook? I can only introduce this question in conclusion with a few notes on what, over the years, I have found to be a significant shift of focus from the classical psychoanalytic outlook to newer perspectives such as my own. These differences will highlight what I meant when I suggested earlier that backward *and* forward, inward *and* outward, downward *and* upward may all be dimensions to be considered in the development of a psychoanalytic model of human existence.

1. SUPER-EGO AND IDENTITY

Talcott Parsons has entered upon an integration of Freudian thought and modern sociology.[1] He emphasizes the usefulness which the Freudian concept of the super-ego (as "the internalization of the social structures") has had for his attempts to link man's inner life and his social world. Let me, therefore, compare the super-ego as an earlier concept—both in the sense that the concept was created earlier in the history of psychoanalysis and that the super-ego originates earlier in life—with the identity concept.

The child internalizes into the super-ego most of all the prohibitions emanating from the social structure—prohibitions, furthermore, which are perceived and accepted with the limited cognitive means of early childhood and are preserved with a primitive sado-masochism inherent in man's inborn proclivities for "turning upon himself" not only the moralistic aggression of his elders but also his own inexpressible rage. (These are aggravated, of course, in cultures counting heavily on guilt as an inner governor.) Thus internalized infantile moralism becomes isolated from further experience, wherefore man is always ready to fall back on a regressive punitive attitude which not only helps him to repress his own drives but which also allows him to treat others with righteous and often ferocious contempt, quite out of tune with his more advanced insights. Man could not become or remain moral without some such moralistic tendency; yet without a further development of truly *ethical* strivings, that is, an absorption of his moralism into the shared affirmation of values, as first envisaged in youth, man could never build the social structures which define his adult privileges and obligations.

Such further development, however, is not taken care of by Freud's "structural" point of view, which is useful primarily in analyzing the extent to which a person has become a system to himself, unable to adapt to and to grow with the actual present. Only a psychosocial theory can explain why adolescents must and can (as children cannot) join each other in cliques and "sub-cultures" and eventually join up with large-scale ideological trends of past or present, even though a few close themselves up in malignant states of individual isolation equally unknown in earlier life. Here the strength of the ego seems to be dependent not only on the individual's preadolescent experience (including the contents of the super-ego) but also on the support it receives from adolescent subcultures and from the living historical process.

But in psychoanalysis, what has thus been learned about a later stage of life, here youth, must always be reapplied to previous observations on earlier stages and disturbances. It becomes obvious, then, that an intricate relation between inner (cognitive and emotional) development and a stimulating and encouraging environment exists from the beginning of life, so that, in fact, no stage and no crisis could be formulated without a characterization of the mutual fit of individual and environment— that is, of the individual's capacity to relate to an ever expanding life space of people and institutions, on the one hand, and, on the other, the readiness of these people and institutions to make him part of an ongoing cultural concern. All this, in fact, prepares and determines the nature of the identity crisis, the solution of which firmly assigns a new and subsidiary place to the super-ego. This, however, is apt truly to return with a vengeance where identity is weakened by personal and historical upheavals. Then the most dangerous and (one regrets to say) the most human admixture of inward and outward aggression, namely, smoldering guilt and open violence, threatens all adaptedness.

2. FROM CASE HISTORY TO LIFE HISTORY

Case histories will reveal much of the "scarcity economics" of an impoverished mental condition, in which much of the available energy has been absorbed by inner conflict. But just because the "economic" point of view was invented to account for such simplified circumstances—simplified by the stereotypy of symptomatic behavior—they serve less well to understand that multiplication of energies which results from the individual's interplay with a widening radius of individuals and institutions. What is at stake here is not more and not less than psychosocial "reality." The clinical world view rightly takes regression and repression as its base lines and endeavors to fill in blind spots, to correct distortions, and to do away with illusions caused by infantile fixations. In thus helping the individual to "face reality," however, therapy creates no more than a minimum condition for dealing with the world "as it is." For man cannot live by what is real in the mere sense that it is undeniable as fact. To give this whole matter another dimension, I have insisted that Freud's "reality" really combines *factuality* with *actuality*—that is, a consensually validated world of facts with a *mutual activation* of like-minded people.[2] Only these two together provide a *sense of reality*. For even among the most intelligent and informed men, there is always a search for a world image shared with those who not only wield the same methods of verification but also think alike and make each other feel active and masterly: only together can they discern some kind of *truth* in experiences of a heightened relevance.

The German word for reality is *Wirklichkeit*. It goes beyond the world of facts (*Dingwelt*) in that it also has "*Werk*" in it as well as "*wirken*" and thus relates the sense of what is real to that which can be realized only by activity. Strangely, psychoanalysis speaks of its own method as one in which memories are "worked through," but case histories rarely take account of the patient's work life, as if ego strength could exist or be restored without the mastery of a section of reality by work and collaboration. Even the most gifted minds must experience verifiable fact by way of a mutual actualization within a unified world image based on some aspect of a period's technology. Only thus does knowledge or competence contribute to a sense of identity. At any rate, the experience of the identity crisis takes place when the world of childhood gives way to that of an ideological universe. Youth gradually becomes equipped with all the cognitive functions which adult man will ever call his own; but it also needs a sense of the future which anticipates what may yet be realized by action—beyond the facts that must be faced.

In the absence of theories including such communal concerns (and in urban settings culturally predisposed to seek roots and sanction in intellectual explanation), some writers and circles can come to cultivate a "reality" and a "normality" oriented toward some psychological utopia: reality then becomes what one has a terminology for. Such considerations give due warning that a science so close to questions of health and ethics must include methods of observing its own functioning in the cultural-historical process and its (intended and unintentional) influence upon it. For mankind will always attempt to absorb new insights as it absorbs other shocking truths, namely, with an adaptation combining overacceptance with deeper resistance.

3. THE INNER AND THE OUTER WORLD

The classical psychoanalytic technique was and has remained our principal research laboratory. How human nature works in "real life" is, by necessity, a matter of the speculative application of clinical findings to the "world outside." In psychoanalysis, it is claimed that only the clinical situation provides the setting that can reveal the true workings of the mind. The authority often quoted in this context is Freud's statement that only a broken crystal reveals a structure which is invisible in intactness. But a living ego organism is not a crystal, and even as anatomy and pathology must yield to physiology and biochemistry in the attempt to reconstruct intact functioning, psychoanalysis must complement its clinical findings with the study of psychosocial functioning. But this means to gain insight into the psychosocial structure of the observational setting itself. The natural sciences have had to take account of the fact that not only the personal equation of old but also all the details of the laboratory arrangements are apt to distort the bit of nature isolated for observation. Psychoanalysis, correspondingly, will have to study what it does to persons as it studies them. Equally important are insights into the world image emanating from a setting which, originating in a special clinical technique, becomes a habitual way of thinking, almost a way of life.

While it is true that no situation affords a better controlled access to the workings of the unconscious than does the psychoanalytic one, the greatest difficulty in the path of psychoanalysis as a general psychology probably consists in the remnants of its first conceptualization of the environment as an "outer world." To a patient under observation, the "world" he records (and, more often than not, complains about) easily becomes a hostile environment—"outer" as far as his most idiosyncratic wishes are concerned, and "outside" his precious relation to his therapist. This reveals much about him and about man; but it seems difficult to account for the nature of the clinical laboratory if the nature of the human environment is not included in the theory which guides the therapeutic encounter.

A related problem is the application of what has been observed in the encounter of therapist and patient to other forms of relationships. In the psychoanalytic situation, early and earliest relations with significant persons are ever again transferred and relieved, relost and renewed, and this (it seems probable) at least partially because of the technical choice of the basic couch arrangement by which the observer and the observed do not look each other in the face, communicate only with words, and thus avoid the earliest and the most lasting mutual affirmation: face to face, and eye to eye. Here, again, what is produced in the laboratory is highly instructive all around. But it presents to some extent an experimentally induced repetition of what in psychoanalytic theory is referred to as the search for an "object" —meaning both the original libidinal attachment to the mother as a whole person and the cognitive capacity to (literally) envisage her as a whole. This is truly basic; but it would seem wise to apply this "object" vocabulary only with caution to the functioning infant, as well as to any other person outside clinical captivity, and especially also to the young person whose needs during the identity crisis demand (besides some "parent substitutes") a vigorous peer group, an ideologically integrated universe, and the experience of a chosen mutuality with newly met persons and groups.

A close study of the original clinical setting as a laboratory would, incidentally, also reveal the fact that, together with locomotion, one elemental aspect of life—namely, violence—systematically escapes the treatment situation, as if the individual would participate in any uses of direct violence (from personal assault to aimless riot to armed force) only when absorbed in the unenlightened and uncivilized mass that makes up the "outer world." But then, as pointed out, the clinical laboratory channels all impulse to act or even move into introspection, so that the cured patient may be prepared for rational action. Thus, the clinician learns much more about the nature of inhibited and symptomatic action than about that of concerted action in actuality—with all its rationalizations and all its shared a-rationalities.

4. THE EGO AND THE I

A final methodological problem may or may not point beyond psychoanalysis. Freud's puritanical self-denial as an observer in the long run prejudiced the very act of observing.

Freud, it is true, went farther than any man before him in revealing systematically, to himself and others, how the observing
mind can learn to become conscious of the repressed. In doing
so, he conceptualized the ego as a psychological part of man's
unconscious inner structure, but he did not question the "I,"
the core of consciousness and of observation. Here, too, it should
be noted, the customary translation of the German *"ich"* by
"ego" deepens the neglect of the fact that *"ich"* also means "I":
in German, then, a subjective Ich = I is conceptualizing an objective Ich = Ego. But who wields this consciousness, so vastly
refined as a weapon and tool in dealing with the unconscious?
In using the word puritanical, I meant to imply that Freud's self-
restraint in this regard was a deeply reverent one: man had
talked enough of his soul, and had for too long congratulated
himself on being "the measure," or the conscious "center," of
the universe. If a man like Kierkegaard could write about the
leap of faith, a doctor and scientist could only grimly and rationally describe with the senses and the methods given to him
what many of the most exalted men as well as the most depraved
had previously refused to acknowledge.

It is one thing, however, to cultivate the proud rationality of
the Enlightenment, of which Freud was probably the last great
representative, and to crown it by insisting that irrationality
and the unconscious be included in the study of what can be
understood rationally. It is another matter to derive from such
study a comprehensive model of human consciousness. Thus, I
have found myself studying in the lives of religious innovators
that border area where neurotic and existential conflict meet
and where the "I" struggles for unencumbered awareness. And
again, is it not in adolescent experience that the "I" can first
really perceive itself as an existential phenomenon? It does so,
as it finds itself both involved and estranged in peculiar states
which transcend the identity crisis as defined in psychosocial
terms, because such states reflect not only the fear of otherness
and the anxiety of selfhood but also the dread of an individual

existence bounded by death. All of this, of course, is easily forgotten when the young adult assumes his responsibilities and
when he is forced to participate in the hierarchies of his society,
with its organized beliefs and cleverly concealed irrationalities.
But in the long run, the "I" struggles to transcend knowingly its
overdefined ego and, sooner or later, faces the dilemma of existence versus politics which I have attempted to approach in my
work on the Gandhian version of truth.

Behind all this may well be another, an existential identity
crisis. Psychoanalysis, in line with the Enlightenment, has offered
a rational explanation for the belief (and the need to believe) in
a deity. It has suggested that the god image "really" reflects the
infantile image of the father, as, indeed, it does in transparent
cultural variations. And yet, it may be for good existential as
well as evolutionary reasons that the ontogenetic parents are over-
endowed with an awe which can later be shared in common beliefs in god images and semidivine leaders. For a community of
I's may well be able to believe in a common fund of grace or
destiny only to the extent that all acknowledge a Super-I that
each I partakes in: a Being that Is. A consideration of this phenomenon could, in fact, begin with the question of what the
image of the great man must accomplish even for a community
of systematic skeptics—and analysts. At any rate, what religion
calls grace and sin transcend the goals of therapy—that is, the
relative comfort of adaptation and the reasonable management
of guilt.

This takes us beyond the identity crisis in its developmental
and psychosocial determinants. But then, this crisis makes sense
only as one of a series of life crises. What does happen, we may
well ask in conclusion, to adults who have "found their identity"
in the cultural consolidation of their day? Most adults, in the
past, turned their backs on identity questions and attended to
the inner cave of their familial, occupational, and civic concerns.
But this, so our questioning youth insists, cannot be taken as an

assurance that they have either transcended or truly forgotten what was once envisaged in the roamings of their youth. The question is: What have they done with it, and how ready are they to respond to the identity needs of the coming generations in the recurrent universal crisis of faith and power? In the end, it seems, psychoanalysis cannot claim to have exhausted its inquiry into man's unconscious unless it asks what may be the inner arrest peculiar to adulthood—not merely because of the burden of pervasive immaturities but as a consequence of the adult condition as such—whether "the times" offer too few final choices of an overdefined kind or too many ill-defined and exchangeable "roles." For it is only too obvious that, so far in man's total development, adulthood and maturity have rarely been synonymous. The study of the identity crisis, therefore, inexorably points to conflicts and conditions due to those role specifications which make man efficient at a given stage of economy and culture at the expense of the denial of major aspects of existence. Having begun as clinical art-and-science, psychoanalysis cannot shirk the question of what, from the point of view of an undivided human race, is "wrong" with the "normality" reached by groups of men under the conditions of pseudo-speciation. Does it not include pervasive group retrogressions, which cannot be subsumed under the categories of neurotic regressions but rather represent a joint fixation on historical formulae mortally dangerous to further adaptation?

PART TWO

In Search of Gandhi

I

On the Nature of "Psycho-Historical" Evidence

FIRST ACQUAINTANCE

A DECADE AGO, I represented one wing of the clinical arts and sciences in a symposium on Evidence and Inference. In order to explain "the nature of clinical evidence," I had to offer some observations of a "markedly personal nature," and this not only from predilection but because the only methodological certainty that I could claim for my specialty, the psychotherapeutic encounter, was "disciplined subjectivity." [1] Of all the other fields represented in that symposium, I felt closest (so I cautiously suggested) to the historian: for he, like the clinician, must serve the curious process by which selected portions of the past impose themselves on our renewed awareness and claim continued actuality in our contemporary commitments. We clinicians, of course, work under a Hippocratic contract with our clients; and the way they submit their past to our interpretation is a special form of historicizing, dominated by their sense of fragmentation and isolation and by our method of restoring to them,

---

The first account of this work was presented to the *Daedalus* symposium on Leadership at the Sterling Forest Conference Center, in 1967.

through the encounter with us, a semblance of wholeness, immediacy, and mutuality. But as we, in our jargon, "take a history" with the intention of illuminating it, we enter another's life, we "make history." Thus, both clinician and patient (and in psychoanalysis, at any rate, every clinician undergoes voluntary patienthood for didactic purposes) acquire more than an inkling of what Collingwood claims history is—namely, "the life of mind" which "both lives in historical process and knows itself as so living."

Since that symposium, the former caution in the approach to each other of clinician and historian has given way to quite active efforts to find common ground. These have been confined for the most part to the joint study of the traditional affinity of case history and life history. But here the clinician is inexorably drawn into super-personal history "itself," since he, too, must learn to conceive of, say, a "great" man's crises and achievements as communal events characteristic of a given historical period. Yet some historians probably begin to suspect that they, too, are practitioners of a restorative art which transforms the fragmentation of the past and the peculiarities of those who make history into such wholeness of meaning as mankind seeks. This, in fact, may become only too clear in our time, when the historian finds himself involved in ongoing history by an accelerated interplay of communication between the interpreters, as echoed by the mass media and the makers of history. Here, a new kind of Hippocratic oath may become necessary.

It is not my purpose, however, to blur the division between therapist and historian. Rather, I would like to try to delineate an in-between field which some of us have come to call the psycho-historical approach. Such a hyphenated name usually designates an area in which nobody as yet is methodologically quite at home, but which someday will be settled and incorporated without a trace of border disputes and double names. The necessity to delineate it, however, becomes urgent when forward workers rush in with claims which endanger systematic exploration. Thus, today, psychoanalytic theory is sometimes applied to historical events with little clarification of the criteria for such a transfer. Such bravado can lead to brilliant insights, but also to renewed doubt in the specific fittedness and general applicability of psychological interpretation. I will therefore attempt to discuss here, in a manner both "markedly personal" and didactic, what parallels I have found between my clinical experience and the study of a circumscribed historical event.

Since the symposium on Evidence and Inference, my study *Young Man Luther* has also appeared; [2] and nothing could have better symbolized the methodological embarrassment on the part even of friendly critics than the stereotyped way in which editors, both in this country and in England, captioned the reviews of my book with the phrase "Luther on the Couch." Now, clinicians are, in fact, rather sparing in the use of the couch except in a systematic psychoanalysis; yet, "on the couch" has assumed some such popular connotation as "on the carpet." And it so happens that Luther all his life was a flamboyant free associator and in his youth certainly often talked as if he *were* "on the couch." His urbane superior, von Staupitz, could we inform him of the new uses of this adaptable furniture, would gladly testify to that. He recognized in the young monk's raving insistence that his repentance had not yet convinced God a "confession compulsion" altogether out of proportion to what the father confessor was ready to receive or to absolve; wherefore he told young Luther that *he* was resisting *God*, not God him. And with the recognition of an unfunctional resistance operative within the very act of "free" self-revelation, the confessor of old had diagnosed at least something analogous to what we find on our clinical home ground.

As noted previously, Freud referred to the phenomenon of *transference* as "neither more nor less than the mainspring of the work of psychoanalysis." [3] And, indeed, for a good historical example of father transference, and, in fact, one clearly divided into a trusting and a mistrustful transference, we need look no further than Luther's relation to Herrn von Staupitz and to the Pope. How Luther succeeded in making these transferences historical in a grand manner is, for the moment, another matter. Transference is a universal tendency active in any relationship in which the other *also* "stands for" a person of the preadult past. This, naturally, plays a singularly important role in the clinical encounter, and yet not only in the patient's attitude toward the clinician. It is also an essential part of what the clinician must observe in himself: he, too, can transfer on different patients images and affects from *his* infantile past. This we call *countertransference*.

All these seeming difficulties, however, are the very tools of the psychoanalyst. To a determined believer in free will, they may all sound like weaknesses, if not dishonesties, while together they are really an intrinsic "property" of the clinical situation. Relived and resolved with systematic care, they are a necessary part of the evidence; and their elucidation is the only way to a cure. But are they also applicable to some aspects of historical research? Here the difficulties of a hyphenated approach become only too obvious, for in the absence of historical training I can only describe the way in which my clinical tools either hindered or helped the endeavor to elucidate a historical event. Yet, it would seem that even the best-trained historical mind could not "live in the historical process" without underscoring and erasing, professing and denying, even loving and hating, and this without trying to know himself as so living and so knowing. I may hope, then, that the predicaments to be described will remind the historian proper of his own experiences. As for historical data proper, I can only try to introduce a psychological dimension into what would seem to be well-established rules of evidence.

Three times in the early sixties, I visited the city of Ahmedabad in the Indian state of Gujarat. The first time I went on the invitation of some enlightened citizens in order to give a seminar on the human life cycle and to compare our modern conception of the stages of life with those of the Hindu tradition. My wife and I occupied a small house on the estate of an industrialist—the city being one of the oldest textile centers of the world. Nearby was the millowner's marble mansion, always open for rest and work to men of public life and of the mind; in its very shadow was the simple house of his sister, a saintly woman known as the Mother of Labor, in whose living room hung a portrait of Tolstoy inscribed by him for Gandhi. It came back to me only gradually (for I had known it when I was young) that this was the city in which Gandhi had lived for more than a decade and a half, and that it was this millowner and his sister (both in their seventies at the time of our visit) to whom Gandhi pays high and repeated tribute in his autobiography. They had been Gandhi's opponent and ally, respectively, in the dramatic event by which labor unionism was founded in India: the Ahmedabad textile strike of 1918.

My fascination was fed by memories. For even as Wilson's image, in Freud's words, "rose above the horizons," only to set in the cruel night of post-Versailles, so it was Gandhi's image which, for my generation, then rose above the horizon—on the other side of the world. As described to us by Romain Rolland, he seemed to have that pervasive presence, always dear to youth, which comes from total commitment to the actuality of both love and reason in every fleeting moment. The strike had been contemporaneous with Wilson's Fourteen Points; and if these Points were (and with variations still are) "Western democracy's answer to Bolshevism," so was Gandhi's *Satyagraha* (begun so locally) the East's answer to Wilson *and* to Lenin.

At the age of forty-five, Gandhi had returned to India "for good" in 1915, after having spent his student years in England and the years of his early manhood in South Africa. He had founded a settlement near Ahmedabad, the principal city of the province in which he had been born, and had found a liberal benefactor in the man whom we shall simply refer to as "the millowner." Gandhi had imposed on himself a delay of political action, his "probation" as he called it. However, once settled, he had immediately begun to travel extensively to become familiar with the life of the masses and to find circumscribed grievances suited to his approach: the nonviolent technique which he had developed in South Africa and had called *Satyagraha*—that is, a method of recognizing and mobilizing the forces of truth and peace in the opponent and oppressor as well as in the oppressed. Then he plunged in. In 1916, he made his famous fiery speech to the students in the Hindu University of Benares (*his* Wittenberg church door). In 1917, he found an opportunity to move in on the system of indigo growing in faraway Bihar in defense of the rights of the peasants there. And in 1918, he accepted, at the millowner's request, the mediatorship in a wage dispute in the principal industry at home, in Ahmedabad.[4] He had studied the situation carefully and had decided to accept the leadership of ten thousand workers, a decision which brought him into public, as well as personal, conflict with the millowner and aligned him on the side of the millowner's sister, who had been deeply involved in "social work" in the widest sense. In the weeks of this strike, Gandhi put into practice his full technique, including a brief fast. The whole matter ended in a manner so Gandhian that his pervasive presence, so far perceived only by a few leading citizens, yet spread parable-like among the people. He broke up his fast, because he had to concede to the millowner that there was an element of blackmail in his putting his very life on the line in a strictly economic issue. And he agreed to what then seemed a somewhat tortured compromise which nevertheless secured to the workers, in the long run, what they had asked for.

This story, then, promised to harbor fascinating public as well as private issues. It seemed significant that Gandhi, in the cataclysmic years 1917 and 1918, would have chosen for the demonstration of his kind of revolution grievances involving first peasants and then workers: for this city of Ahmedabad was not only the oldest manufacturing city in India, with an ancient guild structure; it also promised to be and eventually did become the most tightly unionized one. And as to the local and personal aspects, Gandhi seemed to be guided by a stubborn genius, in that he insisted on being a prophet first in his own country and in his own language, Gujarati. Visualize, in contrast, the global activities of other charismatic leaders in the concluding years of World War I. And, indeed, at the time, the mill strike was scarcely noted: "We cannot see what Mr. M. K. Gandhi can win, but we can well see that he might lose everything," wrote the leading newspaper in the area. Other contemporary observers, in fact, made fun of the convoluted conclusion of the whole affair, calling it a typical "bania" deal—referring to the bargaining habits of the dominant ethnic group in the region. And in his autobiography, written a decade later, the Mahatma makes relatively light of the whole event—a diffidence which he apparently transmitted to his biographers. Yet the very next year after the strike, he would lead the first nationwide civil disobedience and become forever India's Mahatma.

A student of Indian politics and a former co-worker of mine, Susanne Rudolph, has reviewed diverse self-images of India under the British Raj, and has summarized what Gandhi was about to do: "He resurrected," she writes, "an old and familiar path to courage, one that had always been significant to the twice-born castes, but had fallen into disrepute. By giving it new toughness and discipline in action, by stressing the sacrifice and self-control which it required, by making it an effective device of mass action, by involving millions in it, he reasserted its worth with an effectiveness that convinced his countrymen. . . . In the process of mastering his own fear and weakness, he reassured several generations that they need not fear those who had conquered them." [5]

Enter the "psycho-historian": Having learned to esteem the millowner and his sister and having become convinced of the historical and biographic significance of the strike as well as of the "resistance" against it, I determined to study both. My liv-

ing witnesses were to be my old Ahmedabad friends and a
widening circle of other survivors of the event to whom they
introduced me. But before I can account for at least my initial
work with them, I must come to grips with Gandhi as his own
witness. For his autobiography has haunted men and women of
my generation ever since the end of World War I. In what he
called his "Experiments with Truth," he conveyed to us his own
image of himself from childhood on, through the stages of his
manhood up through the period of Ahmedabad.[6] I will, then,
first review the leader's account of himself as a child, in order to
see how these accounts of himself read today. Thus, we once
more come up against that circular chronology, which forces
us to begin with Gandhi's general situation and state of mind at
the time when he wrote the autobiography for purposes both
political and spiritual. Only then can we follow him back into
his childhood, as seen from that vantage point. And only in
having established a number of themes reaching from the dim
past of his origins to the days of historical greatness can we begin to guess what the Ahmedabad event meant to him. After
that, we can begin to attend to those who joined him in that
event, and primarily to the millowner, who, in fact, found himself joined in battle with him in his own domain.

GANDHI'S AUTOBIOGRAPHY

The "presence" of Mahatma Gandhi rarely comes through in
the printed word available to us. There are "sayings" which
make a point with finality, and there are unforgettable record-
ings of his voice. But such self-revealing texts as his autobiography were written in his native Gujarati, a language spoken
by only a fraction of his countrymen. For the vast majority of
them, it had to be translated into other regional languages. And
for us it was translated into English by his faithful secretary,
who sacrifices to an almost schoolboyish fidelity much of the
passion, the poignancy, and the humor that (so I am told) shine
through in Gandhi's Gujarati as well as occasionally in his own

use of English. This accounts for some, but not all, of the haze surrounding the intimate events of his first fifty years which are recorded in his autobiography, the standard history of his beginnings. Out of this text there has emerged a stereotyped Gandhi who is almost too open to fragmentary psychoanalytic interpretation, while in many ways he fails to make psychological sense. I have tried to visualize him and to "hear" him in his middle years, just before he became the Mahatma. In what I have perceived, he stands out almost hauntingly as a man who, while small and ascetic, was of impressive agility and energy, totally serious and yet of an infectious gaiety, always himself and yet attuned to each counterplayer, and most of all utterly and always *there*. Such a man, of course, can on occasion be mortally depressed as well as demonstratively tired and desperately sick. And he is by no means always likable. The level of "liking," however, seems hardly to apply, unless one has special reasons (and surprisingly many Indians do) to totally dislike him. But after having read him and having talked to men and women who knew him in his middle years, it comes as a shock almost conducive to tears to hear his clear, calm, and maternal voice on a noisy old record or to see him move about gaily in a jerky amateur movie.

I have also tried to visualize the child who was to be that man, and have been similarly moved by stiffly posed photographs depicting little Moniya or young Mohandas. One senses that he was more exquisitely put together than the sum of the stories told about him would suggest. Who can describe, who "analyze" such a youngster? Straight, and yet not stiff; shy, and yet not withdrawn; fearful, and yet determined; intelligent, and yet not bookish; willful, and yet not stubborn; sensual, and yet not soft: all of which adds up to an integrity that is, in essence, unexplainable and without which no evaluation holds. Imagining the life that was ahead of that boy and that young man, one cannot help thinking that the funeral pyre that consumed his remains to the bones was an elemental event of pity and charity, compared to the totem meal by which his memory is now devoured by friends and adversaries alike. Many feed on him, deriving pride from having owned him, or from having intelligently disposed of him, or from being able to classify the lifeless pieces. But nobody thereby acquires (for that is the archaic illusion of a totem meal) that grace which held him together and which gave him—and, through him, millions—a special and most rare kind of aliveness.

Gandhi's references to himself as a child, especially, can sound deadeningly repetitious to the Western ear. He was, we are told, not a good student, but somehow did quite well without half trying. Most jealously watching his own character, he became tearful when doubted. Very shy and seemingly uncritical of elders, he was intensely aware of their foibles, and attached to them by *his* wish to serve *them*. Not given to playful levity, he preferred fantasies and stories extolling devotion to parents. Married at thirteen to a girl who would not be taught by him to read and write, he made her accept him as a husband driven by carnal desire of an alleged magnitude that might have debilitated them both for life. He tried desperately to reform his friend and "evil genius," a Muslim boy who went to unbelievable lengths to counter-reform him in the worldly ways of meat-eating and visiting prostitutes. Such a stereotyped record is all that many a reader will remember. Some scenes stand out and must be read with a fresh eye by any would-be interpreter: they concern the ailing father who had been invalided in an accident on the way to the boy's wedding and whom the boy nursed passionately. They are climaxed by an account of the father's death. This is (to use Kierkegaard's word) the Curse in the story, for the father died in an uncle's arms while Mohandas, instead of watching over him, had sought his marital bed, to lie with his (pregnant) wife.

Since the "reconstruction" of leaders as the children they have been has become an inescapable pursuit, I propose to reevaluate here Gandhi's version of his childhood and youth. Psychoanalytic usage has bequeathed to us a certain grammar and syntax of what may be called traumatology, which makes it almost impossible, given some good will seasoned with some basic therapeutic intent, not to see, first of all, what went basically "wrong" with somebody. In applying my métier to young Luther, I have attempted to understand also the fabulous restorative energy of youth which helped his native genius to reaffirm Christian faith with new liveliness and power much over and beyond what would at times appear to be a pathological hate of the papacy. In studying middle-aged Gandhi, I must try to trace indications that such a leader started to develop his singular effectiveness along with his unique concerns rather early in life, and how both matured with the deepened conflicts of each subsequent stage. Just because the time has come when man must understand the danger as well as the nature of what he calls greatness, it is not enough to equate that phenomenon with some kind of extraordinary defect.

Some great men, it is true, do appear to have pervasive neuroses. Their mortal conflicts, however, do not seem containable within a set of symptoms, even if (or just because) they themselves oblige us by offering flamboyant confessions resembling the kind of data seen in case histories. The varieties of great confessions, and their varying impact on their times, certainly call for the interpretation of a William James. There is always some naïve self-revelation in any outpouring of autobiographical data. Yet each given medium (diary or conversation, correspondence or autobiography) has its own formal laws and serves tradition and personal style. As to unconscious motivation, we must always remember that the autobiographer has not agreed to a therapeutic contract by which he promises to put into words all that "comes to his mind."

Memories are an intrinsic part of the actuality in which they emerge. Our first concern must be with the stage of life in which a given medium was used to retell, relive, or reactivate an earlier stage for the purpose of heightening some sense of ac-

tuality in the telling. At best, memories connect meaningfully
what happened once and what is happening now. If they are
painful, they at least recover from the defeats of the past the
stragglers of unlived potentials. All confessions seek to settle a
(big or small) curse.

First, then, we consider Gandhi's autobiography as a historical
event in its own right. I have pointed to the Indian language
problem which gives it a certain opaqueness. But biographers are
also apt to ignore the honest methodological statements with
which Gandhi himself introduces his autobiography. "I have no
spare time. I could only write a chapter week by week. Something has to be written for *Navajivan* every week. Why should
it not be the autobiography? . . ."

So the autobiography was written as a series of "columns"
over the course of several years, and this for a weekly with a
marked pedagogic message. Each column concludes with a
moral, the full meaning of which can be grasped only by a
reader who knows how Indian elders speak to children and
youth and how the young are inclined to react.

Gandhi, at the time, was in his late fifties, and thus, maybe
somewhat precociously, speaking out of a stage of life that has
(or had) a definite connotation within the Hindu life cycle:
"What I want to achieve—what I have been striving and pining
to achieve these . . . years,—is self-realization, to see God face
to face, to attain Moksha." *Moksha* means final renunciation and
withdrawal; and his testamental tone is further explained in the
expressed resolve that ". . . only those matters of religion that
can be comprehended as much by children as by older people,
will be included in this story." Only against this background can
we search these confessions for revelations of hidden motivation.
And never assume without good reason that a man like Gandhi
is revealing "unconsciously" what is welcome evidence to the
spying modern eye. It is, for example, futile to think that one
can "expose" feminine conflicts in a man who says with an utterly relaxed smile that he aspires to being "half a woman"—and

who, indeed, remains a leader with equal appeal for women and men. At any rate, autobiographies are written at certain late stages of life for the purpose of re-creating oneself in the image of one's own method; and they are written to make that image convincing.

Susanne Rudolph has enlarged on the astonishing fact that such "confessions" could be politically effective because an Indian audience "felt further reassured that the conditions of his political potency had been long preparing and had been severely tested." One could point here to Western examples of the singular impact of famous confessions of diverse kinds, from St. Augustine's to Rousseau's, each a work that gave a radical new view of man's struggle with his own passions and of his search for some revelatory truth. To these I would add Freud's *Interpretation of Dreams*, written toward the turn of the century, in which confession transcends itself in methodical self-analysis. "If Gandhi lived his private life in public," as Rudolph has put it, "and if his private restraint became a matter of public concern, it was because both he and those who observed him believed that a man's claims to be just, to command others, and to attain the wisdom of a statesman, were proportional to the capacity for self-restraint." [7] This emphasis is significant in a civilization permeated with ancient concepts concerning the "sublimation" of life-creating semen into the power of thought—and into political potency. If Gandhi's ascetic self-revelations, furthermore, seem sometimes characterized by a florid obsessiveness, so are the opposite extremes of his culture—for example, the exhaustive inventory of copulatory variations depicted on voluptuous temple façades or listed in pedantic handbooks.

But autobiographies are also written at specific periods of public life. In 1925, Gandhi was "politically silent." His career was then, at best, a plateau reached after a steep ascent and stretching toward a nebulous horizon: whether it would lose itself there or another ascent loom ahead was then hard to know. Let us summarize events up to the writing of the memoirs.

Gandhi had spent two decades in South Africa where he had developed the method of *Satyagraha,* or "truth force." First negatively translated as "nonviolence," *Satyagraha* constitutes the faith that he who can face his own propensities for hate and violence "in truth" can count on a remnant of truth in the most vicious opponent, if he approaches him actively with the simple logic of incorruptible love. Gandhi had been in his middle forties when, in 1915, he returned to India, and only in 1918 had he begun to apply his method, first locally (in support of peasants in the Himalayan foothills and of the workers in Ahmedabad) and then nationally in the form of widespread civil disobedience. This latter undertaking he had to call off himself because he felt that the Indian masses were not ready. In 1922, as he had proudly demanded, he had been sentenced to six years in jail but had been released after two. He had found the political climate changed, and what unity he had been able to create between Hindus and Muslims had already been decisively weakened. In fact, his leaderless followers in nonviolence and noncooperation had acquired the nickname "Non-Changers." He had withdrawn from politics and devoted himself to the purification of himself and of India, both to be achieved by spinning, praying, and self-control, and this according to the faith that never left him— namely, that purity is (and brings) freedom, even as truth is (and results in) nonviolence. He had witnessed the danger of redoubled violence in the wake of ill-applied nonviolence and wanted to work his way into the people's hearts "silently so far as possible, even as I did between 1915–1919." He was often depressed. He fasted to unite his followers. Concluding a twenty-one-day fast, he said a prayer in which he asked God to make him His instrument if he should again "enter the world of strife," reminding Him (strangely enough) of Napoleon, "who planned much and found himself a prisoner in St. Helena," and of the "mighty Kaiser, who aimed at the crown of Europe and is reduced to the status of a private gentleman."

The relationship of each installment of his autobiography to the detailed course of historical events is being clarified as the monumental publication by the government of India, in chronological order, of *The Collected Works of Mahatma Gandhi* [8] includes each stage of his life. In the meantime, the general mood of that period should caution us against accepting at face value the memories concerning the child who became that man. But the peculiarities of the autobiography must also be underscored because the occasionally priggish tone and the monotonous references to "lust" create a barrier between the originator of *Satyagraha* and today's and tomorrow's fighters for peace. For what is at stake is the future of what he called "truth force" in a technological world predictably much more affluent and much less ascetic, and the relationship of a more sovereign sensuality (including, maybe, its more sovereign sacrifice) to creative peacefulness.

To sum up: at the time when Gandhi wrote the autobiography, he had behind him a probationary period during which he had become one of the living mahatmas, followed by a meteoric rise to *the* Mahatmaship—a position entirely reformulated by him as one uniting politics and religion. Having then withdrawn from politics, he was in some danger of continuing as nothing-but-the-Mahatma in a religious sense. In his utterances of these years, he consolidated the Mahatmaship exactly midway between the creation of a new secular religiosity and a fresh political beginning, this time on the more solid basis of a wide appeal to the masses. And while at the conclusion of the autobiography he had reached the end of the plateau and saw that a new ascent was ahead of him, he ended with words reminiscent of the beginning: "I must reduce myself to zero." Zero, however, as Joan Bondurant has recently re-emphasized, is a number powerful indeed in Indian thinking. To those who would take out of such a context and isolate any scene either as "factual" or as a distortion of memory inviting interpretation, one is inclined to recommend a psycho-historical criterion. An item in an autobiography should be judged first for its meaning in the *stage of the recorder's life*, and secondly, for its meaning in the *course of his whole life history*. And this means that at the same time it must be seen in the immediate context of *contemporary history* and in the *historical process* of which that period is but a stage. Only then can one turn to the "remembered" item itself, and see what set of criteria would give it a certain convincing probability.

A LIFELONG TRAIT

We will now turn to one of the idiosyncratic trends that are recognizable throughout his *Story of My Experiments with Truth*—and throughout the course of Gandhi's life. His most readable biographer, B. R. Nanda, can say: "What was extraordinary was the way his adventures ended. In every case he posed for himself a problem for which he sought a solution by framing a proposition in moral algebra." [9] Such judgment agrees with Gandhi's dominant "line," but, one must ask, is it compatible with a man's, any man's, development? In projecting this experimental spirit backward, does the aging man make his childhood conform to the needs of his old age? Or do the traumata of his childhood now, indeed, exact an irreversible forfeit? Or do the old man *and* the child now meet each other in a mutual recognition that may be an intrinsic potential of the human life cycle—and possibly a kind of psychological euthanasia? If Gandhi was an existential experimentalist all his life, this propensity must have had precursors suited to the capacities of a little boy and of a young man. For surely (and this is our second set of criteria for a valid psycho-historical item) an early event should be *compatible with the developmental stage* at which it is said to have occurred. And there should be a plausible *developmental continuity* between the pervasive experimentalism of little Moniya and of young Mohandas, of Mr. M. K. Gandhi and of the aging Mahatma.

Here, as pointed out, we are interested not only in the traumata that drive a man into particular avenues of greatness but in some of the very ingredients of that future greatness—that is, in the kind of active tension that he maintained at each stage even where and when he seemed diffident, and by which he cultivated in himself a secret propensity for leadership even when, and perhaps just when, he seemed to be failing. He was once a child with limitations set by the limits of development, and yet the saying "The child is father of the man" makes particular sense for special men: they, indeed, strive to become their own fathers and, in a special way, their parents' fathers while not yet adult.

Just because any childhood scene, however, nowadays fits into a stereotyped scenery of infantile complexes, it is doubly important to take the time to visualize the actual setting of childhood events. Here the world owes a lasting debt to Pyarelal (Nayar), who was Gandhi's secretary for nearly three decades, and who has undertaken to write a comprehensive biography.[10] It contains some vivid descriptions that have the ring of plausibility.

The earliest available photograph suggests that Moniya was, indeed, a small child with "a cheerful, sweet face, and lovely eyes." Pyarelal omits mention, however, of the improbably big ears that were always to detract from Gandhi's countenance. "Unlike other children he was not given to crying. He had a hearty ringing laughter, and everybody liked to fondle him." The youngest and last son of a young mother (twenty-five) and a much older father (forty-seven), he was born into the typical large family crammed into a house in the port city of Porbandar on the Arabian Sea coast of the peninsula of Kathiawar, a shining "white city" with narrow lanes and crowded bazaars. Thus, like many great leaders, he was born on the periphery of his future "domain," and in a setting that would provide a strong regional identity to build on. Kathiawar is a fisherman's and a sea trader's world, renowned for its toughness and shrewdness, for from here, as from the larger port of Cambay, the ships went back and forth between India and Arabia and the east coast of

Africa—down to South Africa. He grew up in a three-story ancestral house which his father shared with his five brothers and their families. The suite allotted to his father (head of the family and prime minister of a small princely state) was on the ground floor and had two rooms, one twenty by thirteen feet, one thirteen by twelve feet, a tiny kitchen, and a veranda. All of this must underscore for us the literal inescapability in the "joint family" system, and the special arrangements any sensitive and self-willed creature must make for some privacy and for some right to move around idiosyncratically.

One of the most instructive passages in Pyarelal's book characterizes the life of a joint family, "where so many people with diverse tastes, habits and temperaments are cooped up day and night in a narrow space, from week to week, month to month and year to year." Along with the virtues of such a family life, which are easily overlooked by Western devotees and victims of small families, he points to sources of bitter ambivalence: "Little things assume big proportions; the slightest suggestion of unfairness or partiality gives rise to petty rivalries, jealousies, and intrigues. To smooth them requires infinite patience, resourcefulness and knowledge of human nature."

The mother, Putali Ba, was an ideal mother of a joint family: "She never made any distinction between her own children and other children in the family . . ." Likewise, the prime minister, as the head of the family, looked after the well-being of every member of his clan well into their adult lives. I would think that the ideal that both mother and father treat everybody's children with equal consideration may also be one of the deepest sources of discontent. In giving to all, the parents, and particularly the mother, may give too little to each, and this may well constitute a style of parenthood responsible for an occasional Indian trait often remarked on by Westerners, namely, a sulking and deeply angry insistence on being granted, sometime, by somebody, an exclusive relationship of preference or of mutual fusion. As Indian fiction also attests, this need may attach itself to an aunt or an uncle who is capable of identifying with lonely children. It adds, I believe, a strong element to the Indian's search for a guru, and to an almost desperate need to be alone with a loved or revered person, or, in the case of special desperation or special meditative gifts, with oneself. A Westerner rarely visualizes the Eastern wish to be isolated (in lonely spots or in the middle of a crowd) against the background of the unavoidable (if often joyful) total immersion in "folks." Life, then, can become a very special arrangement of parallel isolation and detached fusion.

Nanda (outdoing Gandhi) ascribes to young Mohandas excessive passivity, verging on a morbid "diffidence." But Pyarelal's account permits us to see how the little boy and youth survived both an early scrupulosity and a large family with all the integrity and the energy we know him to have possessed later. Moniya had a quality of tenacious and clever attachment which, so it seems, made his parents feel that their relationship to him was a special one, and made him, in turn, feel that his was the fate of an elect being. For the nature of his early relationships, one word suggests itself which expresses the infantile and playful side of what the aging advocate of *Moksha* calls "experiments with truth." The word is "testing." For the little boy was driven to test people around him by a resourcefully varied number of methods, and his parents seem to have had enough humor to agree to being teased rather than to punish him for the stubbornness and the implicit cruelty that are common ingredients of all provocation. Outstanding, also, throughout his life, was Gandhi's locomotor restlessness, a not uncommon characteristic of great men. Paired with insatiable curiosity, this provides energy for testing the unknown. But it also "tested" those who were supposed to keep an eye on him while his mother was busy; his older sister describes him as a mercurial teaser. He would try to make friends with animals, sometimes overdoing it by "twisting dogs' ears." This childlike perverseness persisted into Gandhi's old age: at least one proud young man told me that he could not forgive Gandhi for having, on first acquaintance, twisted his ears rather painfully when *he* was a child. The older sister, at any rate, did not have it easy. It was good to get Moniya out of the house, for when his father was not there he would usurp sacrosanct rights—for example, by removing the image of the ruling prince from a stool and seating himself in its place. He also used to scatter the utensils of worship and to "write" on the floor. When his mother tried to forbid this, he (in Pyarelal's words) "stoutly dissented." (Was this the onto-genetic origin of the sit-down?) On the other hand, he strongly dissented also from any necessity of being watched out of doors. So his sister was told to keep out of sight when watching him, a considerateness at variance with the suggestion that his father wanted to squelch his son's adventuresomeness—at least in child-hood. But while he was playful and without fear when amusing himself, he proved uninterested in all competitive games with other boys. For this he blamed his "shyness." Yet he later took on the role of peacemaker when playmates quarreled among themselves. This, Pyarelal says, was the "passion of his life," from the school in Rajkot to the councils of the British Raj. One could also say that he would never "play" unless he was in a position of such moral dominance that he could represent his power to himself and to others as maintained "for their own good." And often (a not unimportant point) it appeared to be just that.

If this teasing, testing, and experimenting is a trait that meets our developmental criteria since it does find a "higher" form on each level, it must also be seen as a highly personalized form of a relevant cultural pattern. And, indeed, mutual teasing holds a prominent place among those more or less spontaneous ritualiza-tions that make life in the joint family bearable and, on occasion, enjoyable. We must then add a further criterion to a psycho-historical item that we have accepted as developmentally prob-able. It must have a high probability *within the contemporary culture* of the community, and (again) *within the history of that culture*. If, then, the teasing of people and of animals in child-hood was one of the outstanding ways in which Mohandas tested his family and the world of Porbandar, we will recognize many somberly reported stories of his later life as, in fact, animated by a gay teasing obvious to all those present at the time. And, to reach far ahead in his life's history, we may recognize a personal inner triumph, as well as a peacemaking gesture, in the story of how the Mahatma teased the Viceroy in his own palace.

It was after the great Salt March in 1930, in which Gandhi had led his *satyagrahis* from Ahmedabad to the sea in order to dramatize the symbolic as well as the practical implications of the salt tax. He had been arrested, and while he was in jail his *satyagrahis* attempted to raid the government's salt works and were brutally attacked by the police. After some compromises all around, Gandhi was invited to talks with the Viceroy. Churchill scoffed at the "seditious fakir, striding half-naked up the steps of the Viceroy's palace, to negotiate with the repre-sentative of the King-Emperor." But the Viceroy, Lord Irwin, has described the meeting as "the most dramatic personal en-counter between a Viceroy and an Indian leader." When Gandhi was handed hot water for tea, he poured into it a bit of (tax-free) salt from a small paper bag hidden in his shawl and re-marked smilingly, "To remind us of the famous Boston Tea Party."

Such a teasing attitude, however, to be historically relevant, must also be shown to be more than a gratuitous quirk, and, in-deed, to be an indispensable quality of a man's influence on the very people with whom he shared the *actuality of a historical situation*. As one can learn from patients and from everyday failures, teasing is one of those spontaneous ritualizations that wilt when the teaser becomes sadistic or the teased masochistic. Seasoned playfulness is long in developing, and I think that in Gandhi's life it can be shown to have alleviated his moral precoc-ity and to have added a significant dimension to his evolving personal and political style. It even seems to be an essential ingredient in nonviolence. If one watches a moving picture of Gandhi's *satyagrahis* marching to the sea, it is, as it were, physiognomically obvious that they express a certain mature and vigorous "teasing" attitude toward the British authorities, implying that surely they could not make a bloody issue out of a people's determination to scoop up the salt out of their own sea, tax-free. That the British (and the Indian constabulary) eventually did react with a brutality multiplied by a sense of being taunted and of "not being able to take it" cost them much of their inner authority in Indian eyes as well as in their own. So even though the march did not lead to immediate and complete formal success (as, indeed, Gandhi's campaigns usually did not), his playful gesture marked a declaration of equality such as is expressed in all successful teasing.

Teasing and testing, then, can be traced forward and backward as two (but, I emphasize, only two) of the ingredients of those early encounters with mother and father, child wife and boyhood friend, that Gandhi makes so much of in his autobiography. Pyarelal says that Gandhi's mother gave him the ideal of "living not only for mankind but in mankind" and that his father provided the "meticulous regard" for the "littlest of the little things" and "perfection in performance." He emerged from his relationship with his mother as a boy given to one intense relationship at a time and this a relationship of ceaseless testing—for the counterplayer's good. When he ran to his mother, it was to serve her, and when he confessed a theft to his father, the father seemed to be a better man for his son's confession. In each case, however, the confrontation avidly sought by the young experimenter showed him his own limits of power, and yet confirmed the moral direction of his peculiar genius. That, as Susanne Rudolph concludes, "Gandhi in his inner being was quite the reverse of the filial model he defends in the autobiography" [11] is a diagnosis pertaining to something Gandhi all his life was himself aware of, to a fault. But it is true that, like all great self-confessors, Gandhi reveals in his childhood memories those basic "complexes" (such as the Oedipus complex) for which only Freud's new confessional discipline has found adequate concepts—if not always felicitous terms. When, at the end, young Gandhi despaired of the possibility of combining the business of salvation with the intense intimacy demanded by the basic cast of characters in human life, he concluded, "He who would be friends with God must remain alone or make the whole world his friend." Thus, bettering even the mother of a joint family, he adopted all of humanity, and bettering the prime minister of Kathiawar, he made himself meticulously responsible for India and the whole empire. But all this is not a mere matter of projecting the conflicts of his childhood on a widening world of concerns—a crank, a fanatic, and a psychotic could manage that—but one of a minute and concrete interplay, of a craftsmanlike series of "experiments" with historical actuality in its political and economic aspects.

HIS OWN WITNESS

To study an event in Gandhi's life that happened before he wrote his autobiography means first to see what he himself said about it. In connection with some themes of his childhood, I have attempted to detail the difficulties encountered in such respectful inquiry. I have postulated that in perusing a man's memoirs for the purpose of reconstructing past moments and reinterpreting pervasive motivational trends, one must first ask oneself at what age and under what general circumstances the memoirs were written, what their intended purpose was, and what form they assumed. Only then can one proceed to judge the less conscious motivations, which may have led the autobiographer to emphasize selectively some experiences and omit other equally decisive ones; to profess and reveal flamboyantly some deed or misdeed and to disguise or deny equally obvious commitments; to argue and to try to prove what seems to purify or confirm his historical role and to correct what might spoil the kind of immortality he has chosen for himself. Confession-like remembrances often seem to be the most naïvely revealing and yet are also the most complex form of autobiography, for they attempt to prove the author's purity by a public emphasis on his impurities and therefore confound his honesty both as a sinner and a braggart. Therefore, observers trained in clinical observation cannot accept an event reported in an autobiography —such as, for example, Gandhi's account of his father's death— either as a factual event or as a naïve confession without asking why the item came to be prominent in *its* autonomous setting, the autobiography; and why a particular form of autobiography was being practiced or, indeed, newly created at that moment in history. Gandhi himself states that he knew an autobiography to be a rather un-Indian phenomenon, which makes his own an all the more elemental creation, comparable to the influential confessions of such men as St. Augustine and Rousseau.

To put all this diagrammatically and didactically, a psycho-historical reviewer would have to fathom—in one intuitive configuration of thought if he can and with the help of a diagram if he must—the complementarity of at least four conditions under which a record emerges.

Functions of the Record

	I. Moment	II. Sequence
1. Individual	in the recorder's stage of life and general condition	in the recorder's life history
2. Community	in the state of the recorder's community	in the history of the recorder's community

Under I–1, then, we would focus as if with a magnifying glass on one segment of the recorder's life as a period with a circumscribed quality. Gandhi's autobiography served the acute function of demonstrating an aging reformer's capacity to apply what he called truth to the balance sheet of his own failures and successes, in order to gain the wisdom of renunciation for him-

self and to promote a new level of political and spiritual awareness in his nation. But we would also have to consider the special
inner conflicts and overt mood swings which aggravated these,
his often withdrawn and "silent" years. Under I–2, we would
consider all the acute circumstances in Indian history which
would make Gandhi feel that he would find an echo for his message in those segments of India's awakening youth who could
read—or be read to. Under II–1, we would remember that confession seems to have been a passion for him throughout life and
that his marked concern with *Moksha* began in a precocious
conscience development in childhood (which, in fact, he shares
with other *homines religiosi*). In II–2, however, we would have
to account for the fact that Gandhi's record, in both content and
style, went far beyond the traditional forms of self-revelation in
India and bridged such confessionalism as St. Augustine's or
Tolstoy's awareness as Christians and Rousseau's passionate and
Freud's systematized insight into the power of infantile and
juvenile experience. From the psycho-historical viewpoint, then,
the question is not, or not only, whether a man like Gandhi inadvertently proves some of Freud's points (such as the power of
the emotions subsumed under the term "Oedipus complex") but
why such items which we now recognize as universal were re-
enacted in different media of representation (*including* Freud's
dream analyses) by particular types of men in given periods of
history—and why, indeed, their time was ready for them and
their medium: for only such complementarity makes a confession momentous and its historical analysis meaningful.

Our diagrammatic boxes, then, suggest the *relativity* governing any historical item—that is, the "concomitant variability" of
passing moment and long-range trend, of individual life cycle
and communal development.

Let me now turn to the autobiography's account of the
strike of 1918—the rough outline of which I have previously
sketched. If, for brevity's sake, I now refer to it as the Event,

the reader, I trust, will not assume (as some critics have) that because it became important for me, I also consider it *the* Event in Gandhi's life. There is, in fact, besides Gandhi's retrospective reflections, only one full account of it, a pamphlet of less than a hundred pages written by the man who was then Gandhi's secretary.[12] Gandhi's own approach to the matter is strangely episodic and, in fact, broken up by the insertion of a seemingly quite unrelated story.[13] This is the sequence: In a chapter (or installment) called "In Touch with Labor," Gandhi reports on the "delicate situation" in Ahmedabad where a sister "had to battle against her own brother." His friendly relations with both "made fighting with them the more difficult." But he considered the case of the mill hands strong, and he therefore "had to advise the laborers to go on strike." There follows a summary, less than one page long, of nearly twenty days of a strike during which he set in motion all the principles and techniques of his militant and nonviolent *Satyagraha*—on a local scale, to be sure, but with lasting consequences for Ahmedabad, India, and beyond. Then the story of the strike is interrupted by a chapter called "A Peep into the Ashram." Here the reader is entertained with a description of the multitude of snakes which infested the land by the river to which Gandhi, at the time of the strike, had just moved his settlement. Gandhi recounts how he and his ashramites in South Africa, as well as in India, had always avoided killing snakes and that in twenty-five years of such practice "no loss of life [had been] occasioned by snake bite."[14] Only then, in a further chapter, does Gandhi conclude the strike story by reporting its climax—namely, his first fast in a public issue, in spite of which (or, as we shall see, because of which) the strike ended with what looked to many like a kind of demeaning compromise. What was at stake then, and what was still at stake at the writing of the autobiography, was the purity of the nonviolent method: the millowner could (and did) consider Gandhi's fast an unfairly coercive way of making the employers give in, whereas Gandhi did (and always would) consider a fast only justified as a means of persuading his own weakening supporters to hold out.

The methodological question that arises here is whether the chapter which interrupts the account of the strike could be shown to signify an inner resistance against the whole story. Such a thought comes "naturally"—maybe too naturally—to a clinical observer, who knows how an adult in psychoanalysis will embark on a seemingly easy progression of free associations only to find suddenly that he has forgotten what he was about to say next or to interrupt his own trend of thought with what appears to be a senseless image or sentence "from nowhere." Some scrutiny can soon reveal that what had thus been lost or had intruded was, in fact, an important key to the underlying meaning of the whole sequence of thoughts. In a patient, we would consider such disruption to be unconscious and symptomatically related to his pathology; and we may feel it incumbent on us to clarify the matter by interpretation. Men like Gandhi, on the other hand, may sense or know quite well what they are doing, and I will later report on Gandhi's expressed awareness of such a disruption in another part of the autobiography.

But what could the nonkilling of snakes have to do with the Ahmedabad strike and with Gandhi's relation to the millowner? Mere symbolic play with themes might suggest that in the first instance peaceful Gandhiites come up against millowners; in the second, against poisonous snakes; and in the third, against millowners again. Do snakes, then, "stand for" millowners? If one can win over poisonous snakes by love and nonviolence, the hidden thought might be, then perhaps one can reach the hearts of industrialists too. Or the suggestion might be more damaging —namely, that it would be more profitable to be kind to poisonous snakes than to industrialists—and here we remember that another Man of Peace, also using an analogy from the bestiary, once mused that big lazy camels might be able to squeeze through where a rich man could not or would not.

There is, however, an explanation closer to historical fact

and to the propagandistic purpose of the autobiography. Gandhi and the millowner, since the strike, had been involved in a public scandal, albeit this time on the same side. Briefly, one year the millowner had noted hordes of ferocious-looking dogs around his factory on the outskirts of the city and had found out that the municipal police, knowing how Hindus feel about killing animals, were in the habit of releasing captured stray dogs outside the city limits. Since hydrophobia had reached major proportions in the area, the millowner had requested the police to kill these stray dogs, and some obliging officer, for reasons of his own, had arranged for the carcasses to be carted away, on a Hindu holiday, through the crowded city streets. Such is the stuff that riots are made of in India. But Gandhi did not hesitate to speak up for the millowner, saying he himself would kill a deranged man if he found him massacring other people. He wrote in *Young India:* "The lower animals are our brethren. I include among them the lion and the tiger. We do not know how to live with these carnivorous beasts and poisonous reptiles because of our ignorance. When man learns better, he will learn to befriend even these. Today he does not even know how to befriend a man of a different religion or from a different country." [15]

In this prophetic statement, we see the poisonous reptiles "associated" with carnivorous beasts; and from here it is only one step to the interpretation that Gandhi, before telling the story of how he had made what seemed to be undue concessions to the millowner at the end of the strike, had to tell himself and his readers that his basic principles had not suffered on that other and more widely known occasion when he took the millowner's side.

Was Gandhi "conscious" of such pleading with the reader? Probably, for the whole trend of thought fits well into the professed aim of his self-revelations: to sketch his "experiments with truth." But factual explanation (and here is the psycho-historical point) should not do away with the underlying emotional actu-

ality. The assumption of a pervasive ambivalence toward the
millowner is inescapable. But even then it is important to see
how the two men, throughout a long life, could accept each
other's economic enmity as part of a mutual and manly acceptance of the Hindu *dharma*—that is, of the assignment to each
man of a place within the world order which he must fulfill in
order to have a higher chance in another life. If, as Gandhi
would put it, "fasting is my business," then making money was
that of the millowner; and Gandhi could not have fulfilled his
role of saintly politician (or, as he put it, "a politician who
tried to be a saint") had he not had the financial support of
wealthy men. This, the Marxists may say, corrupted him, while
the Hindu point of view would merely call for a clean division
of roles within a common search for a higher truth. The
Freudian point of view, however, would suggest that such a
situation might also harbor "transferences" to later relations in
life of earlier unresolvable conflicts.

Young Gandhi had, in varying ways, forsaken his caste and
his father when he left India to become an English barrister;
and he had forsaken his older brother, who had wanted him
to join him in legal work, when he became a reformer. Such
deviations from one's ancestral *dharma* are a grave problem in
the lives of many creative Indians. At any rate, when he returned
and settled down in Ahmedabad—the city in which both his
native language and the mercantile spirit of his ancestors had
reached a high level of cultivation—and when he again deviated
grievously by taking a family of Untouchables into his ashram,
the millowner alone continued to support him. The millowner,
thus, had become a true brother; and anyone familiar with
Gandhi's life will know how desperate at times was the "Great
Soul's" never requited and never fully admitted search for somebody who would sanction, guide, and, yes, mother *him*. This is
a complex matter, and it will be enough to indicate here that
without the assumption of such a transference of the prime actor
in my story to the principal witnesses, a brother and sister, I

could not have made sense of the meaning of the Event in Gandhi's life—nor of his wish to "play it down."

AUTOBIOGRAPHER AND REVIEWER

Nobody likes to be found out, not even one who has made ruthless confession a part of his profession. Any autobiographer, therefore, at least between the lines, spars with his reader and potential judge. Does the autobiographic recorder, then, develop a kind of transference on the potential reviewer of his record? Gandhi did, as we shall see.

But before reporting this, let me ask another question: Does not the professional reader and reviewer, who makes it his business to reveal in others what they may not know about themselves, also feel some uncomfortable tension in relation to them? Yes, I think that he does and that he should know that he does. There are, of course, some who would claim that, after all, they are voyeurs merely *in majorem gloriam* of history or humanity and are not otherwise "involved" with their subjects. But such denial often results only in an interpretive brashness or a superior attitude toward the autobiographer who seems to reveal himself so inadvertently or to hide his "real" motivation so clumsily. A patient offers his motivation for full inspection only under the protection of a contract and a method; and the method is not complete unless the "doctor" knows how to gauge his own hidden feelings. If it can be assumed that the reviewer of self-revelations or of self-revealing acts and statements offered in nonclinical contexts also develops some form of irrational countertransference, that, too, must be turned to methodological advantage not only for the sake of his work but also for that of his friends and his family, who, indeed, may find him to be somewhat narcissistically involved during the period of his preoccupation with a dead—and immortal!—man's life.

I hope to have aroused just enough discomfort in the professional reader to make him share the sting I felt when in the course of my study I came once again across the following passage midway through Gandhi's autobiography: "If some busy-body were to cross-examine me on the chapters which I have now written, he could probably shed more light on them, and if it were a hostile critic's cross-examination, he might even flatter himself for having shown up the hollowness of many of my pretensions." [16] Here we seem to have an analogue to what I described above as a disruption of free association; and, indeed, Gandhi continues with a momentary negative reaction to his whole undertaking: "I therefore wonder for a moment whether it might not be proper to stop writing these chapters altogether." After which he recovers, luckily, with a typically Gandhian form of self-sanction: "But so long as there is no prohibition from the voice within, I must continue the writing." There seems to be an awareness, however, of having given in to something akin to free association, though dictated by a higher power: "I write just as the spirit moves me at the time of writing. I do not claim to know definitely that all conscious thought and action on my part is directed by the spirit." Again he recovers, however, and sanctions his own doings: "But on an examination of the greatest steps that I have taken in my life, as also of those that may be regarded as the least, I think it will not be improper to say that all of them were directed by the spirit." Now he can dismiss his "hostile" reader: "I am not writing the autobiography to please critics. Writing it itself is one of the experiments with truth." And he can distribute the blame for writing at all: "Indeed, I started writing [the autobiography] in compliance with their [his co-workers'] wishes. If, therefore, I am wrong in writing the autobiography, they must share the blame." This concluding remark is, I think, typical of the Gandhian half-humor so easily lost in translation; and humor means recovery.

To say more about this sudden disruption, I would have to know (according to my own specifications) exactly in what period of his life Gandhi wrote this particular installment of the autobiography. Was there a real snooper—or even a Freudian?—

in his life at the time? Or was the imaginary one an externalization of another inner voice, one temporarily at odds with the one that inspired his every effort? Much speaks for the latter assumption, for the disruption follows a chapter called "A Sacred Recollection and Penance," in which Gandhi describes an especially cruel outbreak against his wife under circumstances (there were many in his life) both sublime and ridiculous. Once, in South Africa, while cleaning her house, which had become a hostel, she had refused to empty the chamber pot of a visitor who was a Christian as well as an Untouchable (*that* combination was too much), and Gandhi had literally shown her the gate. After such extreme and extremely petty moments something could cry out in him: What if all his professions of universal love, all his sacrifices of those closest to him by family ties for the sake of his identification with the mass of others—the poor, the victims, the Untouchables—were a pretense? So here the reader and reviewer become an externalization of the writer's self-doubt; and I felt so directly appealed to that I began to think of how I might have explained these matters to him in the light of our clinical knowledge. Not without the sudden awareness of now being older than he had been when he wrote that passage, I wrote the next chapter of my book in the form of a letter to him, explaining that, as a student of another lover of truth, a contemporary of his on the other side of the world, I had a more charitable term than "pretense" for the psychological aspects of his dilemma—namely, "ambivalence." I confronted him with another instance of petty and righteous cruelty—this time toward some teen-agers—and attempted to formulate a pervasive ambivalence: that his marriage at the age of thirteen to a girl of the same age, and fatherhood in his teens, had prevented him from making what later might have been a conscious decision, at an informed age, for or against married life; that this "fate" had been foisted on him in the traditional manner by his father, whom he had never forgiven for it. Thus, a lifelong ambivalence toward his wife and children, not to speak of sexuality in general, had perpetuated a predicament in his life as well as in that of many of his followers: Are *Satyagraha* and chastity insepa- rable? That such conflicts in the lives of saintly men are more than a matter of mental hygiene I need not emphasize here. Gandhi, I think, would have listened to me, but probably would have asked me teasingly why I had taken his outburst so per- sonally. And, indeed, my impulsive need to answer him "in per- son" before I could go on with my book revealed again that all manner of countertransference can accompany our attempts to analyze others, great or ordinary.

And what, we must ask (and he might have asked), legiti- mizes such undertaking in clinical work? It is, of course, the mandate to help paired with a continuous search for new insights into the irrational in man. And even as we demand that he who makes a profession of "psychoanalyzing" others must have learned a certain capacity for self-analysis, so must we presup- pose that the psycho-historian will have developed or acquired a certain self-analytical capacity which would give to his deal- ings with others, great or small, both the charity of identification and a reasonably good conscience. Ours, too, are "experiments with truth."

A final criterion for a certain degree of probability in this kind of reconstruction is, of course, the interpreter's inclusion in his own method of the inescapable fact that his interpretation is subject to the *mood of his own life,* and heir to a given *lineage of conceptualization.*

I have confessed that since the days of my youth Gandhi's "presence" has appeared to me to have been of a quality rarest among men. But my testamental attitude has now become bound to a field and a method. The state of the psychoanalytic method, so I believe, demands that we learn to proceed from the case his- tory to the life history, from the symptoms of human conflict to the signs of human strength, from man's adaptive and defensive maneuvers to his generative potentials. In working along *these* lines, we may at times understate the severe limitations and the

destructive potentials of a leader like Gandhi. Historical rein-
terpretation has always been thus bound to mood and method,
but a certain discipline of self-awareness may yet make a difference.

I can offer, for such an ambitious aim, only another schema,
which lists the minimum requirements for what a reviewer of
a record and of an event should be reasonably clear about:

Functions of the Review

	I. Moment	II. Sequence
1. Individual	in the stage and the conditions of the reviewer's life	in the reviewer's life history
2. Community	in the state of the reviewer's communities	in the history of the reviewer's communities

Under "communities" I here subsume a whole series of collective processes from which the reviewer derives identity and
sanction and within which his act of reviewing has a function:
there, above all, he must know himself as living in the historical
process. Each community, of course, may call for a separate
chart: the reviewer's nation or race, his caste or class, his religion or ideological party, and, of course, his professional field,
which provides a certain "name"—and a good income.

As far as my position as reviewer is concerned, I can refer
the reader to my own autobiographic account, which leads back
to the days when I first heard of Gandhi and of Ahmedabad and
maybe even of the millowner—all of which remained latent until, at the time of my visit, it "came back to me" almost sensually
in the occasional splendor and the pervasive squalor of India. In
my youth, I belonged to the class of wandering artists, who—as
some alienated and neurotic youths can and must in all ages—
blithely keep some vision alive in the realities of political and
economic chaos, even though, by a minute slip in the scales of
fate, they may find themselves among the uniformed to whom

killing and being killed become a sacred duty, or they perish ingloriously in some mass furor.

Just as Freud's post–World War I transference to Wilson was dominated by an adult skeptic's hate of Christian pretenses (and thus, one may assume, of a disavowal of his own infantile fascination with the splendor of Catholic ceremony), my transference to Gandhi no doubt harbored an adolescent search for a spiritual fatherhood, augmented by the fact that my own father, whom I had never seen, had taken on a mythical quality in my early years. Finally, I should add that, having vicariously lived out some of my "protestant" impulses in writing *Young Man Luther*, my pursuit of the stages of the life cycle seemed to call for just such a figure in his middle years, whose biography (so my students suggested) might be entitled "Middle-Aged Mahatma."

But I do not think that I set out merely to "apply" to Gandhi what I had learned from Freud. Great contemporaries like these two men, in all their grandiose one-sidedness, converge as much as they diverge; and it is not enough to characterize one with the methods of the other. As Freud once fancied he might become a political leader, so Gandhi thought of going into medicine. All his life, Gandhi ran a kind of health institute, and Freud founded an international organization with the ideological and economic power of a movement. Both men came to revolutionize man's awareness of his wayward instinctuality and to meet it with a combination of militant intelligence—and nonviolence. Gandhi pointed a way to the "conquest of violence" in its external and manifest aspects and, in the meantime, chose to pluck out the sexuality that offended him. Freud, in studying man's repressed sexuality, also revealed the internalized violence of self-condemnation, but thought externalized violent strife to be inevitable. And both men, being good post-Darwinians, blamed man's instinctuality on his animal ancestry—Gandhi calling man a sexual "brute" and Freud comparing his viciousness (to his own kind!) to that of wolves. Since then, ethology has fully described the intrinsic discipline of animal behavior and most impressively (in this context) the pacific rituals by which some social animals—yes, even wolves—"instinctively" prevent senseless murder.[17]

When I came to Ahmedabad, it had become clear to me that man as a species cannot afford any more to cultivate illusions either about his own "nature" or about that of other species, or about those "pseudo-species" he calls enemies—not while inventing and manufacturing arsenals capable of global destruction and relying for inner and outer peace solely on the super-brakes built into the super-weaponry. And Gandhi seemed to me to be the only man who had visualized *and* demonstrated an over-all alternative.

If all this sounds self-indulgently personal, it is spelled out here only far enough to remind the psycho-historian that his choice of subject often originates in early ideals or identifications, and that it may be important for him to accept as well as he can some deeper bias than can be argued out on the level of verifiable fact or faultless methodology. I believe, in fact, that any man projects or comes to project on the men and the times he studies some unlived portions and often the unrealized selves of his own life, not to speak of what William James calls "the murdered self." The psycho-historian may owe it to history, as well as to himself, to be more conscious of what seems to be a *re-transference* on former selves probably inescapable in any remembering, recording, or reviewing and to learn to live and to work in the light of such consciousness. This, incidentally, also calls for new forms of collaboration such as the father of psychoanalysis may have had in mind when he met the brilliant American diplomat.

To confound things a little further, there are also *cross transferences* from one reviewer of the same subject to another. For example, in a book on Gandhi's main rivals for national leadership, Tilak and Gokhale (both of whom died before his ascendancy), S. A. Wolpert [18] calls Gandhi a disciple of Gokhale, and, worse, calls Gokhale Gandhi's "guru." Now, Gandhi, while comparing Tilak with the forbidding ocean and Gokhale (his elder by three years only) with the maternal Ganges, and while sometimes calling Gokhale his "political guru," certainly kept *the* guruship in his life free for his own inner voice: an important step in Indian self-conception. But why should Wolpert want to call *his* Gokhale *my* Gandhi's guru with such monotonous frequency—and why should this annoy me? The italics indicate the answer, which (as I would judge from my perusal of the literature on Luther) points to a pervasive aspect of a reviewer's identification with his subject.

SURVIVORS AS WITNESSES

And here I had witnesses: the survivors of a generation of then young men and women who had joined or met Gandhi in 1918, and whose life (as the saying goes) had not been the same since—as if one knew what it might have been. They included, besides the millowner and his sister, individuals now retired or still in the forefront of national activity in industry, in the cabinet, or in parliament. These I set out to meet and to interview on my subsequent visits to India.

In India, professional as well as literary travelers could always count on being lodged with friends of means or with friends of friends, and the millowner related the sayings of many interesting house guests—among them Gandhi. He had offered me a terrace as a study, saying quietly, "Tagore has worked here." But to be a guest in a man's house is one thing; to be a reviewer of his place in history is another. When I returned to Ahmedabad to interview the millowner regarding the mill strike, he became strangely distant and asked me to meet him at his office in the mill. This, he made clear, was business: What did I want?

I should say in general that the clinician-turned-historian must adapt himself to and utilize a new array of "resistances" before he can be sure he is encountering those he is accustomed to.

There is, first of all, the often incredible or implausible loss or absence of data in the post-mortem of a charismatic figure, which can be variably attributed to simple carelessness or lack of awareness or of candor on the part of witnesses. Deeper difficulties, however, range from an almost cognitively ahistorical orientation—ascribed by some to Indians in general—to a highly idiosyncratic reluctance to "give up" the past. Here the myth-affirming and myth-destroying propensities of a post-charismatic period must be seen as the very stuff of which history is made. Where mythmaking predominates, every item of the great man's life becomes, or is reported like, a parable. Conversely, those who cannot commit themselves to this trend must disavow it with destructive fervor. I, for one, have almost never met anybody of whatever level of erudition or information, in India or elsewhere, who was not willing and eager to convey to me the whole measure of the Mahatma as based on one sublime or scandalous bit of hearsay. Then there are those whose lives have become part of a leader's and who have had to incorporate him in their self-image. Here it becomes especially clear that, unless they become professional Gandhians as reformers or politicians, writers or religionists, they considered Gandhi's memory as an invested possession to be shared only according to custom and religion, personal style and stage of life. The interviewed, not being a client, does not break a contract with either himself or the interviewer in not telling the whole truth as he knows or feels it. He has, in fact, every right to be preoccupied with the intactness of his historical role rather than with fragmented details, as patients and psychotherapists are—often to a fault. After all, the millowner had been Gandhi's counterplayer in the Event, and he had (as Gandhi knew and took for granted) used all the means at his disposal to break the strike. About this he was, in fact, rather frank, while he seemed "shy" about those episodes which had proven him to be a gallant opponent and faithful supporter. What kind of "resistance" was *that?*

Let me be diagrammatic: The old man's insistence on anonymity turned out to be a lifelong one. In old newspapers, I found more than one reference to his charitable deeds, which in feudal manner he had always considered his own choice and his own affair. "This is business, not charity," a union official quoted him as saying when he handed him a contribution; and it will be remembered that he did not identify himself when, as a young industrialist, he left money at the ashram gate. Here was a life-long trend, possibly aggravated by some sense of *Moksha*, which supervenes both good deeds and misdeeds. It is not so easy to judge, then, what a man (and a foreigner) does not want to remember or does not want to say or cannot remember or cannot say.

By the same token, the millowner's pointedly businesslike attitude was later clarified in its most defensive aspects as resulting from a previous experience with another inquisitive foreign visitor, while in general it seemed to reflect a sense of propriety, as though he wanted to delineate clearly what in this matter was "my business" and what his. I have already indicated that this same attitude pervaded even Gandhi's sainthood. When, during the strike, Gandhi said to his friends, who wanted to starve themselves with him, "Fasting is *my* business," he added, "You do yours." But then, both he and the millowner belonged to a cultural and national group referred to in India (admiringly as well as mockingly) as *banias*—that is, traders. And while the whole strike and its outcome are often considered a *bania* deal by Gandhi's many critics (whether Marxists, Maharashtrians, or Bengalis), there is little doubt that Gandhi chose to unfold his *Satyagraha* technique first in a locality familiar to him and with people who spoke his language and shared his brand of mercantile shrewdness. And behind such life styles there is always India and that larger framework of cosmic propriety which is called *dharma*—that is, a man's preordained place in the cyclic order of things and their eventual transcendence. *Dharma* can excuse much wickedness and laziness, as can Fate or God's will. But it will help determine, from childhood on, what a man considers

proper and what out of line; above all, it provides the framework within which the individual can knowingly take hold of
the law of *karma*, the ethical accounting in his round of lives.

I felt, then, literally "put in my place" by the old man's "resistance." In fact, when he asked me after our first interview, not
without a bit of mockery, what, if anything, I had learned, I
could only say truthfully that I had got an idea of what Gandhi
had been up against with him and he with Gandhi. Only after-
ward did I realize how right I was and that the cause of my
initial annoyance had been due to at least one parallel between
Gandhi's and my relationship to the millowner. Had not Gandhi
gladly accepted his financial support when he came back from
South Africa, in many ways a newcomer to India after twenty-
five years of absence? And had I not gladly accepted the
wealthy man's hospitality when I was a newcomer to India so
that I could venture out into the turbulence of the city and the
vastness of the land from an initial position of comfort and
sanitary safety? Here a Marxist could find an opening for legiti-
mate questions; and while he is at it, he might well consider the
rarely vented relationship of the recorder to the foundations
which support him. The common factor which interests us here,
however, is the unconscious transference on any host—that is,
the attribution of a father or older-brother role to anyone in
whose home one seeks safety or in whose influence one seeks
security. I should add that in my case this theme seems to be
anchored in the infantile experience—and, strictly speaking, this
alone makes a real transference out of a mere thematic transfer—
of having found a loving stepfather in an adoptive country.
Every worker must decide for himself, of course, how much or
how little he should make of such a connection, and how little
or how much of it he should impose on his readers. But first we
must become aware of it.

Now an equally brief word on the other side of the coin—
namely, the often sudden and unsolicited revelation of such
highly personal material as dreams, memories, and fantasies in

the course of interviews. In my case, these were offered by a number of informants in the more informal settings of social get-togethers. Accepting them with much interest, I was always determined to make use of them only as an auxiliary source of insights, not to be attributed to individuals. I do not know, of course, whether revelations of this kind are common in such work or appeared in mine because my interviewees knew me to be a psychoanalyst. If this most personal data eventually proved to have some striking themes in common, I cannot say whether these themes are typically Indian or typical for men who had followed Gandhi. Here are the themes: a *deep hurt* which the informant had inflicted on one of his parents or guardians and could never forget, and an intense wish *to take care of abandoned creatures*, people or animals, who have strayed too far from home. I had secured from each interviewee the story of how he first met Gandhi only to learn with increasing admiration how determinedly and yet cautiously Gandhi had induced his alienated young followers to cut an already frayed bond with their elders and to utilize a certain passion for doing good. Tentatively, then, I saw these revelations as an indirect admission of the obvious fact that followers can develop a more or less conscious sense of having vastly outdistanced their original life plan by serving a man who had the power to impose his superior *dharma* on his contemporaries, making a modernized use of the traditional need for a second, a spiritual, father. A resulting powerful ambivalence toward him is often overcompensated by the submissive antics of followership. And followership divides too: Gandhi's disciples had to accept what was his own family's plight—namely, that he belonged to all and to no one, like the mother in a joint family. Gandhi's was a unique maternalism, happily wedded in his case with a high degree of paternal voluntarism, but not always easily shared or tolerated by others.

Followers, too, deserve a diagram. Whatever motivation or conflict they may have in common as they join a leader and are joined together by him has to be studied in the full complementarity of:

Coordinates of Followership

	I. Moment	II. Sequence
1. Individual	the stage of life when they met the leader	lifelong themes transferred to the leader
2. Community	their generation's search for leadership	traditional and evolving patterns of followership

As to the last point, Gandhi was a master not only in the selection and acquisition of co-workers but also in assigning them to or using them in different tasks and ways of life—from the position of elect sons and daughters in his ascetic settlements to that of revolutionary organizers all over India and of aspirants for highest political power, including the prime ministership, for which he "needed a boy from Harrow."

The aforementioned edition of Gandhi's works [19] undertaken by the government of India (and now under the charge of Professor Swaminathan) permits us to follow Gandhi's acts, thoughts, and affects literally from day to day in speeches and letters, notes, and even dreams (as reported in letters), and to recognize his own conflicts over being invested with that charismatic cloak, the Mahatmaship. That publication will permit us for once to see a leader in a life crisis fighting on two fronts at once: the life cycle which marks every man as a defined link in the generational chain, and historical actuality.

The psychoanalyst, it seems, makes a family affair out of any historical event. Does anybody, one may ask, ever escape his internalized folk and learn to deal with the cast of his adult life on its own terms? The answer is yes and no. Certainly, where radical innovation depends on very special motivations and is paired with strong affect, there its impetus draws on lifelong aspirations and involvements. It is true that the psychoanalytic method rarely contributes much to the explanation of the excellence of a man's performance—which may be just as well, for it permits the factor of giftedness and grace to escape classification and prescription—but it may indicate what freed him for his own excellence or what may have inhibited or spoiled it. It so happens that the Ahmedabad Event *was* something of a family affair, not only in that Gandhi's counterplayers were a brother and a sister but also because Gandhi here tried to be a prophet at home. The proverb, too, may gain a new meaning if we can locate the difficulty in the prophet's own conflicts and not only in his "country's" diffidence. The very intimacy of my story may seem inapplicable to large events; yet the way Gandhi used his provincial successes to establish himself nationally would seem to go to the core of his style as a leader. A man's leadership is prominently characterized by his choice of the proper place, the exact moment, and the specific issue that help him to make his point momentously. Here I would like to quote from a political scientist's work, which has aroused curiosity and on which I have been asked to comment because it uses some "classical" psychoanalytic assumptions rather determinedly.

THE CHOSEN MOMENT

Victor Wolfenstein, in discussing Gandhi's famous Salt *Satyagraha* of 1930, asks bluntly: "But why did Gandhi choose the salt tax from among his list of grievances as the first object of (nationwide) *Satyagraha?*" [20] This refers to the occasion when Gandhi, after his long period of political silence, chose (of all possible actions) to lead an at first small but gradually swelling line of marchers on a "sacred pilgrimage" from Ahmedabad to the Arabian Sea in order to break the law—by extracting salt from the ocean. And, indeed, the choice of issues worthy of a *Satyagraha* campaign must interest us in past as well as in ongoing history, and Gandhi's choice of the salt tax has always impressed me as a model of practical and symbolic action. It pointed to a foreign power's interdiction of a vast population's right to lift from the long shorelines surrounding their tropical subcontinent a cheap and nature-given substance necessary for maintaining work capacity as well as for making bland food palatable and digestible. Here Gandhi's shrewdness seemed to join his capacity to focus on the infinite meaning in finite things —a trait which is often associated with the attribution of saint-hood.

Wolfenstein's diagnosis concerning this choice is threefold: First, Gandhi "believed that of all British oppressions the salt tax was the most offensive because it struck the poorest people hardest . . . By undertaking to serve or lead the lowliest self-esteem is raised." The expressed implication here is that Gandhi and other revolutionary leaders overcome some sense of guilt by acting not for themselves but for the exploited. Wolfenstein, secondly, points to the fact that "the tax on salt constituted an oral deprivation, a restriction on eating." And it is true that Gandhi was all his life fanatically preoccupied with dietary prohibitions and dietary choices. But then Wolfenstein intro-duces a more purely symbolic issue, which must be quoted more fully: "Another line of interpretation, which is consonant with the view I have been developing of Gandhi's personality, is suggested by Ernest Jones' contention that one of the two basic symbolic significances of salt is human semen. If it had this un-conscious meaning for Gandhi, then we may understand his depriving himself of condiments, including salt, as a form of sexual abstinence, involving a regression to an issue of the oral phase. In the context of the Salt March, Gandhi's taking of salt from the British can thus be seen as reclaiming for the Indian people the manhood and potency which was properly theirs."

Wolfenstein's suggestion—that the power of the salt-tax issue is attributable to an unconscious sexual meaning of salt—undoubtedly has a certain probability if viewed in cultural con-text. Anybody acquainted with the ancient Indian preoccupation with semen as a substance which pervades the whole body and which, therefore, is released only at the expense of vitality, acuity, and spiritual power will have to admit that if there is an equation between salt and semen in the primitive mind, the Indian people's imagination might be assumed to make the most of it. I suggest, however, that we take a brief look at what Ernest Jones really said and what the place of his conclusions is in the history of psychoanalytic symbolism.

Jones's classic paper, "The Symbolic Significance of Salt in Folklore and Superstition," was written in 1928.[21] It really starts with the question of the meaning of the superstition that the spilling of salt at a table may bring ill luck and discord to those assembled for a meal. Jones brings together an overwhelming amount of data from folklore and folk custom which indicate that salt is used in some magic connection with or as an equivalent of a most precious substance—semen. A peasant bridegroom may put salt in his left pocket to ensure potency; tribesmen and workmen may abstain from both salt and sex during important undertakings. Christian sects (to turn the equation around) may be accused of "salting" the Eucharistic bread with semen—and so on. Jones's conclusion is that to spill salt "means" to lose or spill semen as Onan did: suggesting, then, the sexual model of an act of supreme waste.

But before we ask how salt may come to mean semen, it is only fair to state that through the ages it has had a powerful significance as itself. When other preservatives were not known, the capacity of salt not only to give pungent taste to the blandest diet but also to keep perishable food fresh, to cleanse and cure wounds, and even to help embalm dead bodies gave it magic as well as practical value. The very word "salary" apparently comes from the fact that this clean, indestructible, and easily transportable substance could be used as currency. That it comes from the great sea, the mythical giver of life, makes salt also a "natural" symbol of procreation as well as of longevity and immortality, of wit and wisdom, and thus of such powers of preservation as one fervently hopes will give some permanence to the uncertain phenomena of friendship, loyalty, and hospitality. The use of salt on its own terms, then, for the ceremonial affirmation of mutual bonds would do quite nicely to explain the superstition concerning the unceremonious spilling.

Jones's conclusion is really rather cautious: "The significance naturally appertaining to such an important and remarkable article of diet as salt has thus been strengthened by an accession of psychical significance derived from deeper sources. The conclusion reached, therefore, is that salt is a typical symbol for semen. There is every reason to think that the primitive mind equates the idea of salt not only with that of semen, but also with the essential constituent of urine. The idea of salt in folklore and superstition characteristically represents the male, active, fertilizing principle."

In psychoanalysis, "deeper" often seems to mean both "sexual" and "repressed," an emphasis which makes sense within Freud's libido theory—that is, his search for an "energy of dignity" in human life that might account for some quantitative factor in the fantastic vagaries of man's instinctuality and thus prove measurable like the commutable energy isolated and measured in the phenomena observed by natural science. In civilization and especially in his day, he would find pervasive evidence of the systematic repression in children of any knowledge of the uses and purposes of sexuality—a repression which no doubt used the pathways of universal symbolization in order to disguise sexual and, above all, incestual thoughts and yet find expression for them. Among these, early psychoanalysis emphasized paternal and phallic symbols ever so much more than maternal ones; yet, if sexual symbolism did play a role in helping Gandhi, as he put it, "to arouse the religious imagination of an angry people," then the Indian masses, with all their stubborn native worship of mother goddesses, surely might have been swayed as much by the idea that they should have free access to salt as a symbol of the fecundity of the maternal sea as by salt as a symbol of the claim to male potency.

The rich symbolism unearthed by Freud in the study of sexual repression, then, should never lead to a simple translation of any phenomenon into one symbolic meaning. Where survival is at stake, where sexuality is not so obsessive as it becomes in the midst of affluence, where sexual repression is not so marked as it became in the more civilized and rational mind—could it not be that the symbolic equation of salt and semen is reciprocal? Could not the ceremonial linking of the two have the purpose of conferring on life-creating semen, a substance so easily squandered, the life-sustaining indestructibility of salt? This is, at the end, a question of determining the place of sexuality in man's whole inner ecology. But in the immediate context of the chronic semi-starvation that has undermined the vitality of the Indian masses, and considering the periodic threat of widespread death by famine, it would seem appropriate to assume, first of all, that salt means salt. In fact, the further development of psychoanalysis will have to help us understand and to find fitting terms for the symbolic representation not only of repressed sexuality but also of the ever-present and yet so blatantly denied fact of death in us and around us.[22] Here Robert Lifton has, with singular courage, done some inestimable groundwork in studying the consequences of man's seeming ability to ignore not only the certainty of his own death but also the enormity of his propensity to destroy life. This becomes central in our time, when the denial of death has contributed to man's capacity to build unimaginably destructive powers into the super-weaponry poised all around to destroy the world we know—literally at a moment's notice.

Sexual symbolism may help, I would agree, to understand superstitions and symptoms such as, say, the often self-destructive food fads Gandhi indulged in. At one time, he excluded natural salt from his diet, while at another his friends had reason to tease him over a veritable addiction to Epsom salts: where salt cleansed, it was more than acceptable. In such matters, however, he was only the all too willing victim of a preoccupation with diet rampant during his student days in vegetarian circles in England and deeply grounded in the tradition of his native country, although, no doubt, he adorned this with his own concerns over the impact of diet on sexual desire. In deciding on the Salt March, however, he was obviously in command of his political and economic as well as his psychological wits. And in any context except that of irrationality clearly attributed to sexual repression, one should take any interpretation that explains a human act by recourse to sexual symbolism with more than one grain of salt.

ANALOGOUS EVENTS

A historical moment, we have been trying to suggest, is determined by the complementarity of what witnesses, for all manner of motivation, have considered momentous enough to remember and to record and what later reviewers have considered momentous enough to review and re-record in such a way that the factuality of the event is confirmed or corrected and actuality is perceived and transmitted to posterity. For recorders and reviewers alike, however, events assume a momentous character when they seem both unprecedented and yet also mysteriously familiar—that is, if *analogous events* come to mind that combine to suggest a plausible direction to historical recurrences. Such a direction may be seen to be divine intention someday to be revealed, or inexorable fate to which man must learn to adapt. It could be a lawfulness which it may be man's task to regulate more engineeringly, or a repetitive delusion from which thoughtful man must "wake up." Psychoanalysis is inclined to recognize in all events not only an analogy but also a ready regression to the ontogenetic and phylogenetic past. This has proven fruitful in the clinical task of treating patients who did suffer from "repressed reminiscences": but out of such habitual and dogmatic application has come what I have called the originological fallacy, which, in contrast to the teleological one, deals with the present as almost pre-empted by its own origins—a stance not conducive to the demonstration of developmental or historical probability.

The diagrammatic formula for a *historical analogy* would be that another event is considered equivalent to the one at hand because it happened:

Coordinates of Analogies

	I. Moment	II. Sequence
1. Individual	to a comparable individual at the corresponding stage of his development	to comparable individuals throughout their lives
2. Community	in a corresponding stage of a comparable community	at comparable moments throughout history

Let me use as an example the thematic similarity between Gandhi's autobiography and that of the most influential Chinese writer of roughly the same period, Lu Hsün (1881–1937).

The memory from Gandhi's youth most often quoted to anchor his spiritual and political style in his oedipal relation to his father is that of his father's death. This passage is often referred to as a "childhood memory," although Mohandas at the time was sixteen years old and was about to become a father himself. One night his father, whom the youth had nursed with religious passion, was fast sinking; but since a trusted uncle had just arrived, the son left the nursing care to him and went to his marital bedroom in order to satisfy his "carnal desire," and this despite his wife's being pregnant. After a while, however, somebody came to fetch him. The father had died in the uncle's arms—"a blot," Gandhi writes, "which I have never been able to efface or to forget." A few weeks later, his wife aborted. This experience represents in Gandhi's life what, following Kierkegaard, I have referred to as "the Curse" in the lives of comparable innovators with a similarly precocious and relentless conscience. As such, it is no doubt what in clinical work we call a "cover memory"—that is, a roughly factual event that has come to symbolize in condensed form a complex of ideas, affects, and memories living on in adulthood as a supreme "account to be settled."

This curse, it has been automatically concluded, must be heir to the Oedipus conflict. In Gandhi's case, the "feminine" nursing of the father would have served to deny the boy's death wishes, as centered in the fantasy of replacing the (aging) father in the possession of the (young) mother, not to speak of the youthful intention to outdo him as a leader in later life. Thus, the pattern would be set for a style of leadership which can defeat a superior adversary only nonviolently and with the express intent of saving him in the very act of paralyzing him.

The writer Lu Hsün, often quoted with veneration by Mao, is the founding father of modern China's revolutionary literature. His famous short story "Diary of a Madman" (1918), the first literary work written in the vernacular Chinese, is a masterpiece not only (we are told) in the power of its style but as a very modern combination of a precise psychiatric description of paranoia (Lu Hsün had studied medicine in Japan) and a nightmarish allegory of the fiercer aspects of traditional and revolutionary China. Later, in an essay entitled "Father's Illness," Lu Hsün again mixes a historical theme—namely, the discrepancy of Western and Confucian concepts concerning a man's last moments—with the ambivalent emotions of a son. The son had spent much of his adolescent years searching for herbs that might cure his father. But now death was near.

Sometimes an idea would flash like lightning into my mind: Better to end the gasping faster . . . And immediately I knew that the idea was improper; it was like committing a crime. But at the same time I thought this idea rather proper, for I loved my father. Even now, I still think so.[23]

This is the Western doctor speaking; but at the time a Mrs. Yen, a kind of midwife for the departing soul, had suggested a number of magic transactions and had urged the son to scream into his father's ear, so he would not stop breathing.

"Father! Father!"
His face, which had quieted down, suddenly became tense. He opened his eyes slightly as if he felt something bitter and painful.

"Yell! Yell! Quick!"

"Father!"

"What? . . . Don't shout . . . don't . . ." he said in a low tone. Then he gasped frantically for breath. After a while, he returned to normal and calmed down.

"Father!" I kept calling him until he stopped breathing. Now I can still hear my own voice at that time. Whenever I hear it, I feel that this is the gravest wrong I have done to my father.

Lu Hsün was fifteen (to Gandhi's sixteen) at the time of his father's death. He, like Gandhi, had come from a line of high officials, whose fortunes were on the decline during the son's adolescence. At any rate, his story clearly suggests that in the lives of both men a desperate clinging to the dying father and a mistake made at the very last moment represented a curse overshadowing both past and future.

It is not enough, however, to reduce such a curse to the "Oedipus complex" as reconstructed in thousands of case histories as the primal complex of them all. The oedipal crisis, too, must be evaluated as part of man's over-all development emphasized under certain historical conditions. It appears to be a constellation of dark preoccupations in a species which must live through a period of long infantile dependence and steplike learning unequaled in the animal world, which develops a sensitive self-awareness in the years of immaturity, and which becomes aware of sexuality and procreation at a stage of childhood beset with irrational guilt. For the boy, to better the father (even if it is his father's most fervent wish that he do so) unconsciously means to replace him, to survive him means to kill him, to usurp his domain means to appropriate the mother, the "house," the "throne." No wonder that mankind's Maker is often experienced in the infantile image of every man's maker. But the oedipal crisis as commonly formulated is only the infantile or neurotic version of a *generational conflict* which derives from the fact that man experiences life and death—and past and future—in terms of the turnover of generations.

It is, in fact, rather probable that uncommon men of out-standing gifts experience filial conflicts with such inescapable in-tensity because they sense in themselves already early in child-hood some kind of originality that seems to point beyond a mere competition with the personal father's accomplishments. Theirs is also an early conscience development which makes them feel (and appear) old while still young and maybe even older in single-mindedness than their conformist parents, who, in turn, may treat them somehow as their potential redeemers. Thus, they grow up almost with an obligation (beset with guilt) to surpass and to originate at all cost. In adolescence, this may pro-long their identity confusion because they must find the one way in which they (and they alone!) can re-enact the past and create a new future in the right medium at the right moment on a suffi-ciently large scale. Their prolonged identity crisis, in turn, may invoke a premature generativity crisis that makes them accept as their concern a whole communal body, or mankind itself, and embrace as their dependents those weak in power, poor in posses-sions, and seemingly simple in heart. Such a deflection in life plan, however, can crowd out their chances for the enjoyment of intimacy, sexual and other, wherefore the "great" are often mateless, friendless, and childless in the midst of veneration, and by their example further confound the human dilemma of coun-terpointing the responsibility of procreation and individual exis-tence.

But not all highly uncommon men are chosen; and the psycho-historical question is not only how such men come to experience the inescapability of an existential curse but how it comes about that they have the pertinacity and the giftedness to re-enact it in a medium communicable to their fellow men and meaningful in their stage of history. The emphasis here is on *re-enactment*—and renewal, which in such cases goes far beyond the dictates of a mere "repetition compulsion" such as characterizes the unfree-dom of symptoms and of irrational acts. For the mark of a crea-tive re-enactment of a curse is that through skillful communication it becomes the joint experience, a liberating event, for each member of an awe-stricken audience. Some dim awareness of this must be the reason why the wielders of power in different periods of history instigate the efforts of creative men to re-enact the universal conflicts of mankind in the garb of the historical day, as the great dramatists have done. A political leader like Mao, then, may recognize a writer like Lu Hsün not for any ideological oratory but for his precise and ruthless presentation of the inner conflicts that must accompany the emergence of a revolutionary mind in a society as bound to filial piety as China. In a man like Gandhi, in turn, the dramatic autobiographer and the leader are united in one person. In all re-enactment, however, it is the transformation of an infantile curse into an adult deed that makes the man.

Common men, of course, gladly accept as saviors *pro tem* uncommon men who seem so eager to take upon themselves an accounting thus spared to others, and who by finding words for the nameless make it possible for the majority of men to live in the concreteness and safety of realities tuned to procreation, production—and periodic destruction.

All the greater, therefore, can be the chaos that "great" men leave behind and often experience in themselves in the years following their ascendancy. For the new momentum, which they gave to their time, may now roll over them, or their power to provide further momentum may wane from fatigue and age. Uncommon men, too, ultimately can become common (and worse) by the extent to which their solution of a universal curse remains too much tied to its ontogenetic version. The author of "Diary of a Madman" at the end of a career as revolutionary writer died himself in paranoid isolation as, in hindsight, one would expect of a man who all his life could hear his own voice yelling into his dying father's ear. And Gandhi, who could not forgive himself for having sought the warmth of his marital bed while his father was dying, in old age indulged in behavior that cost him many friends. In Lear-like fashion, he would wander through the tempest of communal riots, making local peace where nobody else could and yet knowing that he was losing the power to keep India united. It was then that the widower (who had never had a daughter of his own) wanted his "daughters" close and asked some of his women followers to warm his shivering body at night. This "weakness" the septuagenarian himself sexualized by declaring it to be a test of his strength of abstinence, thus opening himself wide to cheap gossip. This story, too, will have to be retold in terms of the stage of life when it was enacted.

What was once united by the power of charisma, however, cannot fall apart without exploding into destructive furor in the leader or in the masses or in both. Here life history ends, and history begins in all its sociological and political determinants. How a leader survives himself and how an idea survives a man, how the community absorbs him and his idea, and how the sense of wider identity created by his presence survives the limitations of his person and of the historical moment—these are matters that the psycho-historian cannot approach without the help of the student of tradition building and institution forming. He, in turn, may want to consider the "metabolism" of generations and the influence of a leader's or an elite's image on the world image and the life stages of the led: John Kennedy's rise and sudden death certainly would provide a modern model for such a study.

To return once more to my original interest in Gandhi: I have indicated what I have since learned about his personal idiosyncrasies as well as about his power of compromise. If some say that his ascendancy was unfortunate for an India in desperate need of modernization, one cannot imagine what other leader at that time could have brought the vast mass of Indians somewhat closer to the tasks of this century.

I see no reason, then, to decide whether Gandhi was a saint or a politician—a differentiation meaningless in the Hindu tradition of combining "works" and renunciation—for his life is characterized by an ability to derive existential strength, as well as political power, by discarding all such specialization. In interviewing his old friends, however, I found ample affirmation of his agile and humorous presence, probably the most inclusive sign of his (or anybody's) simultaneous mastery of inner and outer events. And it is in his humor that Gandhi has been compared to Saint Francis. Luther understood such things even if he could not always live them; and at least his sermons formulate unforgettably the centrality in space, the immediacy in time, and the wholeness in feeling that lead to such singular "events" as survive in parables—a form of re-enactment most memorable through the ages, although, or maybe just because, most effortless and least "goal-directed." Now, a man has to be dead for quite a while before one can know what parables might survive him. In Gandhi's case, one can only say that the stuff for parables is there. Let me, in conclusion, compare two well-known scenes from the lives of Gandhi and Saint Francis.

Teasing, as we have seen in reviewing his childhood, was a gift and a habit with Gandhi throughout his life; and I have pointed out the affinity of teasing to nonviolence. And I have recounted the unforgettable incident when, after the great Salt March, Gandhi was invited to talks with the Viceroy, and came with a small paper bag of tax-free salt hidden in his shawl "to remind us of the famous Boston Tea Party."

If we choose to insist on the symbolic meaning of salt and would see in this gesture a disguised act of masculine defiance, so be it. But such meaning would be absorbed in the over-all artfulness with which personal quirk (Gandhi would not touch tea anyway) is used for the pointed abstention from and yet ceremonial participation in the important act of sharing tea at the palace, and yet also for the re-enactment of a historical defiance, pointedly reminding his host of the time when the British taxed tea itself and lost some colonies which, in independence, did rather well.

Whatever combination of overt and hidden meanings was enacted here, the analogy that comes to mind is a scene from

St. Francis's life, when he was asked for dinner to his bishop's palace.[24] A place on the bishop's right was reserved for the ethereal rebel, and the guests were seated along well-decked tables. But Brother Francesco was late. Finally, he appeared with a small sack, out of which he took little pieces of dry dark bread and with his usual dancing gestures put one beside each guest's plate. To the bishop, who protested that there was plenty of food in the house, he explained that for *this* bread he had *begged*, and that therefore it was consecrated food. Could there be a more delicate and yet finite lesson in Christianity?

The two scenes bespeak an obvious similarity in tone and artfulness; but in order to make them true analogies, comparison is not enough. Other lifelong similarities in the two men could be enumerated and their respective tasks in their respective empires compared. Gandhi was no troubadour saint, but a tough activist as well as an enactor of poetic moments; and he was a strategist as well as a prayerful man. All this only points to the psychohistorian's job of specifying in all their complementarity the inner dynamics as well as the social conditions which make history seem to repeat, to renew, or to surpass itself.

II

Freedom and Nonviolence

When, in the summer of 1968, I was invited by the Students' Organisation of Cape Town University to give that year's T. B. Davie Memorial Lecture "on a theme related to academic freedom," I was working on my book *Gandhi's Truth,* and it seemed appropriate to share with young South Africans some thoughts on the meaning of Gandhi's method of militant nonviolence, which he had, in fact, created in his South African days. En route, in Johannesburg, some "coloured" men of Indian descent helped me to locate Gandhi's old Tolstoy Farm, now merged into the Afrikaner countryside. On arrival in the commanding Jameson Hall in Cape Town, I found myself part of a yearly ceremony held in full regalia. An academic procession was led by the head woman student of the university carrying, upside down, the "extinguished torch of Academic Freedom." The introductory speeches culminated in a joint recital of a dedication which declared, "Without consultation with our University, without its consent, and, in our view, for no sufficient reason, a law has been passed authorising the Government to impose restrictions based on colour." The dedication concluded: "*We dedicate ourselves to the tasks that lie ahead: to maintain our established rights to determine who shall teach, what shall be taught, and how it shall be taught in this University, and to strive to regain the right to determine who shall be taught, without regard to any criterion except academic merit.*"

As a foreigner, I had felt it proper to prepare an
address dealing with matters of freedom in a theoretical way. The lecture was titled "Insight and
Freedom." As I learned later (but not before I was
about to leave), its substance was of more acute
relevance than all but a few among those present
could have known. For the student leaders were then
planning their country's first academic sit-in in protest against a racial issue.

To STAND BEFORE YOU at this commanding panoramic spot at the
tip of this continent in order to deliver the Davie Lecture is a
momentous task, to be assumed only with humility. Such senti-
ment can only be underscored by the ceremony of which you
have permitted me to be a part; for I am only too aware of the
fact that I am a foreigner to your political actualities, and thus,
to your special anguish over the fate of your freedoms. So I can
only do what previous Davie Lecturers have done: I can only try
to help to demarcate, from the vantage point of my field and of
my present preoccupations, some irreducible aspect of academic
freedom.

And as you look at me, wondering what I may have to say,
you, in turn, must be thinking of my country, marked as it is by
the cruel fact that so recently one of our most vital leaders,
Robert F. Kennedy, who stood and spoke in this very spot two
years ago, was felled by an assassin—as was his great brother, our
president, a few years before him, and, more recently, our black
leader Martin Luther King, unforgettable for his passionate belief in nonviolence. And today's date is the date of Hiroshima.

I come from a country, then, which in all its wealth and
power, freedom and talent, is at the mercy of armed hybris—on
a gigantic technological scale made possible by the best scientific
minds, and on a petty and psychopathic scale, where the smallest
of men may feel driven to wipe out the greatest with little hand
weapons. But my country is also—in spite of all the politics-as-
usual of a campaign year—vigorously reassessing the ethical basis
of its national policies abroad and at home, and this, if for no

other reason, because our academic youth insists on it with all manner of involvement and of nonviolent (and occasionally violent) challenge.

If nonviolence is one of my main themes today, however, it is not because of any acute or recent relevance it may have in either your country or mine. When your invitation arrived, I had on my wall a map of South Africa which I had carefully traced for more intimate acquaintance; and I was studying a book which contained, in its opening pages, a description of Cape Town as "situated at the foot of the Table Mountain which is neither too high nor too low . . . Young and old, men and women, fearlessly move about the whole mountain, which resounds every day with the voices of thousands. Its tall trees and flowers of fine fragrance and variegated hues impart such a charm to the mountain that one can never see too much of it, or move too much about it." [1]

While undoubtedly more exuberant descriptions exist of the beauty surrounding the place where I now stand, even this much exuberance is unique in the works of the man who wrote it: Mohandas Karamchand Gandhi, a resident of South Africa at the turn of the century and then a "coolie barrister" destined to attract rather wide respect in the years to come. I was studying the origins of nonviolence in the life of this man, and this in the wider context of my present preoccupation, which is the psychoanalytic approach to life history and to history. And in Gandhi's book *Satyagraha in South Africa* I had found descriptions of how all the detailed methods of civil disobedience now so familiar to us—from card burning to oath taking to marching—were first improvised in such localities as the mosque in Durban, or the Jewish Theatre, so called, in Johannesburg, or in such frontier stations as Volksrust. But even the most relative triumph of such methods must always be shared by those against whom they have been initiated. And Gandhi's principal opponent, General Smuts, did not fail to rise to the occasion—occasionally. You probably know this story: When Gandhi, who liked to tease friends and opponents alike, left South Africa for good, he sent to General Smuts a pair of sandals which he had made when put in jail by the general's orders. They fitted, and the recipient cherished them, and returned them well-worn twenty-five years later on the Mahatma's seventieth birthday. At that time, the general somewhat ruefully reviewed the outcome of his first encounter with the then hardly known Indian leader:

. . . Gandhi himself received—what no doubt he desired—a period of rest and quiet in jail. For him everything went according to plan. For me—defender of law and order—there was the usual trying situation, the odium of carrying out a law which had not strong public support, and finally the discomfiture when the law was repealed.[2]

I hope before this lecture is over to have given you some proof that South Africa may have every reason to be as proud of this export, the Gandhian method, as it is proud of its gold, its diamonds, and its stamina; for whatever the long-range political fate of militant nonviolence may be, the spirit of its origin has, I believe, added lasting insights to our search for truth.

The word "insight," you have noted, is in the title of this lecture. In order to explain my use of the word, let me contrast it (maybe somewhat unduly) with knowledge. "To know" can mean many things; but knowledge has increasingly come to mean that which can be observed and communicated through methods which attempt to make things definable and comparable, countable and manageable—and this anywhere, and in any language. But knowledge alone can make man—academically free man—the slave of his own methods. Even worse, knowledge as such can become the slave of political and economic power: in the name of the pursuit of knowledge, learned men can help to forge the machineries of exploitation and destruction. Knowledge, then, needs the balance of insight, by which I mean an over-all inquisitive approach by which we learn something essential about ourselves even as we master the facts around us. And who but the universities could be the guardians not only of definable and teachable fields of knowledge but also of those almost intangible and yet so powerful changes in man's awareness of himself which are the domain of insight?

By insight, of course, I mean more than the awareness of the "personal equation" of old; that is, of the distorting effect which idiosyncrasies in the observer's sensory equipment can have on his observations. Such distortion we can study and correct by additional observation. Insight, however, turns inward, and occasionally gives us an inkling of the influence which our central emotions and motivations have on the very choice of and the final evaluation of what we are observing. And since our motives are always partially unconscious—that is, resistant to our very reason—this elusive capacity for insight forces us to face formidable methodological problems. Yet these cannot be shirked; and when my Webster tells me that insight is the power or act of seeing into a situation *or* into oneself, I would unhesitatingly talk back even to Webster and say that true insight is the power or act of seeing into a situation *and* into myself *at the same time:* for the two are, in fact, one power, one act. Now, before you begin to worry about the introspective or self-analytical demands I may intend to make on you, let me assure you that youth is one stage of life naturally (and sometimes even morbidly) open to insight, because insight emerges from passionate experience as much as from the structure of things: which is the reason, I think, why Socrates addressed himself to youth, and why the Athenians felt they had to use violence—in one of its judicial forms—against him.

Socrates confronted the young men he had snared into a dialogue with inescapable logical dilemmas all marking the limits of knowability. Thus, he made them face insights which, as he said, "are the last things to be perceived . . . in the world of knowledge," and yet without which, he insisted, "one cannot act with wisdom either in one's own life or in matters of state." Socrates' has for long been the prototypal method by which the truth in a given matter is revealed: confrontation leads through dialogue

to joint recognition. Here I can be brief. You have often imagined him, as he ignored ordinary procedures of learning, and
buttonholed—or whatever one did with Greek attire—his prospective students in the middle of other activities. His was not
the voice of authority imposing sharp distinctions. Instead, he
invited inquisitive minds to a kind of mental wrestling, which,
for reasons to be spelled out presently, I would call nonviolent.
That such nonviolent challenge can arouse murder in the hearts
of those whose self-deceit is thus exposed—that Socrates no
doubt foresaw and accepted as an essential part of the point
which it was his fate to make.

Since Socrates' time, knowledge has in each generation conquered new worlds beyond the credulity of the previous one.
But problems of insight have thereby not become less significant
or less decisive. On the contrary, we have more proof than we
can manage that a man can know many things most accurately
and yet prejudge their meaning; can help to master nature and
yet also to destroy man; can become well adjusted, pious, and
productive and yet be dangerously insensitive to the point of
deepest alienation not only from those whom he assigns to the
periphery of his world but also from those who are closest to
him, including the closest: himself.

What, then, have we learned about human nature since Socrates? Let us take a second look at his famous analysis of a certain
type of man. This man thinks that he is "master of himself," a
phrase which Socrates first calls absurd because it assumes that
the man is both his own master and his own subject. But then
he explains:

I think the phrase means that within the man himself, in his soul, there
is a better part and a worse; and that he is his own master when the
part which is better by nature has the worse under its control. It is certainly a term of praise; whereas it is considered a disgrace, when,
through bad breeding or bad company, the better part is overwhelmed
by the worse, like a small force outnumbered by a multitude. A man in
that condition is called a slave to himself and intemperate.[3]

I must leave it to the philosophers among you to decide how much of all this and what follows is said with Socratic tongue-in-cheek. He proceeds to spread before us the views which "go together" with the bold assumption of self-mastery:

> It is also true that the great mass of multifarious appetites and pleasures and pains will be found to occur chiefly in children and women and slaves, and, among free men so-called, in the inferior multitude; whereas the simple and moderate desires which, with the aid of reason and right belief, are guided by reflection, you will find only in a few, and those with the best inborn dispositions and the best educated.

It comes as rather a shock that the image of man which we are invited to ponder is limited to members of the male species, and then only to an elite among the free. And as to the state or the state of things, he adds:

> Do you see that this state of things will exist in your commonwealth, where the desires of the inferior multitude will be controlled by the desires and wisdom of the superior few? Hence, if any society can be called master of itself and in control of pleasures and desires, it will be ours.

One may see in this description of interdependent traits and opinions an ideal soundness of character and outlook, or one may detect in it a rather ominous "syndrome" of preconceptions. We note that the right man's dominant and dominating part is associated not only with a good disposition but also with good breeding, good company, and the right beliefs. He is both temperate and reflective, adhering to the wisdom of the superior few. So far he is just like me and thee. We may become decreasingly certain of his and our virtue, however, as we see his lower nature, which he has so well in hand, associated not only with multifarious pleasures, bad company, and the inferior multitude but also with those classes of human beings who are disadvantaged by the involuntary state of childhood, womanhood, or slavery. For we recognize here the human propensity to bolster one's own sense of inner mastery by bunching together and prejudging whole classes of people. We may even suspect that such a man's conviction of his own mastery over himself may come to rely so heavily on the concomitant conviction that those who are dependent on him are inferior that he would do everything in his power to keep unchanged and, in fact, to deepen in others inferiorities which are so essential to his own superiority. About the inner dynamics of such prejudging, then, and about its resistance to insight—about that, so I will claim, we do know more today.

In case you are now already lustily berating your favorite adversary and *his* self-serving prejudices, I must warn you that insight demands first of all the recognition of the fact that a human propensity such as has just been described is shared in some more or less subtle form by all of us.

If I place the responsibility for this trend on something as evolutionary-sounding as man's division into "pseudo-species," the term denotes the fact that while man is obviously one species, he appears and continues on earth split up into groups (from tribes to nations, from castes to classes, from religions to ideologies) which provide their members with a firm sense of God-given identity—and a sense of immortality. This demands, however, that each group must invent for itself a place and a moment in the very center of the universe where and when an especially provident deity caused it to be created superior to all others, the mere mortals. One could go way back into prehistory and envisage man, the only erect and yet also the most naked animal, adorning himself flamboyantly with feathers, pelts, and paints and elevating his own kind into a mythological species, called by whatever word he had for *"the* people." At its friendliest, "pseudo" only means that something is made to appear like what it is not; and, indeed, it is man's capacity for grasping and ordering facts and yet also for make-believe that endows him with the inventiveness needed to create roles and rules as well as legends, myths, and rituals that bind his group together and give to its existence a super-individual significance. This, to be sure, can inspire loyalty, heroism—and poetry. What renders this process a potential ailment of the species as a whole, however, is the fact that in times of danger and upheaval such imagined precedence by providence is reinforced by a mortal fear and hate of other pseudo-species. That these others must be subjugated or kept in bondage by periodical warfare or conquest, by stringent legislation or local custom, becomes a periodical (and, of course, often reciprocal) obsession.

At its unfriendliest, then, "pseudo" means that somebody is trying with all the sincerity of propaganda to put something over on himself as well as on others; and I am afraid that I mean to convey this, too, wherever under the impact of historical and economic displacements a group's self-idealization becomes defensive and exclusive and where, out of fear and pride, existing knowledge is denied, insight prevented, and possible alternatives ignored. And here we can unhesitatingly follow history to the present day, for remnants of the pseudo-species mentality do not necessarily yield to (but, in fact, can imbue) the very conquests of mercantile, industrial, and technological progress. You need only to think about a nation founded by migrants and transmigrants in search of freedom as well as abundance; of the creation by such men of a new, a frontier identity tuned to the wide open spaces and to unlimited possibilities in natural resource and labor supply. You could follow such a people into a way of life divided between grim settling down, continued migration, and mercantile expansionism. Such a country may have been able to overcome its initial—and, in a way, perpetual—uprootedness only by an almost mystical belief in a reconstituted future guaranteed by a sacred book and always handy weapons. Such a vision, and such habituation, would for the longest time obscure the cruel paradoxes of unfreedom built right into unprecedented freedom and progress. I am speaking, of course, of my country; but you may be aware of vague parallels with others—vague because the dimensions differ. At any rate, modern nations can harbor a mystical adherence to the mentality of the pseudo-species; and civilized, pragmatic, and erudite Germany provided the example of a total victory of this mentality in a cruel dream of a thousand-year dominance of one pseudo-species.

But I must remind myself that there are students of culture among you who can judge the social and historical evolution of this pervasive human trend ever so much better than I can. As a psychologist, I can only say a word about some inner consequences of this mentality for "the man" who bases his whole sense of identity and security on it; to his children who must absorb such a sense in their immature years; and to his "inferior" whose powerlessness seems to confirm an implicit prophecy of inescapable bondage.

Guided by Socrates' diagnosis, we saw that even the wisest representative of a dominant pseudo-species—here the free adult male—is apt to support his stand by a dogma which first splits himself into a judging and a judged self. From this, he derives the license to view and to treat all others as if they were no better than the worst in himself, whether these others are not-yet-adults or such other classes of dependent persons as he judges to be "no better than children." Let me, for a moment, speak of (and for) them. Children are too helpless to question the right of their parental masters to make them manageable by making them feel "bad"; they cannot question it until, maybe, the accumulation of resentment finds expression in revolt—if, when, and where history allows. In the meantime, they can only try to become like their parents; attempt to share what fulfillment, protection, and affluence they provide; and accept as God-given the existence of those outgroups that can serve *their* need to be continually convinced that there is always somebody lower than they are at their worst. Thus, "the system" is built into the generations.

The most frightening aspect of pseudo-speciation as a self-fulfilling prophecy is the fact that any group living under the economic and moral dominance of another is apt to incorporate the world image of the masters into its own—largely unconscious —self-estimation; that is, it permits itself to become infantilized,

storing up within (and often against) itself a rage which it dare
not vent against the oppressor and, indeed, often dare not feel
in its naked force. This, too, can become a curse from generation to generation until all the latent rage explodes into riotous
manifestation when and where historical circumstances seem to
invite and to sanction it. It should not surprise us that such ri-
otousness can be as childishly gay as it is carelessly destructive:
for the oppressed endure their oppression only by cultivating in
themselves both the warmth of childlikeness and the irresponsi-
bility of childishness, some belief in the masters' values, and
whatever fragmented primitivity may be their own cultural heritage. It stands to reason, then, that where there is an emphasis on
pseudo-speciation—as in colonial history—the development of
every single individual is endangered by various combinations of
secret guilt and repressed rage—a combination which surely be-
clouds the outlook for insight or foresight.

As I speak of the impact of the master's judgment on those
who are dependent on him, I recall some recent psychological
investigations done at Harvard which demonstrate a frighteningly
simple effect of ordinary prejudice. Behavioral scientists conceived of the possibility that the performances of subjects under-
going tests or of students receiving instructions were, in fact,
decisively influenced by what different experimenters or teachers
have been led to expect of them. In one school, teachers were
provided with a list of children and given the discreet information that dramatic intellectual growth could be expected of them
—although these children had actually been chosen at random.
Here a strikingly high percentage of the children not only performed as suggested but later also showed marked increases in
I.Q. Similarly, in some other psychological experiments the subjects performed in accordance with expectations which, as it
were, had been "planted" in their experimenters, although these
expectations were not objectively justified by the subjects' previous performances. The implications of such studies for situations
in which subjects or children, by dint of some exterior character-

istics, arouse negative expectations is clear, and this especially where testers or teachers are biased in favor of particular styles of intelligence. But when we face the issue of that mysterious "communicative behavior" by which experimenters thus influence their subjects—there we come up against all the unaware, unintentional ways which express our judgment of others. How pervasive such influence is you may judge from the fact that even animals are sensitive to it. Another group of experimenters were told that one group of rats had been bred for "maze-brightness," the other for "maze-dullness," although *all* the rats really came from the same strain. And, alas, the "bright" rats did perform more cleverly and animatedly and the "dull" ones more stupidly and lethargically. But the only communicative behavior which suggested itself as operative in these results was the observable tendency of experimenters to treat promising rats more tenderly—and with fewer words. The principal researcher, in fact, also "wonders what was said to the animals by those experimenters who believed their rats to be inferior." These simple but fundamental observations, verifiable by ordinary experiment, should indicate the striking need for and the potential power of insight.

Now that I have given you at least a fleeting indication that there is an experimental as well as observational access to the involuntary effect of the untruths and half-truths shared by the most knowing and the most knowledgeable of men, I can at last come back to the man who gave to his autobiography the alternate title *The Story of My Experiments with Truth*. And indeed, Gandhi made of his own life history an existential experiment, and that existential experiment became a political one. About this I would like to tell you something in Freudian terms. But whether it reassures you or disappoints you, I am not going to "psychoanalyze" him. Rather, I will try to do something even more preposterous—namely, compare his *Satyagraha* with the psychoanalytic method; for I believe that the insights and methods created by that young Hindu lawyer in South Africa and those created at about the same time by the young Jewish doctor in Vienna promise to rate high among the century's correctives of the untruths adhering to the pseudo-species mentality.

Incidentally, in comparing the life histories of these two so strikingly different men, we can see a certain crossing of Hippocratic and political as well as of meditative and activist elements. If Freud once wanted to be a politician, Gandhi had thought of becoming a doctor. As it turned out, the Mahatma ran his communes (ashrams)like (sometimes quacky) health institutes, while the great doctor founded a professional empire of peculiar power. And if each man invented his own truth method, the Eastern saint, by some strange ideological and economic reversal, became an activist, while the Western doctor opened up a new form of systematic meditation.

Now, what Gandhi meant by truth would be impossible to discuss in brief—if at all. "God," he said, "occurs to you not in person, but in action"; and if I understand him, he meant that only when you probe a vital issue by engaging your opponent in nonviolent action can divine truth reveal itself. And this truth is determined by what joint human awareness is ready in you *and* in your opponent at your moment in evolution and in history. But *mutuality* remains of the essence. Correspondingly, Gandhi insisted that only "that line of action is justice which does not harm either party to a dispute," and also that "only that which transforms both partners in action, is truth."

A prime requirement for nonviolent encounter is, of course, the choice of issue—and of opponent. Gandhi would not even contemplate as an adversary anybody with whom he did not already share a communality in a joint and vital undertaking, be it Indian labor and South African economy at the turn of the century, or the Indian masses and the British ruling class within imperial India. I will never forget how that deeply religious African, Mboya, once visited in a seminar of mine, and how, when asked whether he would have employed nonviolence against, say, the Belgians, he indicated that his people and the Belgians had far too little in common for that. Nor would Gandhi decide on a nonviolent campaign without having studied the grievances in minute detail and formulated the minimum demands dictated by reason and dignity, such as, for example, the right of all Indians to extract the vital salt from the blue sea surrounding their subcontinent without paying taxes to an empire centered way off in the foggy north. He then would inform his opponent of his conclusions, of his minimum demands, and of the prospective place and time of his "attack." There would be little vindictiveness in such militancy. He made every effort to avoid making his opponent suffer unnecessarily: on one occasion Gandhians who had occupied a temple road in India in an attempt to have it opened for the transit of Untouchables left their post every noon so that the British police on duty would not be exposed unduly to unaccustomed tropical heat. "Truth," Gandhi said, "excludes the use of violence because man is not capable of knowing the absolute truth and therefore is not competent to punish." Nor would Gandhi be guided by a wish to do away with his opponent, or even to weaken or to shame him: for this would only result in maintaining the pernicious cycle of violent "solutions." Instead, a gradual and bilateral recognition of the truth inherent in a historical moment must eventually reveal the "moment of truth." The nonviolent challenger, however, would take all the risks of injury or insult upon himself, giving his opponent a maximum opportunity for informed choice and for the courage to change. What makes this approach so psycho-logical is precisely the fact that here the challenger assumes as present in himself as well as in his opponent those fears of being debased by surrender, and of thus losing manhood and identity, that have always marred man's ability to be at least as magnanimous as it was given to him to be. All this the challenger has the moral courage to face and to set aside in himself, and thus, maybe, to "cure" in his opponent—fully aware that there really can be no victory and no peace where lasting and often mortal resentments are perpetuated by agreements concluded without the assent of both parties.

But how about the challenger? Can anybody but a childish optimist, a born masochist, or an undernourished Asian be so passive as to abstain from violence—*and* from feeling and voicing resentment? The fact is that one of the most successful nonviolent campaigns ever was carried out by a group of Muslim warriors in the Himalayas. In fact, the designation "nonviolence," like its precursor, "passive resistance," is altogether too negative a term, suggesting an abstention or aberration from what seems most natural to man or beast: to fight to the bitter end. The basic attitude of *Satyagraha*, rather, depends on the militant recognition of a common humanity; and as to its choice as a weapon of the weak, Gandhi himself sometimes wondered whether nonviolence did not call first and foremost for a soldier's code and courage. But he foresaw that one day manliness might be defined more by its positive humanity than by its defensive maleness, and that the fighter of some distant but bright future might refuse to view any other human being as a mere target in a gunsight—small, distant, and as expendable as vermin. To this end, insight into human nature sooner or later must replace in modern mankind the fear of being judged weak by the standards which have guided the military, the colonial, and the moralistic masters of a past era.

My remarks on Gandhi's methods are not made here in the spirit of a blanket advocacy of a particular policy of resistance, least of all in any country not my own and under circumstances unfamiliar in all detail. I have described this method as a new kind of ritualization of conflict, born in your country, and posing for all mankind an alternative to the cynical view of human nature which ever again pits armed power against armed power —or against unarmed weakness. And it must be more than obvious that the very super-machinery of annihilation achieved in our day (and first used by my country) will sooner or later demand an all-pervasive change in our intellectual and spiritual orientation toward the use of armed and sanctioned violence.

I said that I have studied some aspects of Gandhi's life with a Freudian method applied to the art of biography. Those of you who are familiar with psychoanalysis and with Gandhi's life no doubt would expect such an approach to focus first on Gandhi's marked struggle with what he at times considered his own inordinate sexual needs and his advocacy of radical asceticism as a precondition for nonviolence. It stands to reason that such a requirement would sharply limit the enthusiasm for the method in parts of the world where the ideal of sexual asceticism is less at home than it is in India; and even in India, Gandhi's attitudes toward human appetites have, on occasion, aroused as much mirth as they awakened awe. I should know; for not a few educated Indians, on meeting an American analyst, refer to this aspect of the Mahatma's life as, of course, neurotic. But my emphasis here is rather on what in a moment of sickness and despondence he himself spoke of as a tendency to terrorize himself, that is, to apply moral violence to his own nature—and, indeed, a friend once suggested to him that he might have to learn to be nonviolent against himself, too.

Here, then, the systems of thought developed by Gandhi and by Freud overlap. But again, I am not advocating or advertising any specific method of treatment which by its very nature may fit only certain well-defined circumstances. Rather, I am trying to bring to your attention another potential instrument of insight which is apt to change the image of man.

What did the Viennese doctor refuse to do to his patients—and what did he choose to do instead? He early came to the conclusion that his hysterical patients, mostly women, far from being degenerates as judged by his contemporaries, were suffering from an oppressive moralism, and a violation of human nature. Having, as children, taken into their consciences the moral dictates of their Victorian keepers (parents and servants alike) as to what a little lady was made of, they had, as it were, become mortally prejudiced against themselves and had repressed more than human nature can tolerate. He also concluded that the very doctors who were to free these patients from their inner repressions only perpetuated their infantile dependence by imposing on them authoritative demands and suggestions, and by circumventing their will through hypnosis. Choosing his patients carefully so that he could trust their truthfulness, the doctor decided on a method which would permit them to relax their own violent censorship over their thoughts and feelings and, instead, learn to let the repressed, literally, come to word so that patient and doctor could study it together. In this, the doctor in his psychiatric laboratory made a decision analogous to the one Gandhi made in his political proving ground—namely, that the training for such a precarious method would have to include insight into the motivation of him who wields such a tool. To understand his patients' dreams, Freud analyzed his own. And since the truth could cure the patient only insofar as the doctor had faced the corresponding truth in himself, he performed on himself a self-analysis and advocated that the psychoanalytic practitioner acquire by treatment as well as by training the readiness to tolerate whatever truth might emerge about his patient and about himself.

It all began, then, with a doctor looking into himself as he looked at his patients, and you will agree (some more happily, some a bit ruefully) that even if some treatments failed (as did, indeed, some nonviolent campaigns), this new spirit proved itself to be part of a universal "therapeutics," which has since pervaded the awareness of man in pursuits reaching way beyond the treatment of patients. These pursuits, of course, share the Hippocratic principle that you can test the truth (or the healing power inherent in a situation) only by action which avoids harming, but they augment it with the requirement that such action maximizes mutual insight and minimizes violence, coercion, or threat. Only what brings insight to both partners in their divided function is truth in action.

"Children, women, slaves," we may now recall, were lumped together in the Socratic syndrome of unfreedom. Surely women seem to be able to take care of themselves, was our immediate response. But let us remember here that Freud's most basic insights were acquired in the clinical study of hysterical women patients and that their symptoms responded only to insights into their childhood history: it was the traumatized child in the woman that had made her a slave to her unconscious. The very word "hysteria," more specifically, designated an enslavement to the uterus in the female species. It was Freud who, in his famous case histories, enlightened the world in regard to those factors in a woman's life history which can keep her in the state of infantility. Let me read to you what he said about Miss Elisabeth von R.:

> The youngest of three daughters, she was tenderly attached to her parents . . . but her mother's health was frequently troubled . . . Thus it came about that she found herself drawn into especially intimate contact with her father, a vivacious man of the world, who used to say that this daughter of his took the place of a son and a friend with whom he could exchange thoughts. Although the girl's mind found intellectual stimulation from the relationship with her father, he did not fail to observe that her mental constitution *was on that account departing from the ideal which people like to see realized in a girl*. He jokingly called her "cheeky" and "cock-sure" and warned her against being too positive in her judgments and against her habit of regardlessly telling people the truth, and he often said she would find it hard to find a husband. She was in fact greatly discontented with being a girl. She was full of ambitious plans. She wanted to study or to have a musical training, and she was indignant at the idea of having to sacrifice her inclinations and her freedom of judgment to marriage.[4]

All this Freud summarized as "the harsher side of her character," and we do not overlook the fact that Freud himself shared some of his period's prejudices against "unfeminine" traits. The main point is that he was the first to listen to such patients and to teach them to listen to themselves: he trusted their capacity for insight and thus established one basic prerequisite for a liberation which we now know to be essential for human survival. For does not history teach us that women, who know so well and so immediately the varieties of human needs, remain enslaved even to those aspirations of men which increase the sum total of human unfreedom? Do they not, on the whole, tend to concentrate their intrinsically nonviolent power on small pursuits in domains assigned to them, instead of learning to take their place as citizens, professionals, and co-planners?

And liberation begins at home. As we saw, it is the moralistic adult, so easily and righteously given to moral sadism, who must learn to educate, without violence—that is, with a recognition of the inviolacy of the counterplayer even if, and especially when, the counterplayer is a child. Here the mere avoidance of physical coercion as such is not enough. It can, in fact, lead to a parental self-inhibition that abrogates all indignation as it pretends to sacrifice all force. We also "do violence" to children and arouse inner rage in them wherever we withhold from them a guidance without which they cannot develop fully, or methods of learning for which their cognitive development is ready.

The therapeutic approach, then, supports strongly the impression that all the members of a given communality—whether differentiated by age, sex, race, or class—are inseparable in their influence on one another: each, by the way he sees himself, will influence the way all others see themselves; and such a simple statement, when multiplied, becomes a whole network of potentially fateful interdependencies which can be blocked by official edicts only at great danger to all.

I have put before you two modern methods of healing, one political and one clinical, either of which is a step toward the abandonment of the mentality of the pseudo-species. But I am not implying by any means that Gandhi became a Freudian, or vice versa. On the contrary, Freud believed in the inexorability of violence as well as in the healing power of Eros; and, indeed, some psychiatric activists believe in the cathartic healing power which the exertion of violence, so long suppressed, may have for the "wretched of the earth." Gandhi, in turn, believed to the last in the potentially malignant nature of sexuality. And both Gandhi and Freud, as good post-Darwinians, still shared the assumption that man owes what is so uniquely brutish and so laughably over-sexed in him to his membership in the "animal kingdom." We have since learned from the ethologists that there is more instinctive and, in fact, pacific discipline in the higher animals than man has ever dreamed of. As to the old naturalistic excuse of human viciousness, namely *homo hominis lupis*, it seems that even the wolves have instinctive ways of preventing murder among themselves. Far from deserving disdain as our ancestors, then, animals could well take exception to their "descendants." No, with his sins, man stands alone among all creatures.

With their respective truth methods, however, Gandhi and Freud served to make tangible some prime dangers to man's freedom: one, the bondage of man to such fear of radical otherness that he must annihilate or suppress others; and the corresponding bondage of feeling so endangered by his own nature that he will attempt to unduly repress it. All this, I repeat, all men have in common; and, as we have seen, his inner and his outer autocracies threaten man in unison. These are as old as social evolution: and yet they must be checked by insight in our, in your time. Such insight is new, hardly proven, untrained, and uncertain in its application. But it has always been the challenge of the so-called universities to bridge the oldest and the newest in man. And where men want to learn about themselves and about each other, they must learn together by facing each other. If insight is the process by which one learns to know oneself as one learns to know others, then mutual insights cannot be forced to exclude any category of men without harm to that intelligence on which shared knowledge and joint planning depend. Nor can we build new social barriers into a dialogue already begun without having our views bounce back as projections and prejudices which become all the more confusing and dangerous if they occur in otherwise well-trained and well-informed men.

In all ages, it has been intellectual youth which has kept open a bridge between privileged insights and the needs of the era's underprivileged, thus maintaining avenues to a future ethics. What I have seen of South African students, here and abroad, has convinced me that you are aware of your singular responsibility in the years to come. There is nothing talkative outsiders like myself can teach you that you have not felt more deeply, more concretely, more dangerously. All we can perhaps offer you is a somewhat new way of thinking about and affirming our common humanity.

PART THREE

Protest and Liberation

I

Reflections on the Revolt
of Humanist Youth

A PSYCHOANALYTIC CRITIQUE of contemporary and controversial behavior is always beset with grave methodological problems; yet I do not see how we can take either our students or our own work seriously without stating "for the record" what prophecy of great changes to come and what retrogression to past visions we are able to discern with our methods in passing patterns of dissent. For youthful behavior, where it arouses ambivalent fascination, always appears to be prophetically inspired by the vigor of a new age—and yet also retrogressive in its insistence on outworn simplicities and, at times, beset with astonishing personal regressions. In the following review, I will attempt to describe certain progressive and retrogressive group phenomena in the light of the place and the function of youth in the human life cycle in all its historical relativity. These group phenomena, I will submit, are analogous to what Ernst Kris has called "regres-

---

From presentations made at a symposium on Higher Education at the Villa Serbelloni, Lake Como, in 1968, and at the *Daedalus* conference on The Embattled University, 1969.

sion in the service of the ego," [1] and Peter Blos, "regression in the service of development." [2] For even as creative and young individuals can relive some of their past in order to recover goals once surrendered to adjustment, so whole generations of young people can reach back into unfinished ideological developments of the collective past in order to gather both the imagery and the energy necessary for a radical reorientation. This can suddenly come to the fore when youth finds itself between an older generation that has not been able to make integrated sense of the ethical ideals it bestowed on youth (as acute problems of race and war revealed in this country) and an adolescence lacking in ideological integration. Whether and how, under such conditions, the prophecy will be translated into truly revolutionary action or institutional transformation depends on political factors, including the availability of emergent leadership: in my book *Young Man Luther*, I have attempted to approach this phenomenon psychoanalytically.[3] But it is vastly more difficult to assess the revolutionary potential in a situation which is not yet quite "historical" and in which we, the reviewers, have found ourselves, at a given stage of our own life cycle and career, as involved witnesses. What has become historical has found some form and formulation; but more recent periods of transitory sensational impact are apt to be followed by malaise and a tendency to repress the passing phenomenon together with the immediate circumstances that seem to have caused it. Under such circumstances, what lawfulness one thinks one can discern with the methods at hand may prove as dated as some of the phenomena observed. And yet, psychoanalytic insight will have a role to fulfill in the critique of the wasteful aspects of cultural and historical change—waste which youth as a generation and mankind as whole can ill afford. I have the impression that some of the leading young revolutionaries are now aware of the danger of emotional exhaustion in radical undertakings which are marked by historical retrogression. On the other hand, in attempting to clarify the motivational roots of youthful dissent, we must concede at the outset that psychoanalysis, like other once "revolutionary" movements, paradoxically enough has let itself be drawn into modern attempts to neutralize powerful inner and outer forces of renewal by helping to make man more superficially and mechanically adjustable. Our critique must not be in the service of such adjustment. In fact (and this always heightens our discomfort with youthful dissent), some of the more prophetic concerns of today's or yesterday's youth could serve to remind us of a liberating vision once inherent in our own beginnings.

Before selecting some circumscribed phenomena of active dissent for psychoanalytic scrutiny, I must present a few speculations on the *changing ecology of youth* in the present stage of history; for phenomena of the kind to be reviewed here reflect such historical and technological changes as, at first, always seem to be a matter of degree until many small differences have come to amount to a frighteningly new over-all quality: then we acknowledge a crisis.

Adolescence has always been seen as a stage of transition from an alternately invigorating and enslaving sense of an over-defined past to a future as yet to be identified—and to be identified with. It seems to serve the function of committing the growing person to the possible achievements and the comprehensible ideals of a viable or developing civilization. In our time, the new requirements of disciplined teamwork and programmed rationality in organizations living in inescapable symbiosis with technological systems appear to offer some satisfying and self-corrective world view to many, if not most, young people. They see no reason to question "the system" seriously, if only because they have never visualized another.

In every individual, however, and in every generation, there is a potential for an *intensified adolescence*—that is, a critical phase marked by the reciprocal aggravation of internal conflict and of societal disorganization. Psychoanalysis, for obvious rea-

sons, has primarily studied those more malignant kinds of aggravation that are the result of unresolved infantile conflict and of
adolescent isolation. Yet, from Freud's patient Dora on, case histories have demonstrated that the epidemiology of a given time is
related to the conflicts between the generations—and thus to the
history of cultural change. If, on the other hand, a special sector
of youth becomes militantly agitated and sets out to agitate on a
large scale, it often succeeds way beyond its numerical strength
or political foresight because it draws out and inflames the latent
aggravations of that majority of young people who would otherwise choose only banal and transient ways of voicing dissent or
displaying conflict—and about whom, therefore, psychoanalysis
knows so very little. We must begin by recognizing our patients
as the inverted dissenters, too sick for the more modish malaise
of their time, too isolated for joint dissent, and yet too sensitive
for simple adjustment.

What, then, are the quantitative changes that seem to have
changed the quality of adolescence in our time? It is said that
there are simply more young people around than ever before;
that they now generally mature earlier; and that more of them
are better informed about world conditions by virtue of a common literacy, of high and higher education, and of a common
imagery transmitted by mass communication. But while such
shared vocabularies and imageries serve to convey traditional
ideals of identity, personality, and competence, such promise can
become rather illusory because of the technological, legal,
and bureaucratic complexities attending the sheer numbers of
persons and things, which are apt to paralyze the initiative of all
but some "insiders." Often, therefore, only to be intensely "with
it" and with one another in moments of prophetic promise provided a sense of individuality and communality in otherwise
paralyzing discontinuities. This, it seems, is expressed vividly
and often devastatingly in songs of shouted loneliness underscored by a pounding rhythm-to-end-all-rhythms in a sea of
circling colors and lights. Such active and joint mastery of a

cacophonous world can be experienced with an emotional and physical abandon unlike anything the older generation has known; and yet—especially where compounded by drugs—it can also camouflage a reciprocal isolation of desperate depth.

But what are the qualitative changes in living which gave small subgroups, such activist elites in the humanist (academic, artistic) youth, at least periodically, the power and the capacity to establish the historical actuality of their concerns and demands in the "free world"? This actuality can be measured by three facts: first, these subgroups succeeded in creating convincing, or at least upsetting, slogans, ideals, and images far beyond their various localities; second, they were able to impose their slogans and ideals on masses of other students whether according to the local student culture they had been previously engaged in some form of activism or not; and third, where these subgroups were not able to achieve their original demands, they nevertheless succeeded in arousing adult responses of such acuity that some instructors, parents, and administrators felt alternately inspired or acutely traumatized and unsure of their obligations to their profession and to society. At the same time, wider sections of society were nostalgically confirmed in their erstwhile liberalism or radicalism or, at least, were made doubtful of their acquired conservatism. Obviously, then, such youthful action would be impossible in both conception and execution were it not for specific adult reactions which seemed to confirm its historical actuality. Let me list a few qualitative changes:

1. A worldwide mistrust on the part of pre-industrial and post-industrial youth in the competency of a parent generation which, with all its righteousness and loudly proclaimed "know-how," really finds itself caught in conditions and actions both unpredictable and unsolvable.

2. A shift in the meaning of the life stages in a fast-changing world of specialization and expertise: where an "adolescentulus" in the past was a creature in a transitory stage, he now becomes more and more the participant in an autonomous stage of life.

This autonomy is vastly increased by the fact that sexual life is becoming more independent of procreation, with a resulting disappearance of the sexual double standard: both women and men can now in principle choose their sexual style before they commit themselves to progeny. This newly won autonomy, however, is counteracted by the necessity for those with some ambition to make earlier commitments to an occupational or professional specialty. The resulting danger of being drawn into early compromises with specialization, conformity, and premature success threatens that capacity for a renewal of humanist or, at any rate, personalized values without which universal technocracy could, indeed, become a new serfdom, malignant precisely because of the affluence it promises. Thus, where apprenticeship and specialization once promised a distinct moratorium as well as a distinct identity within a defined occupational ethos, it now often seems to demand an early standardization of experience, with a blunting of both ideological awareness and ethical decision. Some young people, then, insisted on creating variable new moratoria, from "dropping out" to the joining of communities or communes fostering dissident life styles.

3. A contrary and yet often compassionate identification with what our government referred to as "the other side"—that is, with the population of "underdeveloped" countries ravaged by the war machines of the superpowers. This identification included new concepts of heroism and martyrdom, such as the guerrilla warfare of unarmed or poorly armed bands against super-armed hyperorganizations.

4. Alternately, warfare as an institution contained by traditions of honorable and humane conduct is losing its authenticity on a large scale, with the result that images of heroism and martyrdom are transferred to internal issues, such as race relations and nonviolent militance.

5. All of these developments permitted and forced privileged youth to engage in a more concerted exercise of the age-old prerogative to take the side of the dispossessed and thus to give

to their own rebellion the (often sincere) cloak of radical altruism. Only that this youth, depending on local conditions, had to search for those masses of dispossessed in their own countries who might welcome liberation by revolution rather than a better deal within the "establishment." In this predicament, activist youth often retrogressed, historically speaking, in the name of a mystical "people" while actually forming standardized and privileged subgroups of their own.

6. Much of the present conflict in academic life itself seemed to be based on a late and yet powerful awareness that literacy in its widest sense has made educated man a transmitter of traditional meanings while robbing him of the "professional" capacity to mean what he says and to say what he "really" means. As always, the difference between old-time morality and new ethics is best expressed by the juxtaposition of the words "It is written, that . . ." and "But I say unto you." The Reformation thus has run full cycle: in demonstrations of protest, the printed and durable pamphlet is often replaced by the painted placard dedicated to the slogan of the moment. For where change was once a transitional stage marked by reformations and revolutions leading to hoped-for equilibria, change is now self-sustaining, and no one can predict or plan what the world will look like next, although strenuous attempts abound to visualize at least the year 2000. But this also means that modern youth feels in need of an ethical flexibility, a capacity for being "with it," and for the inspiration of big and small "happenings" which convey a festive depth and yet also often a passing illusion of a passionate fellowship here and now.

To come back once more to us, the very participant observers: Perhaps we learn most as we become aware of what social change is doing with (and to) our theories of youth. I have, for example, conceptualized within the stage of youth a *psychosocial moratorium*—a period when the young person can dramatize, or at any rate experiment with, patterns of behavior which are both juvenile and adult, and yet often find a grandiose alignment with traditional ideals or new ideological trends. A true moratorium, of course, takes the pressure out of time as it provides leeway for timeless values. If, by definition, it must end, it is expected to be followed by a period of energetic and goal-oriented activity. In the past, adults have often mourned the end of the moratorium as an irrevocable loss of potential identities sacrificed to the necessities of life. In our day, young leaders in speech and song declared the world beyond youth to be totally void and faceless. But a moratorium without end also disposes of all utopias—except that of an infinite moratorium. The large-scale utopias that, in the postwar period, were to initiate a new kind of history—the war that would end all wars, the socialism that would make the state wither away, the thousand-year Reich, a true league of nations, or the advent of militant nonviolence—have all been followed by holocausts as coldly planned as were the gas chambers and Hiroshima, or as shockingly planless as mass riots; and they have been superseded, on both sides of all curtains, by bureaucratic-industrial systems of sometimes negligible ideological differentiation. Thus also ended the unquestioned superiority of the fathers, whether they had obeyed and died or survived and thrived. If, then, as it always must, rebellious youth borrowed roles from past revolutions, it yet had to avoid the temptation to settle for any previous consolidation. The mere thought of what political and economic form the world might take after the next revolution seemed in itself counterrevolutionary.

A moratorium without some kind of utopian design, however, can lead only to an ideological promiscuity that both adopts and disposes of the old revolutions. There is, of course, the Marxist model. Some of our activists liked to resemble Marxist revolutionaries in appearance and in vocabulary, but they could not possibly share either their erstwhile historical chance or, indeed, their intellectual discipline and political competence. They needed a proletariat to liberate, but few groups of workers today could be led for long by intellectual youths with no blueprint. Thus, youth had to appoint *itself* a kind of proletariat—and "the people" often came to mean primarily young people without ties to any community of adults.

A viable model was, at least episodically, the Gandhian one, anticolonial and nonviolent. There is hardly an item in the arsenal of modern protest—from card burning to mass marching —that Gandhi did not invent as part of the revolutionary method of militant nonviolence. Originally a revolt of those who happened to be unarmed, it came through him to mean above all the method of those who *choose* to remain unarmed. Yet (except for such activist groups as the civil rights marchers and the draft-resisting dissenters in America who made their point by taking determined total chances with themselves), today's youth has lacked the continuity that could elevate nonviolent protest to the level of truly national campaigns. Nor is there much evidence that the remaining victims of colonialism in the world care to count on the youth of affluent countries. Therefore, youth had to appoint itself also the corporate victim of colonialism; and the mere dependence on an older generation came to symbolize a despised "colonial" bondage.

Gandhi was by no means unaware of the cathartic function of violence; the psychiatrist Frantz Fanon was its spokesman. By emphasizing the therapeutic necessity of revolutionary violence, Fanon forms an ideological link between anticolonialism and the "Freudian revolution," which has counterpointed the methods of political suppression with a systematic exploration of man's inner repression. Some of our young people, combining emotional license with alternately violent and nonviolent confrontation and with both intellectual and anti-intellectual protest, attempted to combine the gains of all revolutions in one improvised moratorium and often succeeded only in endangering and even mocking them all.

Out of the combined revolutions of the oppressed and the repressed, of the proletarians, the unarmed, and the mental sufferers, there seemed to emerge a *revolt of the dependent*. That to be dependent means to be exploited is the ideological link between the developmental stage of youth and the sex-typed status of women, the economic state of the poor, and the political state of the underdeveloped. This, at least, could partially explain the astounding similarity of the logic used in the patterns of confrontation both by privileged youth and by the underprivileged rebels. And has humanist youth not learned from psychoanalysis to look at man's prolonged childhood dependence as an evolutionary fact artificially protracted by adults in order to subvert the radiance of children and the vigor of youth and to press both into the "confirmations" of traditional adulthood?

The revolt of the dependent, however, directly challenged all those existing institutions that monopolize the admissions procedures to the main body of society. These confirmations, graduations, and inductions have always attempted to tie youthful prophecy to existing world images, offering a variety of rites characterized by special states of ceremonious self-diffusion. All this, too, dissenting youth sought to provide for itself in newly improvised and ritualized self-graduations, from musical happenings and the "human be-in" to communal experiment and purely demonstrative revolt.

I have now indicated a few aspects of the revolutionary inheritance which past generations and especially the charismatic leaders of the postwar period have bequeathed to youth. But I have also pointed to the fact that, in the meantime, industrialization has changed all basic premises; and the majority of young people remain engaged in the invention and perfection of techniques that by their immense practicality seem to assure safety, rationality, and abundance, even as the exploration of space could promise a new type of heroic adventure and limitless celestial leeway. But even technological youth at times heard the prophetic quality of the two questions agitated youth seemed to ask: When, if not now, in this post-ideological period in history and before cosmic technocracy takes over altogether, will man attempt to combine his timeless values, his new insights, and his coming mastery in one all-human outlook? And who, if not they, the young people assembled in the prolonged moratorium of academic life, will study, live, and rebel for the sake of that outlook? For there is still one more quantitative change that has altered the quality of human life.

Modern youth has grown up with the fact that an affluent civilization can learn to become relatively peaceful and neighborly in limited areas of its existence and yet delegate the greatest destructive power that ever existed to the political determination of nuclear monsters scientifically created and loyally serviced by well-adjusted experts and technicians. Not that most young people, any more than most adults, can for any length of time maintain a sense of reality in contemplating these facts—unless, periodically, they pay total attention to them. Much as we have learned about the consequences of instinctual repression, we do not yet possess systematic terms and concepts adequate to deal with the split in human awareness (Lifton speaks of "psychic numbing") that makes the coexistence of consumer affluence and of minutely planned "overkill" possible, nor with the emotional price exacted for this split.

And yet we must realize that the specter of nuclear war changes the whole ecology of what we have come to view as the over-all instinctual economy of man. As long as wars can (or could) provide ideologically convincing reasons for the massive deflection of hate on external enemies, much interpersonal and intergenerational conflict could live itself out in periodic states of war. As communication makes the enemy appear human, and as technological developments make war absurd, unrelieved self-hate as well as the hateful tension in families and communities may well cause new and bewildering forms of planless violence.

No wonder, then, that the *legitimacy of violence* became the greatest single issue in the ideological struggle of youth today; and nowhere was youth more convincingly united than in the civil rights and peace marches that emphasized their solidarity with the victims of racial serfdom at home and with the victims of a total war abroad—a war that grew out of a colonial rear-guard action. The illegitimacy of technocratic violence, of course, came to sharpest awareness in those young men who had to be prepared to see themselves or their friends inducted into a "service" that legitimized what appeared to be a senseless war. Most of them decided to fulfill traditional expectations of duty and heroism. Some who objected "conscientiously" either were forced to link their conscience to a belief in the prescribed kind of God or had to face jail under conditions that negated even a traditional sense of martyrdom. A few turned violently against the system; but if on occasion they seemed totally committed to a negative utopia in which the existing world must come to an apocalyptic end before anything could live, one should remember that they had grown up in a setting in which adult happiness-as-usual did not exclude the minute-by-minute potential of a nuclear holocaust—and an end of mankind as we know it.

The cognitive facts established by Piaget make it plausible enough that youth tends to *think* ideologically—that is, with a combination of an egocentric, narcissistic orientation determined to adapt the world to itself and a devotion to idealistic and al-truistic schemes and codes, whether or not their feasibility can be proved or disproved. Correspondingly, it is the all-or-nothing, or what I have called the *totalistic*, quality of adolescence which permits many young people to invest their loyalty in simplis-tically overdefined ideologies. In periods and intervals of mini-mized revolutionary potential, in turn, youth is led into beliefs and actions in which the psychological borderlines between ad-venture and political drama, youthful prank and potential crim-inality, are often hard to draw—even as it is difficult to discern where in the personalities of potential leaders hysterics and his-trionics blend with true charisma.

All this is well known; but there is much to learn about the developmental position of youthful enactments midway between the play of children and the ritualized aspects of adult society. Infantile play, among other accomplishments, re-enacts experiences and anticipations of a traumatic character in the microcosm of the toy world, and the promises of its make-believe provide a necessary balance against the combined pressure of an immature conscience, a vague drivenness, and an often bewildering social reality. The need for such a balance is multiplied in adolescence, when the grown-up body, the matured genital equipment, and a perceptive mentality permit actions on the borderline of mere playfulness and utterly serious reality, of passing prank and irreversible deed, of daring pretense and final commitment. In negotiating these borderlines together, young people may be able to share transient conflicts that might otherwise force each individual to improvise his own neurosis or delinquency, but they obviously also can lead one another into permanent involvements out of line with their self-image, their conscience—and the law. Most "outgrow" this, but it is important to visualize how much the adult world, too, with its ceremonial habituations in areas of the greatest and most lasting relevance, continues to express the need for ritual make-believe, which "before you know it" can turn into historical disaster.

But we are concerned here with the retrogressive aspects of youthful re-enactments. Transitory regression, we saw, can be part both of creativity and of development, as is implied in Kris's and Blos's aforementioned formulations. Blos, in fact, considers the "capacity to move between regressive and progressive consciousness with . . . ease" the unique quality of adolescence.

And, indeed, having sketched the universal reasons for the vagueness of today's world images, I would reassert that at least some of the adolescent processes described so readily as regressive have the distinct adaptive function of reviving and recapitulating the fragmentary conflicts of childhood for the sake of recombining them actively in a new wholeness of experience. Such unification must obviously count among the workings of the ego. But it is also accompanied by a new sense of "I," as well as a new experience of "we." The fate and function of such a sense and such an experience in the sequence of life stages have so far eluded conceptualization in psychoanalytic terms. At any rate, that a specific wholeness of experience may be irretrievably lost once adolescence has passed is the fear which gives much of adolescent behavior a certain desperate determination. And this, too, could become a source of identification with the under-privileged, anywhere, who have missed their chance and, if led by ideological youths, might, indeed, find a new one.

2

I will select for a more detailed discussion of progression and regression one strand of development investigated by L. Kohlberg [4] and others, but little discussed in psychoanalysis—namely, that of progressive moral and ethical orientation. I will speak of *moral learning* as an aspect of childhood; of *ideological experimentation* as a part of adolescence; and of *ethical consolidation* as an adult task. As we know from the study of psychosexuality, the earlier stages are not replaced, but develop according to an epigenetic principle—that is, they are absorbed into a hierarchic system of increasing differentiation. As the individual proceeds developmentally from the moralism of childhood through the ideology of adolescence to some adult ethics, the characteristic gains and conflicts of the early stages are not abandoned but, in the best of circumstances, renewed and reintegrated. If the child, then, learns to be moral, by which I mean here primarily to *internalize early prohibitions*, his moral conflicts continue in adolescence, but come under the primacy of ideological thinking. By ideology, in turn, I mean *a system of commanding ideas* held together to a varying degree more by totalistic logic and utopian conviction than by cognitive understanding or pragmatic experience. The ideological and moral orientations are, in turn, absorbed, but never quite replaced, by that ethical orientation which makes the difference between adulthood and adolescence—"ethical" meaning a *universal sense of values assented to* with some insight and some responsible foresight.

Such step-by-step development guarantees to this whole value structure a gradual synchronization with economic and political realities, but it also results in a persistent liability that can always lead to individual regressions and joint retrogressions. In adulthood, this can be seen either in a partial arrest on the ideological level or a ready backsliding to infantile conflicts over moral interdicts. As we shall now elaborate in detail, aggravated and especially agitated youth, although highly sensitive to ethical positions and ready to put themselves on the line when a gifted leader seems to master the historical moment, in the absence of ideological synthesis sometimes retrogressed to the logic, albeit inverted, of the *moral* position: protests are, as it were, hyper-moralistically turned against the establishment's morality. To clarify the developmental aspects of this phenomenon, I will subdivide this position, in descending order, into an *anti-moral* position that militantly negates all punitive authority and, with it, all *guilt;* an *amoral* position that flaunts accepted norms and primarily discards *shame;* and, finally, a *pre-moral* position that denies any need for strenuous morality: it denies the *separation* from paradise. While the last attitude could be, at least on the surface, quite angelic in its advocacy of love as the governing force, the moral pressure resisted in the other positions could manifest itself, paradoxically, in a turning around of moralistic fury against the established wielders of punitive power as enemies of childlikeness and of youthfulness—and, of course, of "the people."

To begin with the ethical orientation: On October 16, 1967, at the Arlington Street Church in Boston, Harvard student

Michael K. Ferber was one of the leaders of an anti-draft ceremony at which he made a statement entitled "A Time to Say
No." He concluded it thus:

But what I want to speak about now goes beyond our saying No, for
no matter how loudly we all say it, no matter what ceremony we perform around our saying it, we will not become a community among
ourselves nor effective agents for changing our country if a negative is
all we share. Albert Camus said that the rebel, who says No, is also one
who says Yes, and that when he draws a line beyond which he will
refuse to cooperate, he is affirming the values on the other side of that
line. For us who come here today, what is it that we affirm, what is it
to which we can say Yes?

If Ferber was speaking in ethical terms for the young who
were acting like himself, there were at his elbows the Reverend
William Coffin, a most affirmative university chaplain, and Dr.
Benjamin Spock, who had used psychoanalytic insight to make
more people say Yes to more babies with more practical awareness than had any single doctor before him. And such company
emphasizes the fact that the most ethical sentiments of the young
are often synchronized with the most youthful sentiments of
concerned adults. Most of all, however, Ferber's statement must
serve here as a motto for the ethical leadership of a regeneration
of *young adults*, who, with exhortation by song or slogan, by
dramatic action or quiet resistance, and by competent social
criticism, have in recent years introduced a new ethical orientation into American life—an orientation already well visible in
the concerns of a new and skillful generation of more autonomous young adults.

I have begun with the Boston Resisters because a group retrogression is least likely to occur where a disciplined civil resistance to a circumscribed nationwide grievance dominates action.
We have heard an equally clear Yes by the students at Cape
Town University who reiterated their and their teachers' determination to open the universities to black countrymen. If, for
principle's sake, one should single out a retrogressive danger in

the area of ethical dissent, it is the arbitrary choosing of rebellious gestures that might not add up to a sustaining Yes, and of methods of action and demonstration not sufficiently coordinated with those of others to amount to a political movement.

Let me now, in all brevity, list those earliest experiences which can re-emerge in juvenile reassertions. Infancy contributes to all later life, together with some fateful vulnerabilities, an undaunted orality and an unbroken sensory eagerness. The infant's *mutuality* of responses with the maternal person leads to the introjection of a benevolent and reliable parent image and thus helps to appease primal anxiety. This, in turn, works for a favorable ratio of *basic trust* over basic *mistrust*, which assures that *hope* will become the fundamental quality of all growth. All this combines to form a first *developmental position* that contributes to all later stages as it reaches higher levels of differentiation. In adolescence, the quality of *fidelity*, the capacity to be loyal to a vision of the future, incorporates such infantile trust, while the capacity to have *faith* emerges as a more focused hope tuned to an ideologically coherent universe. This first developmental position, then, can reappear in youth and young adulthood as a vital contribution to a larger vision of love and "beauty"; it can reassert itself regressively in isolated, addictive, or psychotic disturbances; or it can manifest itself in the collective isolation of a utopian or revivalist community life of a markedly childlike, trusting, and mystical spirit.

In contemporary patterns of dissent, it must be obvious that the group style generally subsumed under the term "hippiedom" was such a totalization of the first developmental position. In the midst of our technocratic world, young men and women encouraged one another to live like the proverbial lilies of the field, with trusting love as their dominant demand and display. In the scheme of moral positions, in turn, such a return to the logic of both infancy and paradise can be seen as a re-enactment of the *pre-moral stage*. These young people seemed to convince themselves (and sometimes us) that the fall from grace and the ex-

pulsion from paradise must count as overexertions of divine rigor
and that basic mistrust is superfluous baggage for a "human
being." This position can be experienced as a reaffirmation of
the indispensable treasure of experience that our technocratic
world is vaguely aware of having sacrificed to the gods of gad-
getry, merchandise, and mechanical adjustment; and, up to a
point, the world was grateful to—or, at any rate, fascinated by
—this tribe from "another world."

Let me insert here one brief story of a "confrontation" of
this kind. Harvard Hall was being repaired behind a large and
ugly wooden fence. Overnight, there appeared a sign on it saying, "This fence needs love." The next day, young people appeared with paint and brushes. They were told to be careful
what they were doing because President Pusey could see that
fence from his desk. Before nightfall, there were big and flowery
letters spelling out, "More pay for Pusey."

But alas, an existing technology has its own methods of ab-
sorbing and neutralizing utopian innovations, and the flower
children, too, suffered—precisely because of their repression of
the necessary minimum of mistrust—from the combined exploitation by microbes, drug pushers, and publicists.

There could be no greater contrast than that between either
the ethical or the pre-moral positions just sketched and the
amoral and anti-moral ones to be considered next. And yet dissent unites, and the hippies and the motorcycle gangs were on
occasion seen to dwell together like the lambs and the lions. I
have heard of one instance when draft resisters linked themselves
together around a conscientious deserter with chains handed
them by one of the black-leathered gangs. If the anti-moral and
the amoral positions are more obviously sinister than the pre-
moral one, however, it is because they champion a belief in the
goodness both of physical violence and of "obscenity."

The amoral position is clearly related to the second stage of
infantile development—that is, about the second and third years

of life. In dogmatic brevity, the libidinal stages of anal-urethral and muscular development have a psychosocial corollary in the sense of *autonomy*, which must outweigh the danger of excessive *doubt* and *shame*. The new, rudimentary strength to emerge from this stage is a sense of *free will*—seasoned by mutual delineation with the will of others. The psychopathological counterpart of all this is, in fact, a malfunction of the will, in the form of inner *overcontrol* manifested in compulsive and obsessive trends or in a willful *impulsivity*.

Adolescence calls for a revival of the second developmental position, as well. Tested in ongoing history, a sense of free will can become part of a collective will, guided by some higher will. Willful impulse, in turn, is subordinated to communal experience, while obedience can become part of a chosen discipline. In totalistic rebellion, however, the re-enactment of this position can lead to a complete reversal. Flaunting any rules of shame, the dissenters may sport shamelessness, obedience may become defiance, and self-doubt, contempt of others. Such deliberate challenges, in turn, can arouse the worst in those challenged, wherefore the militant amoralist found himself, sooner or later, confronted by uniformed men, paid to do the "dirty work" for nice people, and, indeed, often apt to behave like the externalized version of a brutal conscience.

I hope that I will not be misunderstood. I am not calling all those who acted out an amoral orientation personally amoral, or devoid of an ethical orientation. On the contrary, the very decision to behave in an amoral fashion, and systematically so, *can* be in part an ethical one, especially where the conviction prevails that the exposure of the hypocrisies of law enforcement as well as of moral orderliness is a first step to national or racial rejuvenation. But here, too, the display of a certain "liberated" shamelessness, in conjunction with a concerted attempt to put the authorities to shame, is both transparent in its retrogression and hazardous in application. Often such a conviction is at least explainable as a reaction to a childhood milieu which was totally overshadowed (as is that of most black people in this country) by the illegal violence of righteous people. Thus, the amoral position can naturally impress many youths as more heroic or even ethical than the stance of many conformists, who enjoy a freedom and a safety they have never had to fight for.

It is well within developmental logic, then, that the retrogression to an amoral state could lead extreme dissenters to play out—no less compulsively for seeming so obvious and deliberate —such infantile patterns of protest as the use of excrement as ammunition or the deft deposition of feces in places to be desecrated. In this context also belongs the indiscriminate assault of authorities with dirty names, including the fanatic use of the appellation "pigs," which certainly showed a strange lack of respect for an innocently muddy animal; and the use of sexual four-letter words—a blatant retrogression from "sexual freedom."

This may be the place to discuss briefly the often heard assumption that such retrogressive acts on the part of privileged youth not ordinarily given to slang expression are simply overgrown temper tantrums due to their parents' "permissiveness." Authentic permissiveness can probably not be learned in a few generations. In the meantime, a kind of paralyzing laisserfaire typical for parents who do not trust their own impulses only results in an all too obvious inhibition of parental anger and especially of genuine indignation. This leaves the rage of both the parents and the children untested and untrained, and survives in a residual apprehension as to when the parents will dare to vent their suppressed rage and prove that they, indeed, can manage their own violence. But problems of child rearing are always part of an intergenerational climate; and it cannot be childhood experience alone that compelled young people to test the limits of the dispassionate fairness claimed by authorities as well as by parents. Where such challenge was met with the deployment of a hired force that did not hesitate to express the annoyance which the privileged lacked the courage to display, the ethical weakness of the elders who thus delegated and sanctioned violence immediately aroused the solidarity even of those larger numbers of young people who would not otherwise be attracted by amoral stratagems.

In the third stage of childhood—that is, the fourth and some of the fifth year of life—the imaginative *anticipation of future roles* is played out with toys and costumes, in tales and games. This initiative is intrusive and locomotor, with an emphasis on invading the parental domain, although in girls it is apt to yield to more "feminine" concerns. If, then, guilt over the sexual and aggressive designs on parent figures (the oedipal constellation) is the negative heritage of the third stage—and this with a marked fear of damage to the executive body parts—it becomes only more plausible that young people would be attracted by charismatic leaders and utopian causes which will sanction and give direction to the re-emergence of vigorous and competitive imagination. What is reawakened, then, is the claim to the right to wield *initiative* of imagination and action—and this with a projection on others of the *guilt* which once deepened the propensity for repression and made the child who had gone too far in play and fantasy so amenable to moralistic pressure.

To ward off the worst, past generations have tried, not without condescension, to assign to male academic youth an area of boisterous, promiscuous, and rebellious re-enactment of phallic pursuits for the purpose of "sowing wild oats" or of "blowing off steam" before adult "reality" will force some sportive exuberance back into obedient channels. Higher education, especially, has always cultivated its style of genteel boasting and sportive competition, but in the long run it has also conveyed the power of ideas as embodied in rebellious men and periods of the great past, and it has thus supported the refusal of aggravated youth to be made subservient to technical and bureaucratic regimentation. The translation of such genteel rebelliousness into revolutionary stances was fascinating to behold; and so was the participation of women students, whose previous rebelliousness had, for the most part, been relegated to different patterns of behavior supporting or complementing the men's needs. But as they came to share the deep concerns over the dehumanization first exemplified by the Vietnam war but then also seen in the treatment of women at home, women also participated in the moralistic outrage to be discussed next.

Among the retrogressive trends associated with the aggravation in youth of the conflict between free initiative and paralyzing guilt, there is the *anti-authoritarian* and yet *hypermoralistic* stance, which was sometimes even stranger to behold than the name I am here attaching to it. Here is a simple and mild example of what I mean. In a college newspaper, a student took a truly distinguished professor to task for an allegedly illogical and unethical point of view. The issue is not so important here as the stance. The writer scolded: "What truly bothers me is the quality and logic of your justification . . ."; "I find thoroughly naïve your attempt to distinguish between . . ."; "Still more ludicrous is the characterization in your letter . . ."; "Even if I were to grant you this point for the sake of argument . . ."; "What most . . . experts lack is a discernible sense of responsibility . . ." This total turning of the schoolmaster tone against a legendary "authority" was typical of the tone sported by some self-appointed revolutionaries, who declared a given man or group to be "guilty," with a fanatic use of "guilt-by-association" logic. The infantile position re-enacted here, obviously, is that of the child's secret hope that someday he will be big enough to tell his parents off; in the meantime, we may be embarrassed to hear a child tell a younger sibling that he or she is "dirty" with a strident voice in which we recognize our own. Conversely, some young people with the clearest intelligence and the most ethical intentions could talk one another into anti-authoritarian slogans, unaware of the probability that in cultivating such stances they were hastening the time when they were to use them against one another for reciprocal moral liquidation.

In the meantime, fanaticism "dared" by agitators can lead to dangerous confrontation precisely because it is staged in places reserved for adult male prerogative. Perhaps the re-enactment of the third developmental position was nowhere more obvious than in the emotional and behavioral side effects of those dramatized confrontations that centered in the occupation of buildings as seats and symbols of established power. The acquisition of a territorial base in the heart of the establishment is, of course, an old revolutionary technique which is as strategic as it is symbolic—and dangerous. In the occupation of a center in the alma mater, however, retrogressive trends were mobilized for the very reason that the conquerors claimed and counted on the relative safety of the academic sanctuary, and the guaranteed exclusion from it (unless they were specifically invited) of the police forces of city and state. Successive mood swings seemed to vary from an undoubted sense of having accomplished a historically valid communal deed comparable to the storming of the Winter Palace to excesses clearly dramatizing themes of a degradation of father figures as guilty usurpers and of the right of the young to claim both license and amnesty, almost before the deed was consummated. And, indeed, faculties tended to make family affairs of such revolts; which made it equally ludicrous to demand and to grant amnesty or to insist on severe punishments for deeds that, in fact, did manage to arouse guilty doubts in the confronted adults and force them, too, to confront one another in prolonged and overdue debate.

We must now, finally, look again at that vast majority of the young who, without such provocation, would be aggravated only in their dreams and who join a revolt only under very special historical conditions. Not that the majority has not always cultivated periodic pranks, raids, and even riots which in some cultures have come to be taken for granted. But even though on such occasions and in some countries lives are lost, these youthful disorders rarely assume the nature of a concerted rebellion. After all, students are not necessarily alienated from an industrial world, or even from a military-industrial complex, so long as their studies promise them active participation and advancement in it, and with it a style of leisure utilizing all the comfort of modern mechanization. It is difficult to ascribe to this majority a tendency to retrogress or to re-enact a previous developmental position, because their aspirations are to a large extent only an extension of the fourth life stage—the *school* age—into a prolonged period of apprenticeship. In other words, their identities remain centered in their work. In our continuum from pre-moral to expressly ethical orientations, this great middle range, on the whole, cultivates a *moral pragmatism*. This dominates, above all, the students of occupational specialties which attempt to come to grips with the concrete complexities of modern life, be they production or distribution, transportation or communication, medicine or law. For them, *what works is good*, and it is man's fate to be in motion and to set things in motion in league with the nature of the universe. Teamwork justifies man's trust in the eventual manageability of all modern complexities, including poverty and race relations, war and the conquest of space.

This general orientation fits questions of morality, ideology, and ethics into world views of methods and techniques which verify themselves, problems of sin or salvation being delegated to a Sunday religiosity never in conflict with habit and reason and guaranteeing rewards to those who help themselves. The result is the promise of a universal technical-cultural consolidation.

If there is anything comparable to retrogression in this orientation, it is rather a fixation on all too early, all too exclusive emphasis on the adjustment to the dominant modes of production and of success; and while those at home in such work discipline are apt to escape the more disturbing forms of identity confusion, they also must live by a certain dissimulation of emotions, the cumulative fate of which in inner or interpersonal life is hard to gauge. Their patterns of dissent differ in countries of different degrees of economic development. Even where the pragmatists occasionally permit themselves to be agitated or led by ideological activists, intellectual youth cannot always foresee whether their temporary supporters want a different system or a more profitable identity within the existing one; for the pragmatists are closer to the power struggles within the political structure than they are to any demands for ideological renewal. But while the pragmatists are young, increased contact with humanist intellectuality is apt to breed radical doubts. Otherwise, a retrogression within the logic of the school age takes the form of "dropping out" for the sake of doing "my thing." Such avoidance of an early submission to the narrow techniques of limited competencies can be of personal value, especially when joined to enriching experiences and exercises. But dropouts are apt to erect a pretense of superiority over all those who work and serve, thus projecting on others a *sense of inferiority* which is the shadow of the school age and dominates the negative identity of the workman. Otherwise, the identity of the competent workman organized with his co-workers in units of economic and political power provides an identity so grounded in tradition and language that the humanist may well envy it. On the other hand, where masses of young persons potentially competent but not specially trained are excluded from such work communality, they may find no other "jobs" to excel in and to protest with but (more or less flamboyant) crime.

Thus, the earlier stages of life bequeath to adolescence and youth circumscribed strengths and conflicts which are variously relieved and transformed during the disengagement from childhood, if, indeed, there is a plausible adulthood to engage in. The barrier often called a "gap," we must now specify, is defined by the dilemma of adulthood as well as by that of youth. Today, it is reinforced on the adult side by a kind of pervasive deficiency in ethical and religious orientations which were still consonant with an identity promised a generation or two ago. In fact, many of the adults most efficient in modern transactions have had the least time to complete or, indeed, to renew their identity development—not to speak of their sense of intimacy or generativity—under the pressure of technological, historical, and political change. Maybe for this reason, some bearded young men and severe young women managed to look and act like veterans of life compared to their loudly successful and boyish-looking fathers and their demonstratively happy and girlish-appearing mothers.

Which brings us to us, the professors. If my diagnosis of the inescapability of some retrogressive trend is correct, then this must be assumed to have its counterpart in us as well. It appeared, I think, in reverberations of our own half-fulfilled youth which can make us idealize the motives of the young; or again, it could appear in the form of an angry rejection of almost all agitated young people. As we perceived that much of youth deeply mistrusted us, we were shocked to note that we mistrusted ourselves and each other, whether we were overcome by a new sense of awe before such blatant eternal youthfulness or by a redoubled fatigue which told us that nothing ever really came of youthful utopias.

Such ambivalence exposed us to a dangerous doubt as to when to be "permissive" and where to "draw the line." And this is exactly where youth, at its worst, wanted us. For if, indeed, a more or less unconvinced and unconvincing permissiveness or grudging moral inaction on the part of the parent generation had anything to do with the unrest of youth, then this particular unrest tested the limits of our permissiveness in order to find the exact point where and when we were going to turn into angry authoritarians anyway or, for that matter, call the police. What was at stake, then, was the authenticity of either our strictness or our permissiveness.

Given the obvious fact that we are a generation of parents and teachers not guided by an acute political ideology, we were asked to prove that our strictness was based on our own ethical commitments and on insights commensurate with our knowledge; that our indignation was more than a retrogression to unreconstructed moralism; that our permissiveness was really more than a forced suspension of our indignation. And, indeed, individuals in parental or authoritative positions, who themselves were treated punitively when they were children, cannot in one generation (or two) overcome the need to relieve their conscience in punitive outbursts for which they often feel guiltier than the young. Such conflict of inner authority is, of course, also built into the younger generations: their very consciences are alternately too permissive and too punitive, and in order to clarify their own wavering, they must challenge ours. This, in turn, called for what firmness we could muster, but it was hard to understand that what was at stake was not our professional stature (their parents' "success" in the world had become less than relevant to some of these young people) but our inner authority as adults.

It is, therefore, of great importance that we should apply what insight we have to our relationship to our own youth: did we not feel that we had, indeed, abandoned some of our creative and ethical concerns for the sake of our advancement? In enjoying academic and professional freedom under the protection of and with massive grants from the "establishment," what deals had we made unknowingly or quite knowingly, and with what questionable profit? And, most of all, what mockery had we made of our student days in trying to remain young in some superficial and ritualized ways, forgetting maybe what universities truly stand for? Were we still "professing" in addition to learning and teaching facts and methods? Were we preserving "universities" as autonomous communities which stand *between* the parents and the state, as guardians and guides of ethical renewal?

I am not saying that most students quite knew what they were demanding, or, indeed, would have known better how to do what we were failing to do. But their challenge and our doubts were two sides of the same universal question: the role of humanist education in a technocratic world. Academic life now seems to depend on a communality of younger faculty and older students, in which the social implications of all specialties must be spelled out continuously through newly created bodies of discourse and planning.

Some militants, looking at us, even refused to concede a need for identity. To them, the very concept was only another attempt to force youth into overdefined roles prescribed by the establishment. Whether or not this is partially true, it is important to concede that there is a hidden ideological connotation to all theories concerning man's nature. Even the most carefully verified observations will prove to have been subject to the ideological polarizations of their historical period. This certainly has been the case with psychoanalytic theories, including that of identity. Yet, in our day, when (to paraphrase McLuhan) the mask is so often the message, we faced young people who, Proteus-like, hid their true identity—in every sense of the word —behind dark glasses and ubiquitous hair, while flaunting a negative identity often beyond their emotional means. This, too, can be part of courageous living; but it can also go together with a stubborn negation of the three developmental necessities marking the completion of youth: an identity tied to some competence; a sexuality bound to a style of intimacy; and the anticipation of becoming, before long, responsible (in whatever function) for the next generation.

We should acknowledge, in conclusion, the advances on the part of many young adults, who once were those youths, to re-enter the establishment with an increased sense of responsibility, a sounder respect for the mastery of technicalities, and a more vital enjoyment of life. They also have made genital freedom a central aspect of greater communal honesty. A vigorous genital culture, of course, depends on reliable contraceptive methods. While the invention of contraceptives not interfering with genital enjoyment was fervently anticipated by Freud, it may be necessary today to be vigilant in the face of an all too ready belief that sexuality and love, and that genital and procreative instinctuality, can be divided so neatly and technically without new kinds of emotional repressions—unless a new ethics, concerned with wider generative aspirations and obligations, continues to develop.

The future, I would submit, will force on young adults not only new styles of direct and extended parenthood but also the responsibility of being, indeed, their younger brothers' and sisters' keepers. After all the remarkable service which some of our young people have rendered to the underprivileged at home and to underdeveloped areas abroad, they may still have to learn that to be a young person under conditions of rapid change means to assume responsibility for younger persons nearby, and this in ways impossible for older people—and often least of all for parents. This, too, was prophetically anticipated in the transient brotherhoods and sisterhoods—even if such passionate caring for one another was at times only a sporadic and romantic phenomenon.

In this mostly "diagnostic" essay, then, I should like to end with this one "therapeutic" suggestion which (luckily, as so often) relies on the prognostically obvious: If the older young people could find the courage in themselves—and encouragement and guidance from the old—to institutionalize their responsibility for the younger young, we might see quite different images of both youth and young adulthood emerge than those we now know. New models of fraternal behavior may come to replace those images of comradeship and courage that have been tied in the past to the comradery of military service and probably have contributed to a glorification of a kind of warfare doomed to become obsolete before long; and they may come to continue the extraordinary work, both inspired and concrete, done in the last few decades by pioneering *and* competent groups of young people on a variety of economic and political frontiers. This, in turn, would make it possible for adults to contribute true knowledge and genuine experience without assuming an authoritative stance beyond their actual competence and genuine inner authority.

In the definition and defense of such a new generational bond, I also see a new role for (well, relatively) young men and women with psychoanalytic training. They have taken the time to add to their formal training years of a systematic introspection that has made them acquainted with timeless inner recesses and processes accessible only to insight. Beyond their function as healers, they could well serve as interpreters of the conflicts that are aroused in those who—on either side of the barrier—remain oppressed by the "super-ego" images and impulses of the "classical" generational struggle. But in supporting this trend, one must also emphasize the Hippocratic obligations implied in it: diagnostic and therapeutic insights cannot, beyond a certain professed partisanship, be subservient to ideological counter-transferences; nor must social critique turn into clinical name calling. In a post-Freudian world, insight must assume a timeless significance and an ethical power of its own.

For adults, too, retrogress under the conditions of the changing emotional ecology described here; or, rather, the manifestations discussed here are already the result of acute and yet hidden adult retrogression. We who know so much about the child in the adult know so much less about the fate of the adolescent in him, whether as a continued source of renewal or as a split-off younger self alternately idealized and repudiated, revived and "murdered"—and, of course, re-projected on the young. That adolescent remnants endure is often especially obvious in the peculiarities of people whose occupation forces (or permits) them to spend their lives with and for youth, not to speak of the adolescents-in-residence on every faculty. But it is eminently clear that adults of ethical stature, while having, up to a point, synthesized their ideological involvements and their moral absolutes, may under pressure fall back on either. Whether the result is generational surrender or renewed generational isolationism, it sooner or later leads to a display of that brittle dignity which is supposed to protect careers. But to many young people, a career that is not worth taking chances with is not worth having.

To share true authority with the young, however, would mean to acknowledge something that adults have learned to mistrust in themselves: a truly ethical potential. To study the psychological foundation of this potential may be one of the more immediate tasks of psychoanalysis.

A new generation, for us, always started again with Oedipus. We took it for granted that King Laius knew what he was doing —for could he not count on the authority of the oracle when he left his baby boy to die, taking no chances with the possibility that a good upbringing might have proven stronger than the oracular establishment? From what we know today, however, we might be inclined to ask: What could you expect of a little boy whose father felt so bound by phobic traditionalism? Nevertheless, our theories are still obliged to confirm the oracle: in them, each new child appears to be a potential bearer of the oedipal curse, and parricide remains a much more plausible explanation of the world's ills than filicide.

Yet it must be clear that all puberty rites and confirmations, as well as all inductions and, yes, all graduations, while they establish a reciprocity of obligations and privileges, also threaten with an element of mutilation and exile—if not in the crude form of surgical covenants, then in the insistence that a person's final identity must be cut down to size: the size of a conventional type of adult who knows his place and likes it.

The discovery of the Oedipus complex made amenable to conscious critique a generational fate grounded both in phylogeny and ontogeny. Such fate does not become obsolete through historical change. But it may well be that different periods of unrest, different epidemiologies of upset, and different forms of revolt offer to our insight new aspects of man's tragic struggle and rare victories. In this wider sense, it may well be that some of the confrontations which rebellious youth insisted upon were prophetically highlighting the fateful consequences of an out-lived patriarchal moralism and the necessity for a more universal and more mature ethics.

II

Once More the
Inner Space

"WOMANHOOD AND THE INNER SPACE" originated in a symposium on The Woman in America of the American Academy of Arts and Sciences in 1963. There, divergent aspects of the main theme were discussed by representative scholars from a number of fields and advocates of a variety of viewpoints. I emphasize this here again, because in these matters context is all—as one quickly learns from the fate of such efforts in times when their subject matter becomes "political." Then, single passages are separated from the rest and isolated phrases assume a slogan-like life of their own. They are not merely quoted "out of context," but forcibly put into a new one. This, at any rate, was impressed on me when on revisiting the Harvard area I heard my essay cited among writings deemed inimical to womanhood.

So if I am now asked whether the woman's movement has

Based on my response to a request from a former student, Jean Strouse, who was editing an anthology of psychoanalytic essays on women, from Freud's early writings on. For each item, she commissioned a contemporary critique. Since I was the last of the reprinted essayists in the volume, and extant, Jean Strouse thoughtfully asked me to write my own critique of the essay "Womanhood and the Inner Space,"[1] and she provided me with some questions which, she felt, the essay raised.

affected my thinking about women, I cannot bypass these developments. In fact, I must take account of them in some detail not only as a personal experience but also as a phenomenon characteristic of some stages in liberation movements. For if we recognize in such intellectual militancy a necessarily ruthless replowing of the ground of consciousness, we must also note that it is apt again to plow under insights into unconscious motivation that seem indispensable to the flowering of any modern liberation. But before I come to that, let me confess that I also have been affected by the more recent and still growing impression that many young women do, indeed, seem to embody a new womanhood—at once competent and thoughtful, outspoken and loving. Here, as elsewhere, new and more universal identities are evolving. I must truthfully say, however, that this has confirmed rather than "affected" what, through a long life in a number of countries, I have learned to feel womanhood can be or would become wherever it will free itself from the mere obligatory and fashionable aspects of the dominant roles, with all their built-in neuroticisms, *and* from mere reactive rebelliousness.

But if it should be now insisted that I enlarge on what I mean by womanhood, I would not know how to answer. The special polarity of the erotic encounter and of lifelong love is so close to the secret of life that only poets would attempt to find words for it. I am son and brother, husband and father to women: each a radiant and unique being, they are part of my existence and essence as I am part of theirs. Our joint experience at its best is an interplay of divergence appreciated and affinity confirmed. And this is true for women in other spheres, where intellectual interplay transcends all differences. At any rate, I could not write about women as a definable category of otherness—except in a clearly comparative subcontext such as the one to which I gave at first the admittedly slogan-like title, "The Inner and the Outer Space." As a matter of fact, wherever in human life a category of others turns into a bunch of "them," there is already something very wrong. And I have come to understand that many young women have been able to face the suddenly high-lighted awareness of their having been implicitly treated as "them" in such a variety of confining (even if sometimes flatter-ing) roles throughout history, only by vindictively lumping men together as "them," and by mistrusting totally what might prove treacherous. But vindication is not yet liberation.

In the symposium on womanhood for which the article was written, my job clearly was to start with a psychosexual theme. I had to explain where and why my own observations could not be fitted into those classical psychoanalytic formulations of wom-anhood which emphasized exclusively the organ that was *not* there. And I had to focus on what was very much there on the inside—visible and touchable only in its vestibular access, but certainly "known" early to all children except the most under-privileged urban elite.

But alas, in the minds of many feminists, I merely seem to have been granting—and with some condescension—a reasonable equivalent to maleness; and, worse, I still seemed to believe in anatomy as well as in the unconscious. And let us face it right now: it is the idea of being unconsciously possessed by one's body, rather than owning it by choice and using it with delibera-tion, which causes much of the most pervasive anger. Here I had to learn that in women's liberation, as in other liberations spear-headed by the educated middle class, a corollary to the attempt to raise consciousness is the determination to repress the aware-ness of unconscious motivation, especially where it demands an adjustment to what suddenly appear to be the physical stigmata of sex, age, or race. Thus, in this post-Freudian era we face not only some of the standard repressions unearthed by Freud but the re-repression of much that has so far been, shall we say, widely half understood and that, more fully understood in a new key, could help importantly in true liberation. To be sure, some of the theoretical paradigms of early psychoanalytic interpre-tation are badly dated. But to continue a once truly revolution-ary enlightenment, to redate systematically what belongs to the passage of time and to sift out what is lasting—that can mean to accept historical responsibility.

So, we turn to my paper and its (partial) fate. Let us see how some sentences, when used for political rhetoric, lost their theoretical half tones and, instead, took on one (inflammable) color. For example, I am asked:

One of the chief points which feminist writers take issue with, in your formulations about womanhood, has to do with the old controversy about nature vs. nurture. You write that, "The basic modalities of woman's commitment and involvement naturally also reflect the ground plan of her body; and that anatomy, history and personality are our combined destiny." Anatomy, feminists would argue, is only destiny insofar as it determines cultural conditioning . . . "Erikson's whole theory," claims Kate Millet, "is built in psychoanalysis' persistent error of mistaking learned behavior for biology." What is your answer to this charge?

My answer is that if even staunch feminists concede that anatomy, to some extent, "determines cultural conditioning," then we really have no basic argument. We could start here as well as anywhere; the question is, only, Where do we think we are going? To clarify *my* direction, I need only ask readers (if in an uncomfortably professorial manner) to take another look at what I am quoted as saying and to mark the little words "also" in the first part of my sentence and "and" in the second. "Also" means that the modalities of a woman's existence reflect the ground plan of her body among other things—as do men's modalities reflect that of the male body. "And" says that history and personality and anatomy are our joint destiny. And if we should go all out and italicize "combined," too, then an all-round relativity is implied: each of the three aspects of human fate— anatomy, history, and personality—must always be studied in its relation to the other two, for each codetermines the others. Such "systematic going around in circles" (as I have called it, so as not to overdo the word "relativity") takes some thought which is indispensable to the study of human facts.

Incidentally, I did not start this destiny business, and Freud did not, either. Napoleon was the "man of destiny" to whom, naturally, history was all. Freud the doctor wanted to make things more concrete (and, no doubt, shake the great usurper's throne a bit) by reminding him of the power of motivations (even some imperial ones) based on anatomy. And I, an heir of ego psychology, asked rather modestly whether we ourselves are not also part of our destiny. I find myself in a body that exists in a particular social place and historical period, and I must attempt to make the most and the best of that, while helping others to make the most and the best of themselves—and of me. A freer choice nobody can claim or grant to anybody, even if it would seem (and I will quote one such suggestion later) that it is implicitly guaranteed by the American Constitution.

In my article, I describe a play procedure which was employed in the context of a long-range study of a large group of California boys and girls. For most of the first two decades of their lives, they were seen twice a year in the Guidance Study of the Institute for Child Development of the University of California, to be measured, interviewed, and tested. On the occasion of their visits during their eleventh, twelfth, and thirteenth years, I asked one child at a time to come into my study, to arrange with given toys on a given table "an exciting scene from an imaginary moving picture," and then to tell the "plot." The story was recorded and the scene photographed. An open-ended observational procedure, then, but not what the critics half-mockingly refer to as an "experiment" meant to find "evidence" for a "theory."

How the *clinical* observation of free play has become an important tool in the recognition of a disturbed or anxious child's central problems is summarized in *Childhood and Society*. What I learned in Berkeley was that children outside of a clinical context, too, would willingly, and some eagerly, invent a toy scene, projecting on the play construction (unconsciously, one must assume) themes which often proved to be significantly related to life themes revealed as central and dominant in a wide variety of other data systematically collected over the years by observers of various theoretical persuasions. The wider implications of such play phenomena I have discussed more recently in my Godkin Lectures, which will appear under the title (suggested by a line from William Blake) *The Child's Toys and the Old Man's Reasons.* Thanks to the wealth of data in the Berkeley Guidance Study's "follow-up," I have, in fact, been able to review a few of those play constructions (now nearly thirty years old) and show their relevance in the light of these subjects' further course of life.

At the time of the original procedure, I was fascinated by what I soon perceived as the "language" of *spatial representation* facilitated by the use of blocks: How the constructions-in-progress moved forward to the outer edge of the table or back to the wall to which it was attached; how they rose to shaky heights or remained close to the table surface; how they were spread over the available space or constricted to a portion of that space. Now, the spatial aspect of the matter probably makes more immediate sense to persons who are visually inclined and who have learned to "read" what children "say" as they move in space and play with things and forms. At any rate, it soon became apparent that these girls and boys tended to use space differently, and that certain configurations as well as themes occurred strikingly often in the constructions of one sex and rarely in those of the other.

Let me restate the main trends here, in order to emphasize that to build with blocks and to arrange toys are modes of spatial action. Where the boys represented outdoor scenes without using any of the blocks, they emphasized the free motion of animals, cars, and people in the open spaces. If they built streets and crossroads, they channeled traffic, which, in turn, might lead to collisions or be stopped by the traffic policeman. Where the boys built structures, they were apt to build relatively high ones, to erect towers, and to add protruding ornaments in the form of cones and cylinders. On occasion, they accentuated such height by playing out the danger of collapse. And their structures enclosed fewer people and animals than did those of the girls.

In comparison and contrast, the girls, when arranging configurations of furniture without building any surrounding walls, emphasized the interior of houses. Where walls were built, the configuration was one of simple and low enclosure. And, indeed, these contained many more people and animals. When the girls added a more elaborate structure, it was apt to be an ornate doorway leading into the enclosure; and there were scenes in which animals and (male) people entered or intruded into the predominantly peaceful interior.

Interestingly enough, some critical writers are teased into playing with the material even as they read about it. Elizabeth Janeway, in referring to my "famous experiment," summarized it thus: "Boys . . . use their toys and blocks to construct outdoor scenes of action where wild animals threaten and automobiles collide. Little girls prefer interiors where their dolls serve each other tea, or play the piano." [2] None of these California children mentioned tea; nor did I. The significance of such reinterpretations seems to lie not only in the attraction of play but also in the readers' inclination to embellish role stereotypes in the play content over the more mysterious spatial configurations on which my analysis of the use of outer and of inner space rests.

If I, then, abstract the configurations more often done by the boys as dominated by height and downfall and by strong motion and its channelization or arrest and those done by the girls as dominated by static interiors which were open or simply enclosed, peaceful or intruded upon, it is obvious that in the actual play constructions there was a rich interplay between form and content, between the spatial position and the narrative themes assigned to the dolls and toys. In the end, however, it would have taken a special effort to overlook the fact that the sex differences in the use of play space did correspond to the morphology of genital differentiation, or, as I put it: "In the male, an external organ, erectable and intrusive in character, serving the channelization of mobile sperm cells: in the female, internal organs, with vestibular access, leading to expectant ova."

But the matter certainly does not rest with this seeming reduction to some basic elements. It begins here. If I concluded that these differences may suggest a "difference in the experience of the ground plan of the human body," which, in turn, "influences the experience of existence in space," I proceeded, in the rest of the article, to apply this assumption to corresponding configurations observed under other conditions, such as in clinical experience, in the observation of animal behavior, and in anthropological accounts. A configurational exploration, then, but no "theory" as yet. But all these wider demonstrations are usually omitted in references to the essay, although they explain the "inner space" as a configuration denoting a series of concentric "surroundings," from the womb of origin and the maternal body and presence to social organization and styles of dwellings, and from the quality of domestic or communal life to the "feel" of the universe.

To some readers, it seems to follow immediately that, on the basis of my "proof," I declare men to *be this* and women to *be that:* as one publication (approvingly) had it, men, to me, are "penetrators" and women, "enclosers"; men are oriented outward, women inward. Likewise, where I claim that "male and female principles in body construction . . . remain relevant throughout life for the elaboration of sex roles in cultural space-times," Janeway (in all her well-known clarity, warmth, and responsibility) concludes that "according to this formula, men are active, women intuitive; men are interested in things and ideas, women in people and feelings." Worse, "there is a limit to learning . . . in Erikson's view, and that limit is involved with the ground plan of the body and is inescapable."

Well, I have been forced to re-read the paper and to clarify it again for myself. Let me add that I feel the need to change very little except a few imprudent words and phrases as well as some ambivalently poetic ones. It was imprudent to say, "the emphasis here is on predisposition and predilection, rather than on exclusive ability, for both sexes (if otherwise matched in maturation and intelligence) learn readily to *imitate* the spatial mode of the other sex." I should have said, instead, "to make use of, to share, and at times to imitate, the configurations most typical of the other sex." Play configurations can mean many things, and a variety of bodily and spatial experiences are shared, in principle, by both sexes. Both sexes, for example, grow up and stand upright, or may be living in high-rise apartments, and therefore have a variety of "reasons" to build tower-like structures, not to speak of the mere pleasure of putting block upon block. Likewise, both have a bodily interior and live in houses, and thus may wish to build enclosures. It is quite probable, therefore, that the play space will at different ages be used variously for the expression of common and of different experiences, even as single children will demonstrate quite individual meanings. This, to me, makes it all the more convincing that our pubertal children demonstrated more clearly how differences in the experience of sexual maturation may appear in the play space. But no matter how the interior and the exterior space are experienced, used, and represented at different ages, the sexual and procreative orientation becomes and remains—that much I must claim—a significant aspect of existence in space.

Now back to the department of clarification by italics. When Kate Millet makes the (horrible) suggestion that I "define" the female as a "creature with a woundlike aperture," she refers to a sentence which claims that "children of both sexes sooner or later 'know' the penis to be missing in one sex, leaving in its place a woundlike aperture" (*Identity: Youth and Crisis*, p. 267). The mere underscoring of the word "children" would emphasize that

234 Life History and the Historical Moment

I am referring to infantile observations made at a stage of development when the inviolacy of the body is a matter of anxious concern leading to the well-known phobic "theories" which (as I insist throughout) are counteracted in the growing child's eventual awareness of a "protective inner-bodily space safely set in the center of female form and carriage."

That, in another passage, I did fail to italicize two even shorter words seems to have invited an even weirder misunderstanding. On page 278 of the same book, I speak as a clinician and note a particular *quality* in the transitory as well as the chronic depressions of women: "In female experience an 'inner space' is at the center of despair even as it is the very center of potential fulfillment. Emptiness is the female form of perdition." Such hurt—and I now italicize—"*can* be re-experienced in each menstruation; *it* is a crying to heaven in the mourning over a child; and it becomes a permanent scar in the menopause." Millet read "it" to mean mourning over each menstrual loss, wherefore she undertook to count how many periods women average in a lifetime and how often, therefore, Erikson thinks, they are crying to heaven over a child not conceived. To older people like myself, the loss of a child by death was once a more expectable experience in family life, whereas in past generations all living children represented a triumph of survival.

Come to think of it, there must be some historical relativity in much that is written about such matters—and in much that is misunderstood. Janeway clarified for me one such issue mentioned in the paper, namely, the special historical dilemma of American women.

To be told in Erik Erikson's words one is "never not a woman" comes as rather a shock. This is especially true for American women because of the way in which the American ethos has honored the idea of liberty and individual choice. We can find, in fact, an excellent description of the psychological effect of these traditional American attitudes in Professor Erikson's own classical study, *Childhood and Society*. "The process of American identity formation," he writes, "seems to support an individual's ego identity as long as he can preserve a certain element of deliberate tentativeness of autonomous choice. The individual must be able to convince himself that the next step is up to him." Very well; but then what about the limiting restrictions of being "never-not-a-woman". . . . it is more than restricting, because it involves women in the kind of conflict with their surroundings that no decisions and no action open to them can be trusted to resolve.[3]

This challenging quotation makes plain the fact that I should not have written about American identity formation without specifying its meaning for American women—a theme I have approached in my recent Jefferson Lectures (*Dimensions of a New Identity*, 1974). But it makes equally clear that such traditional oversight cannot now be corrected by focusing on the fate of women exclusively, instead of studying the *correspondences* in male and female experience in different historical periods.

To make this systematic will be a gigantic job, since correspondences, in any instance under discussion, can counterpoint sameness as well as difference, mutual complementation as well as irreversible antagonism, compensatory rewards as well as irretrievable sacrifices.

I can touch here on only a few of these correspondences. For example, if the reiteration (by a man) of such a verity as "never-not-a-woman" appears to be shocking, one must consider that a man is never-not-a-man, either. If to this some may respond with conviction the corresponding fact "but that is what he wants to be!" it should be remembered that a boy, under certain cultural conditions, is not even permitted to *think* that he might ever *want* to be not-a-man or not-quite-a-man with all the proud trimmings of manhood in his culture. In America, this has meant to want to be or to make like being a *self-made man*, made in America, an ideal most invigorating and unifying under historical conditions which permitted and demanded a new national identity made out of a multiplicity of immigrant identifications, on a wide continent of expanding opportunities. That eventually a stance developed which maintained, at all cost, the

semblance of self-chosen roles, sometimes to the point of carica-
ture—all this only parallels other national stereotypes; and one
could, no doubt, relate the unfreedom of women in this as in
any culture to the kind of freedom enjoyed by some men and
barely lived up to by most. But in America, the emphasis on
choice in all social roles has become an ideological faith which
Janeway seems to feel is violated by any suggestion "that
woman's role differs from man's because women are born differently." Her crescendo of complaint can make a man feel quite
guilty (somewhat like a mean older brother) for ever having
brought up the subject; for such a suggestion, Janeway says,
"destroys any value that can be derived from the notion of roles
. . . it knocks to the ground the idea of the role as a means of
learning, of getting things done, and of communicating by
means of behavior . . . it seems a sad waste to throw away such
a valuable concept simply to put women back in their place." [4]

If here the self-made role is at stake, together with its time-
honored method of convincing oneself that the next step is always up to the individual's choice, then, indeed, it must be said
that American women have not only not enjoyed equal political and economic rights but have also been forced to assume
(and learn to flourish as best they could in) roles which were
meant, above all, to *complement* the male ideal of self-madeness
and mobility in a "man's world" which thus by and large did
dictate "woman's place."

Janeway, as you can see, alternately calls a role a "notion,"
an "idea," and a "concept." And, indeed, it seems important to
differentiate between the role concepts which emerge in a given
country (such as Talcott Parsons' in this country) and the role
ideology dominant in it. No true role *concept* would ignore the
fact that functioning roles, if ever so flamboyant, are tied to
certain conditions: a role can only provide leeway within the
limits of what bodily constitution can sustain, social structure
can make workable, and personality formation can integrate. A
role *ideology*, however, would induce persons to convince them-

selves and each other at all cost that their role choices can sur-
mount all or some of these limitations. Women in America, having for so long lived in and with the ideology of the self-made
man without partaking of it except vicariously, may plausibly
feel that in this very country of liberty and equality they have in
some ways further to go than women in some other democracies,
and this not only in the mere acquisition of the right and chance
to participate equally in the game of economics and politics.
For the very nature of that game, as is obvious in its procedural
and verbal habits, excluded all but exceptionally adaptable and
insistent women from being "one of the boys." And one may
well ask whether women *should* play the game, even if they
could, without changing its nature. Even where political and
economic liberty provides the belated right to join men in self-
made stances cultivated in American history, it will soon become
obvious to liberated women that the American male must now
learn to adjust to a limitation of *his* aspirations and dreams,
namely, where they have led not only to the overexpansion of
goals but also to the corruption of means, to the mechanization
of motives, and to a restriction of personality potentials.

Equal opportunity for women, then, can only mean the
right and the chance to give new meaning and a new kind of
competence to (so far) "male" occupations. Only thus can
women really influence future work conditions and marriage
arrangements, life styles, and forms of communal collaboration.
At the end, only a renewal of social creativity can liberate both
men and women from reciprocal roles which, in fact, have exploited both.

In my essay, I concentrated on those aspects of the "inner
space" which mark its central importance—relatively neglected
in psychoanalytic literature—for the woman's positive identity,
and more or less unconsciously envied by men. If one then in-
quires about the fate of those *negative self-images* which the girl
inevitably absorbs as she grows up under conditions in which, as

Jean Strouse emphasizes, she cannot fail to make the "observation that the qualities associated with having a penis (action, adventure, change, fighting, building, aggressing) are valued more highly than those associated with having a vagina," we must learn to think of them, too, in *correspondences*. This means we must evaluate the negative as well as positive elements in the identity formation of both sexes, and this not only in their importance for the "inner *economy*" of the individual person, as clinical thinking all too easily suggests, but rather as part of the emotional *ecology* shared by persons of both sexes. Where one sex harbors negative images of the other, the resulting mutual defensiveness leads not only to acknowledged antagonisms but also to attempted resolutions in (more or less conscious) *social deals*. Incidentally, I have learned to like this word "deals" because it suggests a reciprocal bartering and bargaining, an apportioning and allocating of rights and duties, and this with varying outcomes, such as square deals, double and fast deals— and, of course, dirty ones. To speak of such deals helps me to relate (or to think we may learn to relate) the inner defenses studied by psychoanalysis and the "political" machinations common in daily life. So let us play with a few correspondences between male and female existence, to see what happens to the negative identities in each.

Readers by now will be fully informed, probably to the point of ennui, of all the proliferations of penis envy. It may provide just relief to remember that males must suffer a corresponding discomfort, namely, the fear of losing or damaging a vulnerable and exposed organ of such magic prowess—and competitiveness. For there are, of course, real and imagined differences in male equipment, too, and a resulting *inter-male* penis envy. But if there is an element of what we call "overcompensation" in men's search for arenas of majestic accomplishment, men are making up not only for a fear of being immobilized and found to be wanting in stature and status but probably also for a deep envy of the maternal capacity to produce what in all its newborn weakness is and remains, after all, the most miraculous human product in the universe: and it breathes!

Boys, of course, have mothers, too, and have internalized mother love with their (or some) milk. But only the girl has it literally in her to become a mother herself. Whether she learned to like or dislike her particular mother and what she stood for, she must transform her own early dependency into her own style of adult dependability. In whatever context she later chooses to be thus depended on, however, there are always deals permitting her to remain in some respects dependent—and to make others overly so. The boy's and man's developmental job is apt to be quite different and yet reciprocal: namely, to doubly compensate for the pull to infantile dependence and to establish male autonomy while also finding ways of becoming clandestinely dependent on women (and men) in the adult scene. At any rate, to the boy and man, womanhood combines the highest as well as the lowest connotations, so that part of his own negative identity—the "effeminate" traits he must suppress in himself as he becomes a man—is in stark conflict with the maternal ideals he received from and continues to seek in motherly persons. Such conflicts, incidentally, creative men and women are able to resolve on a grand scale because they learn to feel and to depict the otherness usually suppressed; and although they suffer some well-publicized agony on the way, they are sure of universal applause. For ordinary men and women love to witness, at least in the printed page or on stage and screen, the playing out of some bisexual freedom (and even the resulting tragedy) denied to them. Modern life may come to permit a much freer inter-identification of the sexes in everyday life: we will return to this point.

If the little girl, then, feels inferior because of the boy's negative attitude to the woman in himself, she also knows that she is going to be assigned superior roles by a compensatory—if variably ambivalent—valuation given her traditionally in the roles of mother and sister, value giver and teacher, lady of the house, mistress, and playmate—all potentially confining roles and yet each endowed with a specific power which forces the man, in turn, to live up to his part. No wonder that, faced with some pained awareness of all this, some individuals of both sexes prefer trying out homosexual or otherwise interchangeable roles. However, without rare gifts or insights, they do not escape transparently analogous role complications.

Does all this express a clinician's habitual pessimism? The point is that these age-old conflicts call not only for liberty in socio-economic matters but also for emotional liberation—whatever comes first. And a specifically psychoanalytic re-evaluation of sexual differences must ask not only what defensive deals individuals make with their own manifold identifications but also what deals men and women have made or are making with each other, in order to complement each other's defenses, and to come to some workable division of roles.

But one must also always allow for the ideal in a given period. Indeed, a strong *ego-ideal* provided by parents, elders, and leaders with consistent values is a prime psychological necessity, and this especially as a counterforce against the (developmentally) more infantile and (collectively) more atavistic *super-ego* which mortgages all choices in life and in history. It is, therefore, especially important to watch, in the sudden shift of awareness brought about by an attempted liberation, the comparative fate of new ideals and of old super-ego pressures. The latter, after all, are always the inner mainstay that helped to secure and to maintain the traditional status quo. Often, it can permit a liberation only at the price of turning old guiltiness into a new and consuming righteousness, and an erstwhile negative self-image into blind accusations against others, now newly appointed enemies. As youth in much of the world captured a great vision of peace (which *has* made a difference), it also vented a moralistic fury on the whole adult generation, and in the name of peace created new and hateful confrontations across the generational border. We are now aware of the moral exhaustion which can follow such moralistic realignment of images. In the women's movement, one can discern a corresponding moralistic projection of erstwhile negative self-images upon men as representing evil oppressors and exploiters. This may be necessary; but it must not replace that cold *self*-appraisal in historical terms which no true revolutionary movement can do without; and in our time such historical self-appraisal must include some "psycho-historical" insight.

Do I mean that women should recognize their masochism in that inner collusion which I have postulated? When it comes to masochism, I again invoke the formula that "only a total configurational approach—somatic, historical, individual—can help us to see single traits in context rather than in isolated and senseless comparison." True, woman is prepared by physical constitution and by tradition to bear some unique discomfort and pain and some special sensitivity associated with her procreative endowment; but this becomes a masochistic love of suffering only when she "exploits pain perversely or vindictively, which means that she steps out of rather than deeper into her female function." So I do not ascribe to a simple female masochism (or, indeed, to a male sadism) the historical fact that woman through the ages has assented to an *accentuation* of the inner space as an over-all confinement and to an *exploitation* of masochistic potentials in roles in which she was "immobilized, infantilized, and prostituted, deriving from it at best what in pathology we call 'secondary gains' of devious dominance."

But so, we must now continue, have men accepted and inflicted on their own kind hardship and slavery, injury and death, for the sake of the defense and conquest of those outer spaces which they needed for their victories. The corresponding exploitation of *their* masochistic as well as sadistic potentials has been hidden only by the imagery of heroism, of duty, and of work. So I should extend to men, also, my suggestion that only a new biocultural history (created by women and men articulately self-observing and communicative) could clarify the evolution of the masochistic potential in our man-made world, and of our overadjustment to it.

The inner psychological division necessary to maintain such a world of accentuated inner and outer spaces as I outlined in my paper harbors, then, negative and positive identity elements in both men and women. It would take more than one essay to specify how all this *develops*, either ontogenetically or historically. But it is clear that where in girls a certain "inner-directedness," and, indeed, a certain self-contained strength and peace, was cultivated, they were also forced to abandon (and sometimes later to overdo) much of the early locomotor vigor and the social and intellectual initiative and intrusiveness which, potentially, girls share with boys; while most boys, in pursuing the male role beyond what came naturally, had to dissimulate and to disavow what receptivity and intuitiveness they shared with girls. How each sex overdeveloped what was given; how each compensated for what it had to deny; how, thus, each managed to get special approbation for a divided self-image; and to what extent "oppressor" and "oppressed" (beyond and behind the overt scene of blatant political and economic exploitation) colluded with each other in both flattering and enslaving each other and themselves—*that* is what I mean by the deals which men and women must learn to study and discuss.

I am asked what effect the relative accessibility of abortion and birth control may have on the identity of women. These two words always strike me as being dangerously negative for an issue which makes mankind face the responsibility for its own life-giving power: "birth control" seems to associate the matter (choose one) with price, pest, or arms control, and "abortion" with the elimination of waste. "Planned parenthood" is better; it emphasizes initiative and thoughtfulness, and assumes that the wish for parenthood exists. And, indeed, among many young adults planned parenthood is becoming a voluntary joint experience of great meaning. For it attempts to give a few children their due, while it applies the energies saved from parental overcommitment to wider communal responsibilities. I have always called the dominant task of adulthood *generativity* rather than procreativity or productivity, because I did want to allow for a variety of activities other than parenthood or the making of goods or money—activities which are, well, "generative" because they contribute to the life of the generations. Here, indeed, is a field of new leadership for young adults privileged enough to have choices and to recognize them.

The ideological leadership of young adulthood also seems all important at this time just because it emphasizes the adventure of new ideals and plays down the grim moralism of old. True, we can see now—now that we can avoid it technologically—how motherhood was used to enslave women by the combined forces of instinctual drive, social tradition, and inner collusion. But, again, the mere attempt to right a wrong by turning it upside down, and to claim that there is no instinctual need for parenthood and that parenthood is *nothing but* social convention and coercion, will not liberate anybody's choices. A choice is free when it can be made with a minimum of denial and of guilt and with a maximum of insight and conviction.

In view of all this, questions regarding birth control, when addressed to *me*, can only mean: If what we have subsumed in the image "inner space" is, indeed, so significant, both as the inner bodily ground of female procreation and as a dominant configuration in self-images and social roles, how can modern woman be aware of this *and* choose to be or not to be a mother if and when it suits her? And we are facing the age-old question all over again, of whether a person or a generation can simply choose to disregard as inconvenient or unnecessary any part of the instinctuality essential to our bodily existence. In other words, on our way to liberate genitality but to restrict procreation, are we about to repress yet another "basic drive"? Or *is* it "yet another"?

Mankind, it is true, has learned to transform sexuality into a source of vital personal expression and into an art of intimate communication. Love has learned to borrow from necessity, and self-fulfillment from a natural mandate. All this—and sublimation—has helped to civilize mankind and has provided much of the fuel for its creativity. But it has also made us frightfully self-indulgent—and I mean indulgent of the single self, licensed by an ideology of individualism.

This is the time, then, to face a simple fact just because it was never more unpopular: not even psychoanalysis, while investigating the power of the libido, has sufficiently accounted for the procreative core of genital activity. In my article, I point to modern investigations of the human sexual response which seem to reveal a vigorous involvement of the inner procreative organs in the erotic excitement due to every kind of sexual act. And, as I have insisted, even the great aim of psychosexual maturation (and of psychoanalytic cure), namely, the "primacy" of genital sexuality, does not, in itself, assure adult maturity, unless genitality, in turn, becomes an intrinsic part of erotic intimacy, and such intimacy, in turn, part of joint generative commitments. In reminding you of this, I realize why both pro- and anti-psychoanalytic liberationists may look at my contributions with mistrust: for how can one be really liberated in one's genitality *and* remain committed to generative tasks?

A theory of the life cycle rather suggests the opposite question: How can one really maintain genital liberation and not come to terms with the deep urges of generativity? In fact, we face here the question (and psychiatry will soon be up against it) whether the need for procreation can be simply ignored or repressed either for the sake of convenience or for that of the most stringent economic considerations, either in the name of "free" sexuality, or in that of fashionable role playing—even as genitality was once unsuccessfully repressed for the sake of, say, Victorian status seeking. I have already given, or implied, my answer: birth control calls for new and combined insights both psychological and political. The hybris of planned progeny calls for a new creedal context: a world order with the provision of an equal opportunity to develop fully for each child chosen to be born, and backed up by the generative commitment of all adults.

Much is being written now by and about the new woman. My impression is that what is published is all too often written by writers, of writers, for writers. I point this out because writers have a shared investment in a specific type of generativity. Fair enough; but one would wish that in matters so close to the core of human life, more writers would include in their awareness the less verbal, or, at any rate, less intellectual masses of women—whether workers or mothers or both—and ask what makes up the sense of existence in their days and nights, their years and stages of life—including their old age. To liberate *them* means to create new and convincing functions and duties as well as rights beyond the mere know-how of birth control.

But to return once more to the men. Considering the brazen way in which, in the essay under discussion, I juxtaposed the inner and the outer space, it will not be too shocking if I now claim that, indeed, *birth control* and *arms control* are two corresponding technological developments which are stirring up both the male and the female self-images in order to combine them in a more all-human identity. As birth control goes to the core of womanhood, the implications of arms control go to the core of the male identity, as it has emerged through evolution and history.

Atavistically speaking, armament originates in the extension of the man's strong right arm as the carrier of weapons and tools employed and perfected in all those righteous wars which the human pseudo-species have waged against each other, wars such as no self-respecting species wages against itself in nature. Warfare, to be sure, has become a self-perpetuating institution, which justifies itself on grounds of technical perfection as well as on political grounds as the logical outcome of former wars and

of the treaties that ended them forever incompletely. But warfare, as we surely have come to realize, also serves the periodical
reaffirmation of uniformed masculinity with its simultaneous
function of making an impression on one another, on woman-
kind, and on the enemy. This, too, has served ideals, inventions,
and deeds which mankind considers part of its proudest history.
In these days, however, we are becoming aware of war's
thoughtless exploitation and the extermination of defenseless
populations anywhere and the periodical and mandatory sacrifice of a generation of fittest sons which our heroic history has
entailed. Today, we suddenly hear Homer in a new key; and
we view with less admiration the sight of full-grown men de-
ploying the age-old stance of armed militancy plus righteousness,
from far jungles and coasts to the Wall Streets and Washing-
tons. But such new awareness, instead of exhausting itself in
perpetual protest, must also lead to an assessment of the warrior's
evolution from the man-to-man fighting spirit to the impersonal
exercise of mechanical warfare and the cold engineering of
annihilation. It now seems that arms control comes first, and that
the economic and motivational investment in super-weaponry
must first be contained in an over-all attitude of mutual deter-
rence which will also deter the deterrer.

This, no doubt, will make, and is already making, specific
demands on the male psyche, and must cause grave bewilder-
ment in young men, whose adolescent mores still reflect the
anticipation of periodic combat with some people of some other
kind. Today, even when there is no war, the availability of
small, manageable weapons at home makes it possible for some
peculiarly crazed young people to appoint any group and any
person to be that "other kind" that must be exterminated. If
birth control, then, frees women for a choice of (alternating or
simultaneous) roles other than motherhood or spinsterhood,
arms control, if understood in all its emotional implications,
would permit men to become freer for roles not originally
defined by a hunter's or a conqueror's imagery. Parenthetically,

the widespread concern with inwardness on the part of many young men may well be pointing to a withdrawal of commitment from a variety of overextended fighting fronts and a new search for anchor in that inner space which we all share.

Which brings me to my conclusion—and I do mean also the conclusion of my previous paper. For (should I apologize?) I still believe what I said there in somewhat creedal terms about the Ultimate residing in the Immediate. But I must apply this now, of course, to both sexes. To put a fuller existence above uncontrolled parenthood, and planned peace above unrestricted war, would call not only for new inventions but also for the redirection of much of human instinctuality. A more conscious and concerted sublimation of generativity from generation to generation cannot rely on the mere avoidance, prohibition, or inhibition of either careless procreation or thoughtless violence. Mankind needs a guiding vision. And fate usually makes it only too clear what the next vision *must* be: today, it must be a world order which would permit all children chosen to be born to develop to an adulthood that may learn to humanize its inventions—experientially as well as technologically. I cannot see how such an adulthood could evolve except through an equal involvement of women and of their special modes of experience in the over-all planning and governing so far monopolized by men.

III

Psychoanalysis:
Adjustment or Freedom?

I TAKE MY CUE for a few reflections on some paradoxical value implications of psychoanalysis from remarks made by Robert Wallerstein. First quoting a provocatively simple definition of the difference between science and ethics—namely, that science is descriptive and demands verification and that ethics is prescriptive and calls for justification—he concluded that the healing professions stand somewhere in between. In aspiring to heal, he said, we cannot avoid prescribing values, "some deliberate and avowed, some unrecognized and unavowed." This formulation would seem to include a whole spectrum from those *explicit values* which we can vigorously declare to be at the very core of our work and which are being continuously reformulated in the professional literature, to those *value implications* which may be hidden in our work or are, at any rate, ascribed to it by others, and which, whether we do or do not wish to call them our own, we may yet have to acknowledge as part of our influ-

Presented in a panel on Ethics, Moral Values, and Psychological Intervention at the meeting of the American Association for the Advancement of Science in San Francisco, in 1974.

ence and of our history. It would, at any rate, be within the psychoanalytic ethos to attempt to be aware of and to avow or disavow what we have come to stand for.

It was the word "unavowed" that first challenged my attention; for being, no doubt, dynamically related to what is repressed, it yet points to a denial specific for the ethical sphere. To consciously avow, furthermore, can also mean to profess; and I am not only a psychoanalyst by training and practice but also was a college professor by choice. In other words, I have helped to teach the tenets of psychoanalysis not only to practitioners who can be expected to take some systematic responsibility for their own motivational awareness, but to large classes of college seniors engaged in the conflicts as well as the sharpened sensitivities of maturation. And psychoanalytic insight must add a new dimension to and a new mandate for teaching. As we delimit our responsibilities, then, from those traditionally reserved for the older professions—divinity, law, medicine—we may ask ourselves what it means to teach something about the unconscious determinants of human behavior to the young.

Here I should record that I accepted my college mandate not from any urge to proselytize young people to the psychoanalytic viewpoint but because I was asked by the then dean of Harvard College to see how one might design a "General Education" course that would help clarify psychoanalysis for students who read the new prolific psychoanalytic literature without systematic guidance and, so he thought, were apt to misread it in significant ways.

We agreed then to convey some of the inner logic of psychoanalytic propositions by offering an intellectual exercise not foreign to youthful rumination—namely, to take a look at the whole human life cycle as experienced and envisaged in retrospect and prospect from the vantage point of one's age, as studied in the field of human development, as pictured in the symbolism of the ages—and as newly interpreted by psychoanalysis. In small group discussion, I became aware of the nature of some of the misperceptions which psychoanalytic readings provoke not only in all those who resist the disturbing assumption of unconscious motivation but also in many who are eager and able to learn, and yet mistake much of what psychoanalysis has to say about human nature as tacit prescriptions for conscious conduct—assumed prescriptions which can have a precipitously liberating effect on some and yet a paralyzing one on others.

As history changes and, with it, the role of psychoanalysis in society, new doubts about the validity of the psychoanalytic kind of enlightenment are added to the "natural" resistance against the recognition of unconscious motivation. And it may well be that we psychoanalysts ourselves carry with us some sense of hybris over being successful practitioners and widely read advocates of what in its beginnings was and in many ways still is and must be a very intimate clinical art-and-science. But one deep and perennial hesitation in letting psychoanalytic insight become part of everyday awareness is typified by a report (which I have not been able to verify) that even freethinking Einstein used what is, at any rate, an old story in order to illustrate what a paralyzing influence psychoanalysis might have on man's actions: the story of the centipede which was stopped in its tracks when somebody asked it to think carefully, before it moved again, which leg it was going to move first, and which of the other ninety-nine next.

Up to a point, this is a good story. But then one begins to wonder by what right man compares himself to an innocent centipede, which, as far as we know, lacks the inhibitions which are our evolutionary heritage and the split into a superconsciousness and an unconscious, which makes our motivation so complex. In fact, when Freud spoke of man as a *"Prothesengott"*—that is, godlike only by dint of having made his extremities and his sensory organs infinitely powerful with mechanical extensions—he made clear what a complicated variety of centipede *we* are: which explains, in fact, why we do need a certain heightened consciousness in order to correct and direct our motives and motions. And as for Einstein's contribution to the human condition, he helped to make us, after all, the kind of curious centipede that studies the relativity adhering to its multiple footing.

But history does appear to validate a certain concern with the unavowed influences of any new discovery on man's motivation—whether the discovery is totally removed from it, as the theory of relativity would seem to be, or most directly concerned with motivation itself, as psychoanalysis is. When Freud founded this radically introspective branch of the Enlightenment, he still could take much of Western civilization and its belief in enlightened progress for granted and was faced with the changing world of technocracy, with world wars and world revolutions, only toward the end of his life. And he may well have foreseen that psychoanalysis would not only continue to be rejected by reactionaries and moralists—*that* he was proud of—but that in some parts of the world it might be widely accepted and, in fact, flauntingly acted out as well as talked out and yet remain covertly resisted in its essence. If informed youth in the second half of this fast-moving century is attempting, by an alternation of revolt and compliance, to manage the memory and the mandate of the revolutionary changes of the first half, the influence of the Freudian enlightenment is part of that burden. And at times youth does seem to claim mastery over the dangerous knowledge of the unconscious by displaying previously forbidden and denied impulses (such as patricidal wishes or bisexual inclinations) with a mixture of passion and mockery, or by challenging the unconscious with precipitate experiences induced by drugs. But if in this stance we detect an attempt to assimilate the insights of psychoanalysis by means of the overt enactment of wishes once described as either repressed or only symbolically expressed, psychoanalytic enlightenment may, indeed, be faced with new Hippocratic tasks which we must attempt to envisage.

At any rate, today the relationship between the generations

and between the sexes can no longer be approached with psychoanalytic concepts without considering the role which these
concepts have played and will and should play in the cultural
and ideological controversies of our time. For we cannot claim
any more merely to heal clients in offices and clinics, and to
enlighten students and readers, without directly intervening in
the processes by which values are formed and transmitted in
society. Rather than deny this fact, we had better find the
proper frameworks for teaching the tenets of psychoanalysis
both in the context of clinical training and in that of humanist
enlightenment. To search in each framework for a style which
enlarges and trains ethical consciousness even as it reveals the
workings of the unconscious—that may well be the answer to
the dilemma of the all too conscious centipede.

As the intervention of psychiatric prescriptions in the values
of the times becomes a conscious ethical issue, however, it must
be recognized that mental healing in any form has always had a
close relationship not only to the prevalent ills but also to the
values of a given era; for ills and values are always two sides of
the same ethos. Whether we think of those possessed who in the
Gospels are cured by faith; or of those ridden with evil spirits
exorcised by tribal ritual; or of the more modern hysterics being
confronted with their repressions; or, finally, of the schizoid
characters of our mechanized day—the new insights and the new
style of confrontation of any therapeutic art-and-science are
first of all defined by the epidemiological disturbances they were
first challenged to alleviate. It then appears that some of the
dominant neuroses and psychoses of any given period of history
contain a kind of *inverted revolt* against the values of the existing
order; and that we, the mental healers, by taking the dominant
symptoms seriously (rather than decrying, suppressing, or pun-
ishing them), accept some validity in that challenge. In establishing diagnostic and prognostic criteria for some typical and yet
vexing kinds of patients and deviants—and in postulating an

etiology and prescribing a cure for their symptoms, a new therapeutic style also postulates what seems normative and essential in human nature; and it helps to prescribe what men owe to each other and what they must avoid doing to each other. Whatever the healing professions advocate, then, is always part of a central value struggle of their times and will, whether "avowed" or not, become ethical intervention.

Patients, in other words, are those members of a given society who—for a variety of etiological reasons—are most inactivated by inner conflicts shared by all. And the public, obscurely aware of this, is so eager for prescriptive slogans defining normal and moral conduct that it will dramatically oversimplify what we conceive to be delicately scientific and therapeutic matters. We may then claim that we have been misunderstood, and that all we wanted to do was to heal specific disturbances or to understand circumscribed aspects of human nature. But perhaps we should take a closer look at the wider applications which our therapeutic enlightenment seems to suggest.

A few brief and simple examples taken from recent history must suffice. Take the matter of "adjustment to reality." Certain types of patients were found to be suffering from partial but distinct denials of verifiable fact. Treatment, we say, must help them to make the reasons for that denial conscious and to bring the whole person up to that level of insight and will power which we attribute to the "intact" part of the personality—that part which, in fact, makes the person treatable. What we really hope for, especially with our more ambitious treatments, is adaptation rather than adjustment, in that the cured patient, while refusing to overadjust, should learn to *adapt to* what is factual and inevitable and yet also strive by a freer participation in actuality to *adapt to himself* (and to those he cares for) what can and should be changed in his environment. It is this active and effective quality of true adaptation which prompted me to suggest, in a lecture on medical ethics, that the Golden Rule in all its classical brevity, when viewed with modern insights, might be seen to direct us to do to another what will further the other's development even as it furthers our own. Mutual activation is the ethical essence of "my" rule; and it implies that true communality permits and demands it. Yet, before we know it, our vocabulary is seen and used to support a general ideal of *adjustedness*—and this often to conditions which we, in fact, do not believe a person *should* be encouraged to tolerate, precisely because they make mutuality and communality impossible and, in fact, enslave the more sensitive and insightful to conditions which strongly favor other, and often more ruthless characters.

Or take the diagnosis of "sexual repression." Our treatment was intended to lift infantile repressions in order to restore to the adult patient the capacity to make conscious choices—that is, to make it possible to tolerate in oneself and to find an interpersonal style for what is deeply needed and truly wanted, and to discard what is neither. At the same time, it was hoped that new forms of child rearing informed by psychoanalysis would help to alleviate rather than to aggravate the human tendency toward repression. Together with the ideal of adjustability, however—and, of course, in line with a general change of mores— psychoanalytic sexology seemed to prescribe "unrepressed" rules of conduct by which that person is considered the "freest" who can engage in an unlimited use of others for the obsessive expression of all the "techniques" suggested by the sex books.

And yet, we would agree that a common characteristic of all ills, sins, and evils, whether they are spelled in small letters and are accessible to therapies of the mind or are capitalized for higher attention, is the use of another as a mere object, whether the other is thus demeaned as an inferior creature, as cheap merchandise, or as a mere mechanical contrivance. Modern technicism, which tends to make a statistic of each person, may be aggravating just such Evil under the disguise of an ethos of efficiency beyond compassion or awareness of guilt.

Finally, let me point to some consequences of the great

clinical invention of reconstructing a detailed *pathogenesis*—the very invention to which we owe the knowledge of early stages and thus the life-historical as well as the case-historical point of view. A resulting emphasis on the earliest "causes" of a disturbance has contributed to decisive insights, and this especially as part of a methodological self-appraisal. However, it can also result in a relative neglect of those conflicts specific for the age of acute onset or aggravation of the disturbance in later life stages. In fact, the general preoccupation with first "causes" has led to a widespread habit of righteous and often vindictive complaints (and this at times on the part of individuals from rather overprotective backgrounds) over having been victimized by progenitors and assorted other exploiters. This, as we have seen, can exhaust itself in a habitual rage not conducive to inner freedom and least of all to a recognition of an adult's responsibility for himself and others.

Historically speaking, then, it seems necessary to be aware of the total moral climate in which psychoanalytic insights take their place in a given period. Certainly, such insights cannot count any more on the particular matrix of an enlightened ethics within the "morality" which Freud "took for granted." No wonder, then, that individual psychotherapy in the classical sense is being complemented by a search for new therapeutic conventions such as therapy in groups or other methods of sharing a wider awareness. But where such search turns to more mystical sources of enlightenment rooted in different civilizations, the question is to what extent they may serve as an escape from the Judeo-Christian heritage which we must come to grips with—even as those civilizations must come to terms with their now internalized values—as humanity enters the technocratic age.

I have concentrated here on psychoanalysis. It will be easy for the listener or reader to apply what I have said to other varieties of psychological intervention, such as the pharmacological one, which suggests a stance of correcting the world's evils by the habitual intake of corrective dosages of some chemical substance; or the behaviorist one, which offers a utopia of conduct so scheduled by implanted controls that ethical conflict is altogether unnecessary. The danger of all such interventions is that they will be absorbed by societal processes for the purposes of ethical short cuts sometimes contrary to the initial intention of the inventors of the method.

Without the systematic vigilance of the healing professions, then, and maybe in spite of it, a society dominated by technocratic habits of thinking is especially apt to turn every bit of new knowledge to the advantage of its prime economic, technological, and ideological inclinations. All this appears to be part of the unofficial evolution of ethics: the question is only what, once we know it, we perceive our further function to be.

And here it must be said that "unavowedly" our terminology colludes with the fashionable oversimplification of our findings. Psychology and psychoanalysis, by trying to link mental science with the older sciences, have tended to use physicalistic and mechanistic terms which in popular parlance easily come to mean the opposite of their original humanist intentions. In a number of contexts, I have pointed to the habitual use of the phrase "love object" which, in our field, has come to denote another person loved as a whole person and loved with one's whole person. Originally, Freud spoke only of the object of a hypothetical libidinal drive which is first directed toward the self but then finds objects in the primary persons; even as Piaget designated as an object what the infantile senses learn to perceive as coherent and persistent personages: two *conditions* for the capacity to love. But if sexual experience is referred to as "satisfaction from one's body and the outside world [one's objects]," the concept of a libidinal object search which originally was meant to denote the bond-creating vitality of Eros unavowedly serves an image of man as an inner bartering system in busy exchange with other such systems in an "outer world."

Certainly, the profoundly humanist milieu in which the ego's "mechanisms of defense" were first conceptualized was every-thing but mechanical in its emotional and intellectual atmo-sphere. One might say that for this very reason there was felt to be ample leeway for such a scientific-sounding term for man-kind's defensive deals with its drives and its conscience. And yet, in the long run, the term may have contributed to an image of man as a robot of inner mechanisms, even as the term "ego," which in psychoanalysis means the orderly and ordering, de-fensive and adaptive core in the center of the person, seemed to acknowledge what in popular parlance becomes egocentrism at its vainest. The point is that such misconceptions are by no means only due to cognitive misapprehensions or unconscious resistances, but are part of the changing moral climate with which an aware ethics must learn to reckon.

A psycho-historical review of the fate of psychoanalytic con-cepts, then, would have to clarify how each owed its original terms to dominant trends in scientific thinking (e.g., the trans-formation of energy), which at the time not only led to the dis-covery of new facts but also promised a heightened sense of real-ity within the laws of the universe; how each denoted a matura-tion or liberation (libido is freed from enslaving self-love) and became a magic formula connoting not only a scientific descrip-tion but also a healing value of great power; how each term thus came to be endowed with an ideological quality imme-diately convincing to insiders ("object" can evoke an image of passion, while "object loss" can denote deep mourning or desperate withdrawal), whereas the term may mean nothing or, in fact, connote the opposite to other listeners or readers.

My own prescription here is, however, not the anxious or righteous avoidance of such paradoxical meanings—for no sci-ence concerned with human nature can escape such fate—but systematic study.

Let me use some of my own concepts as examples of how certain terms can evoke extreme and contradictory responses not only in those who accept, and, in fact, appropriate them, but also in those who refute them on mixed ideological and conceptual grounds. By "ideological," I mean here a highly charged attitude rooted essentially in a general need for a world view coherent enough to attract one's total commitment and to render forever unnecessary the upsetting swings in mood and opinion which once accompanied identity confusion. Such needs endow, of course, the earliest commitments to professional as well as to political philosophies and persist in adulthood, even after first commitments may have become successively attached to changing creeds: wherefore our basic scientific concepts as well as our ethical precepts are often endowed with an ideological fervor which keeps them—and us—young at best and a bit juvenile at worst. But our commitment gets in the way of our investigatory ethos whenever and wherever we begin to prescribe to others what they must observe so as to guarantee the right conclusions or what they must avoid observing lest they might conclude the unmentionable.

Having begun (as teacher, clinician, and researcher) with the direct observation of the phenomena of childhood and youth, I have found it natural as well as necessary to add to the array of specific vulnerabilities diagnosed by clinical observation some suggestions concerning the potential strengths built into each stage of life—and this not just in the sense of a reasonable adjustment, but also in that of a vigorous adaptation with some energy to spare for subsequent stages. Taking my cue from Freud's dictum that education can do no more than underline what is given in development, I inquired what potential sources of human strength may be built not only into the stages of individual life but also into the constituent elements of society by and within which human lives must unfold. The rationale for this is the assumption that the life cycle (in all its promise and vulnerability) and social institutions (in all their corruptibility and indispensability) have evolved together. This trend of thought has been both welcomed and decried as "optimism" contrasting with Freud's grandiose pessimism, and as advocacy of a general acceptance of society as such. This, some warned, can only lead to a prescription of adjustment to the "establishment."

Such evaluation of a person's work according to its ideological mood is of some importance for the ethical area under discussion here, for it stands to reason that any mere emphasis on what can and will go wrong, while essential to a clinical science, can, in its application to daily conduct (i.e., to the maintenance of "mental health"), lead to ideological attitudes of prevention often marked by phobic avoidances. But it is equally true that an "optimistic" attitude may help to re-repress the painstakingly unearthed fateful aspects of human childhood.

If I, furthermore, postulate a built-in developmental aim of adult maturity in the individual life cycle and an intrinsic socio-evolutionary goal of one specieshood for mankind, I may, again, remind you that Freud pointed to the recurrent self-assertion of Eros as a power binding larger and larger units of mankind together, and this just when he was tragically aware of the periodical and ever more efficient destructiveness of Thanatos. The existential mood, then, which in balance can be said to have been dominant in a great innovator's scheme, is difficult to assess; what is clearer is the totalistic need of those who follow to assign to it over-all utopian or fatalistic, progressive or reactionary, individualistic or collectivistic values. As for my assumedly optimistic variant, both my most effusive friends and my grimmest critics tend to overlook or slight the fact that for each psychosocial step I posit a crisis and a specific conflict denoting, in accord with psychosexual theory, a lifelong anxiety (basic mistrust, shame, guilt, self-doubt, confusion, isolation, stagnation, disgust, despair), and this not merely because I must concede its existence but because there is no human strength without it. Thus, only the near psychotic forms of identity confusion in some youths and the panic of widespread identity loss pervading historical periods can reveal the dynamic reasons for the extent to which identity formation is crucial in the life history—and in history.

But again, friends and critics alike will interpret this psychosocial term either as a nothing-but prescription of an obedient fusion with an available set of social roles—or else, on the contrary, as a total individualistic identification with the self. And between these extremes, there is always the technicist assumption that anybody, having studied the matter somewhat and surveyed his chances, can decide on his favorite identity and proceed to "achieve" it.

In pointing to some of the "unavowed" ways in which even once radical psychoanalysis has been made subservient to major trends of the times, I have merely indicated what can and does happen to any and all revolutionary ideas: political, therapeutic, spiritual—and scientific. The basic paradox to be understood is that even as great thinkers detect new universal laws and thus provide unexpected new masteries for mankind, the "rumor" of these laws awakens some basic disorientation for all but those who can verify and understand them in their strictest meaning, and that means in a communality of expertise. To others, even science might need to be taught not only with logical persuasion but also with an understanding for man's deep motivational and emotional investment in all those (previous or emerging) world images which govern the values conveyed through the generational process.[1]

To return, for a moment, to Einstein, I have elsewhere suggested (or agreed, from a dynamic viewpoint, with those who suggest) that the theory of relativity, too, has been drawn into the process of *pseudo-ethical assimilation* which I have here tried to sketch: for it was and is being perceived as an advocacy of ethical relativism, even as older theories such as causality, the conservation of energy, or the survival of the fittest have become rationalizations of human (and inhuman) conduct. Psychoanalysis, again, may have the built-in correctives for such a predicament, precisely because it knows how to study the importance of oversimplified world views for the management of anxiety in each person and community, and especially so as it becomes aware of its own historical fate in such changing world images.

In conclusion, I would like to repeat in this context what I have suggested elsewhere concerning a developmental differentiation between morality and ethics. The use of the word "evolution" may be somewhat incautious: it is intended above all to connote infinitesimally slow change as compared to historical and technological changes. And if I speak of an evolution of ethics, I use the word in the sense postulated by Waddington when he called man "the ethical animal." But that upright human creature with a highly variable instinctual life, the creature marked by language and culture, must, during an especially long period of infantile and juvenile dependence, learn to become ethical—and this exactly because he is not regulated by a reliable set of instinctive patterns fitting a given section of nature.

The first requirement for a psychoanalytic study of moral values and ethics, then, is the *epigenetic* point of view which postulates that the ethical core which is built into all of us phylogenetically must evolve in each of us ontogenetically—that is, through the mediation of the generational process. Developmentally speaking, we must, then, differentiate between an earlier, *moral* conscience and a later, *ethical* sense. What psychoanalysis graphically calls our super-ego, that part of our conscience which forever lords it over us (and at times seems to crush us), is primarily the ready recipient of prohibitions driven into us in childhood by frowning faces and mortal threats, if not beaten into us by physical punishment—and this before we can possibly understand the meaning of it all. In later life, this remains our most moralistic side—that side of us which takes pleasure in turning on others and condemning those who are doing what we dare not do, or in hating or wishing to do away with those who, so we claim, are endangering the moral fiber of our kind of mankind.

Morality and ethics thus must evolve in each person in a

step-by-step development through ever more differentiated and insightful stages. Even as each earlier stage lives on in all the later ones, each later stage can represent a re-integration of all earlier ones on a higher level. But this also implies a continuing and inexorable *dynamic conflict* between the earlier and most primitive, and the later, more mature values in each person—and in all communities.

I have, I think, indicated sufficiently the *ideological* step which, in youth, intervenes between infantile morality and adult ethics. Here, I would like to enlarge briefly on.the step from ideological to ethical avowal in young adulthood.

The other day, I had occasion to speak on the nature of vows and oaths to a graduating medical class which was divided over the validity of the customary Hippocratic declaration.[2] An oath, at its best, is an occasion for the free and joint affirmation of a commitment which has become part of a shared identity within a communal tradition. Because of the indispensability of such commitment (in some form) in young adulthood, an oath can be used by the "establishment" to maintain what has become trite, overused, or corrupt, and therefore will be resisted precisely by those who take it seriously. Thus, any formula that is worth attesting also delineates what one must detest and what is worth protesting. An oath, in the form of a vow, then, is a knowing and mutual commitment of fidelity to one's chosen intimates, and this for the sake of those who depend on one's joint care. But only in early adulthood can we avow systematic values which seem to be confirmed in daily practice and in concrete competency.

The *adult* pole of our ethical nature, then, is an affirmative, because more informed and experienced, sense of what one human being owes to another in terms of the developmental realization of the best in both—and in their dependents. But alas, our most ethical, most ideological, and most moralistic modes tend to make deals with each other—deals which eventually permit man to commit or, indeed, to passively agree to the enslavement or annihilation of other human "species" in the name of the highest values. And as to what we do to our own kind, consider the "crime of punishment" by which we righteously and legalistically incarcerate society's deviants (and suspects) and by which we excarcerate dissenters, and both with no more logic than the thoughtless moralism with which we repress parts of ourselves within ourselves. It is this above all that insight must help us to resolve sufficiently to counteract the special potentialities for evil in a worldwide technology. It is for us to increase the margin of ethical choice by gaining and giving insight into the blatant deals which not only virtue and vice but also the ethical, the ideological, and the moral are attempting to make within us and right in front of us.

This, finally, may help us to understand the way in which the dynamics of moral and ethical conflict are built into the values themselves. Consider only that Truth is more than not lying—a difference beyond all legal indictment or impeachment. Similarly, to have Courage is more than not to be cowardly, Faith much more than the absence of existential doubt. At any rate, the strengths which potentially emerge from each developmental crisis in life can also be seen to serve the evolvement of a truly ethical sense.

In conclusion, we should realize where our mandate in matters of ethics places us as a mental healing profession—namely, squarely between that which changes most slowly in mankind and that which changes fastest: the phylogenetic and ontogenetic processes governing the unconscious, and technical mastery. Insight into unconscious motivation has come into its own only very recently and, so it seems, has some difficulties in delineating its place between the factual nature of medical science on the one hand and the ethical kind of truth on the other. The word "clinical" once did refer to the bedside services a priest administered to the dying, even as healing once meant to make a person whole, in body, mind, *and* soul. Ours, I think, is the specific obligation to heal by gaining and giving insight into the unconscious sources of irrational anxiety in order to free the energies and the shared pleasures of a sensual existence. Only such mastery of the irrational frees us for the capacity to fear discerningly those factual dangers which demand competent action. Beyond anxiety and fear we may face that existential dread which awakens universal resources of faith and fellowship.

NOTES / INDEX

Notes

BACKGROUNDS AND ORIGINS

1. "IDENTITY CRISIS" IN AUTOBIOGRAPHIC PERSPECTIVE
(PAGES 18–45)

1. Stuart Hampshire, in the *London Observer* (December 1, 1968).
2. Peter Blos, *On Adolescence* (Glencoe, Ill.: Free Press, 1962).
3. Sigmund Freud, *An Autobiographical Study, The Complete Works of Sigmund Freud* (London: Hogarth, 1959), vol. 20, p. 40; also in Norton Library (New York: Norton, 1963). Originally appeared in 1925, in a volume on the state of medicine as revealed in the autobiographies of its leaders.
4. Mircea Eliade, *The Myth of the Eternal Return*, Bollingen series, no. 46 (New York: Pantheon, 1954).
5. Erik H. Erikson, "The Nature of Clinical Evidence," in *Insight and Responsibility* (New York: Norton, 1964).
6. Anna Freud, *The Ego and the Mechanisms of Defense* (New York: International Universities Press, 1946).
7. Heinz Hartmann, *Ego Psychology and the Problem of Adaptation* (New York: International Universities Press, 1958).
8. Erikson, "The First Psychoanalyst," *Yale Review*, 46 (1956); revised in *Insight and Responsibility*. See also the reviews of Freud's posthumous work in this volume.
9. Erikson, *Childhood and Society* (New York: Norton, 1950, 1963).
10. Merton M. Gill, ed., *The Collected Papers of David Rapaport* (New York: Basic Books, 1967).

2. FREUD'S POSTHUMOUS PUBLICATIONS: REVIEWS
(PAGES 50–96)

1. Ernest Jones, *The Life and Work of Sigmund Freud*, vol. 1 (London: Hogarth, 1953; New York: Basic Books, 1953), pp. 287 ff.

2. Page numbers refer to American edition.
3. December 13, 1966.
4. New York *Times,* December, 1966.
5. Jones, *Life and Work of Freud,* vol. 3 (1957), pp. 150, 151.
6. Alexander and Juliette George, *President Wilson and Colonel House* (New York: Dover, 1964).
7. Sigmund Freud, *The Interpretation of Dreams,* Standard Edition (London: Hogarth, 1953), vol. 5, p. 483.

3. POSTSCRIPT AND OUTLOOK
(PAGES 101–103)

1. Talcott Parsons, "On Building Social System Theory: A Personal History," in *The Twentieth-Century Sciences: Studies in the Biography of Ideas,* Gerald Holton, ed. (New York: Norton, 1972).
2. Erik H. Erikson, *Insight and Responsibility* (New York: Norton, 1964), p. 159.

IN SEARCH OF GANDHI

1. ON THE NATURE OF "PSYCHO-HISTORICAL" EVIDENCE
(PAGES 113–168)

1. Erik H. Erikson, "The Nature of Clinical Evidence," in *Evidence and Inference,* Daniel Lerner, ed. (Glencoe, Ill.: Free Press, 1959); revised and enlarged in Erikson, *Insight and Responsibility* (New York: Norton, 1964).
2. Erikson, *Young Man Luther* (New York: Norton, 1958).
3. Sigmund Freud, *An Autobiographical Study.*
4. Mahadev Desai, *A Righteous Struggle* (Ahmedabad: Navajivan, 1951).
5. Susanne Rudolph, "The New Courage," *World Politics,* 16 (1963), 98–127.
6. M. K. Gandhi, *An Autobiography; or, The Story of My Experiments with Truth,* translated from the original in Gujarati by Mahadev Desai (Ahmedabad: Navajivan, 1927).
7. Susanne Rudolph, "Self-Control and Political Potency: Gandhi's Asceticism," *The American Scholar,* 35 (Winter, 1956), 79–97.
8. *The Collected Works of Mahatma Gandhi* (Delhi: Government of India, Ministry of Information and Broadcasting, 1958–).
9. B. R. Nanda, *Mahatma Gandhi: A Biography* (Boston: Beacon Press, 1958).
10. Pyarelal, *Mahatma Gandhi: The Early Phase* (Ahmedabad: Navajivan, 1965); and *Mahatma Gandhi: The Last Phase,* 2 vols. (Ahmedabad: Navajivan, 1956–1958).
11. Rudolph, "Self-Control and Political Potency."
12. Desai, *A Righteous Struggle.*
13. Gandhi, *Autobiography,* part 5, chaps. 20–22.
14. An old Indian friend recounted to me an event taken almost for granted in those early days—namely, how young Vinoba Bhave (the man who in all these years has come and remained closest to Ghandi in spirit, style, and stature) sat by the ashram grounds and a big and poisonous snake

crawled under his shawl. He kept still, and another ashramite quietly folded up the garment and took it to the riverbank.

15. Louis Fischer, *The Life of Mahatma Gandhi* (New York: Harper, 1950), p. 238.

16. Gandhi, *Autobiography*, part 4, chap. 11.

17. Erik H. Erikson, "Psychoanalysis and Ongoing History: Problems of Identity, Hatred and Nonviolence," *American Journal of Psychiatry*, 122 (Sept., 1965), 241–50.

18. Stanley A. Wolpert, *Tilak and Gokhale: Revolution and Reform in the Making of Modern India* (Berkeley: University of California Press, 1962).

19. *Collected Works of Gandhi*.

20. Victor Wolfenstein, *The Revolutionary Personality* (Princeton, N.J.: Princeton University Press, 1967).

21. Ernest Jones, *Essays in Applied Psychoanalysis*, vol. 2 (London: Hogarth, 1951).

22. Robert Lifton, *Death in Life: Survivors of Hiroshima* (New York: Random House, 1968).

23. Translated by Leo O. Lee for my seminar at Harvard from *Lu Hsün ch'ü-chi* (Complete Works of Lu Hsün [Peking: 1956]), vol. 2, pp. 261–62.

24. See Joan Erikson, *St. Francis and His Four Ladies* (New York: Norton, 1970).

2. FREEDOM AND NONVIOLENCE
(PAGES 171–186)

1. M. K. Gandhi, *Satyagraha in South Africa*, in *The Selected Works of Mahatma Gandhi* (Ahmedabad: Navajivan, 1968), vol. 3, pp. 7, 8.

2. Louis Fischer, *The Life of Mahatma Gandhi* (New York: Harper, 1950), p. 118.

3. Plato, *Republic*, 4.431.

4. Sigmund Freud, *Studies on Hysteria*, Standard Edition (London: Hogarth, 1955), p. 135.

PROTEST AND LIBERATION

1. REFLECTIONS ON THE REVOLT OF HUMANIST YOUTH
(PAGES 194–206)

1. Ernst Kris, *Psychoanalytic Explorations in Art* (New York: International Universities Press, 1952).

2. Peter Blos, "Character Formation in Adolescence," in *The Psychoanalytic Study of the Child*, vol. 23 (1968).

3. Erik Erikson, *Young Man Luther* (New York: Norton, 1958).

4. L. Kohlberg and R. B. Kramer, "Continuities and Discontinuities in Childhood and Adult Moral Development," *Human Development*, 12 (1969), 93–120.

2. ONCE MORE THE INNER SPACE
(PAGES 225–236)

1. Erik H. Erikson, "Womanhood and the Inner Space," in *Identity: Youth and Crisis* (New York: Norton, 1968).

2. Elizabeth Janeway, *Man's World Woman's Place* (New York: Morrow, 1971), p. 8.

3. *Ibid.*, p. 93.

4. *Ibid.*

3. PSYCHOANALYSIS: ADJUSTMENT OR FREEDOM?
(PAGES 260–262)

1. See the Jefferson Lectures (*Dimensions of a New Identity* [New York: Norton, 1974]), and the Godkin Lectures (in press).

2. "On Protest and Affirmation," *Harvard Medical Alumni Bulletin*, 46 (1972), 30–32.

Index